MEASURING CHANGE IN COUNSELING AND PSYCHOTHERAPY

Measuring Change in Counseling and Psychotherapy

Scott T. Meier

THE GUILFORD PRESS
New York   London

© 2008 The Guilford Press
A Division of Guilford Publications, Inc.
72 Spring Street, New York, NY 10012
www.guilford.com

Printed in the United States of America

This book is printed on acid-free paper.

Last digit is print number: 9 8 7 6 5 4 3 2 1

Library of Congress Cataloging-in-Publication Data

Meier, Scott T., 1955–
   Measuring change in counseling and psychotherapy / Scott T.
   Meier.
      p. cm.
   Includes bibliographical references and indexes.
   ISBN: 978-1-59385-720-2 (hardcover)
   1. Psychodiagnostics.   2. Psychological tests.   I. Title.
   [DNLM: 1. Psychological Tests.   2. Mental Disorders—
therapy.   3. Outcome and Process Assessment (Health
Care)   4. Psychotherapy—methods.   WM 145 M511m 2008]
   RC469.M428   2008
   616.89'075—dc22

                                          2008020686

Preface

The central goal of this book is very ambitious: to help the reader understand how measurement issues affect clinicians who must cope with daily concerns regarding provision of psychological care. To do so, it is necessary to explore in some detail how the fields of psychology, psychological testing, and psychological treatment arrived at their current condition. Such an exploration lays the groundwork for describing (1) important measurement, testing, and assessment concepts, and (2) contemporary progress and problems in both measurement and psychotherapy domains.

Although a seemingly straightforward scholarly task, describing problems related to psychological testing and assessment can quickly turn controversial and heated. Debates about the usefulness of criticism of psychological testing are long-standing: Even early psychologists such as Cattell and Jastrow disagreed about the merits of debating testing's strengths and weaknesses (Cronbach, 1992). Let me make clear that I do not believe that use of educational and psychological tests should cease or that such a cessation is desirable or even possible. On the contrary, I share the view that "psychological tests often provide the fairest and most accurate method of making important decisions" (Murphy & Davidshofer, 1988, p. xii). And despite occasional suggestions to the contrary (cf. Paul, 2004), the domain of psychological testing is clearly a science. The typical psychological test is based on psychometric evaluations and has a theoretical perspective; a distinct body of literature exists that focuses on concepts related to educational and psychological measurement and assessment. I think it is important, however, that both clinicians and testing experts continue a respectful discussion about research and theory that contributes to scientific progress in both measurement and psychotherapy domains.

The inadequacies of our approach to measurement may in part be due to how complex constructing and performing valid testing really is. Another goal of this book, therefore, is to present this material parsimoniously. I have emphasized the conceptual, not the statistical; I use simple frequency distributions and visual displays rather than more complex data sets and tables of numbers. Cronbach (1991a) stated that

> one need not be a skilled mathematician to advance methodology; you call upon an expert once you know what to call for. The crucial contribution—which mathematicians cannot be expected to make—is an adequate formal description of an interesting set of social or psychological events. (p. 398)

My approach has been to describe the problems of measurement and assessment from the perspective of psychological theory. The hope is to reconnect measurement with substantive theory.

When data are based on sound clinical measurements, this enhances clinicians' ability to be compassionate in day-to-day decisions about clients/ patients. A goal of this book is to help readers draw that connection between sound data collection and compassionate clinical choices. This goal dovetails with requirements by the American Psychological Association and other professional organizations that students learn about methods of assessment employed for evaluating the efficacy and effectiveness of interventions.

Organization of the Book

In Chapter 1, I begin with an introduction and further rationale for this book. The next four chapters provide an in-depth examination of how measurement and assessment concepts and controversies have evolved, or in some instances, failed to progress, over roughly the past 100 years; portions of these chapters are based on Meier (1994). Chapter 2 covers the history of the concept of "traits"—psychological traits—and the ascendancy of traits as the object of what we are trying to measure with psychological testing. Knowledge of measurement's historical issues is important because lack of such knowledge is a reason some domains have not progressed much in the subtlety of their approach to measurement. Chapter 3 describes the effects that method variance, self-reports, and ratings by others have on test validity. Psychological states have been shown to be probably as influential as traits in human behavior; consequently, they have significant impact on test validity. That point is the subject of Chapter 4. Chapter 5 concludes the first group of chapters, emphasizing that problems with the testing *context* give rise to the problems described in Chapters 2, 3, and 4.

With this foundation, I then turn to cutting-edge work in the area of measuring change in counseling and psychotherapy. Most texts on this topic marginalize or ignore clinical measurement and assessment, but recent developments in assessing change have great potential to improve psychotherapeutic practices and outcomes. In Chapter 6, I describe the state of the art in nomothetic measurement of therapeutic change; these advances include change-sensitive tests and the use of feedback to improve outcomes. Chapter 7 describes current work with idiographic methods. One such method is deriving measures from single case conceptualizations. Narrative- and language-based approaches fall into the idiographic category as well. Chapter 8 summarizes both sections of the book.

Pedagogical Features

Graduate students often reference reading material in terms of "the book" rather than "the author," as in "The book says. . . ." This is telling. Matarazzo (1987) observed that the textbooks employed in psychology courses are more responsible than other sources for transmitting psychological knowledge to the next generation of students. Therefore, I think it is important to expand the scope of topics typically presented in a text on psychological measurement and assessment. Students who undertake a standard measurement and assessment course are likely to learn the basics of psychometrics, followed by an overview of and practice with a few well-known instruments such as the Weschler Adult Intelligence Scale (WAIS) and the Minnesota Multiphasic Personality Inventory (MMPI). In contrast, the aim of this book is to provide readers with a set of concepts and activities needed to evaluate their intended testing purposes, current and future, against available and potential tests and other operations.

For example, the book includes a series of writing assignments to help students learn how to identify, evaluate, and report on tests' psychometric information. These assignments are designed to help students learn, with the help of their instructor, where to locate information about tests, how to do a basic literature review related to test information, and how to apply what they have learned about tests to actual test use. Instead of defaulting to standard practice in the field (which often lags behind current research and theory), students should learn how to think critically and flexibly about tests. To do so, they need to be able to conduct a time-limited, but reasonably thorough, review of the available literature on tests of interest. Thus, students need to know:

1. Where to find information about tests from such diverse sources as publishers' websites, *PsycINFO*, *Tests in Print*, *Mental Measurements Yearbooks*, and *Test Critiques*.
2. How to locate tests to measure particular constructs.
3. Theory and theoretical definitions related to constructs they wish to measure.
4. The purposes for which tests were designed and have been employed.
5. How different samples (normative and intended) might affect test scores.
6. How to locate and evaluate reliability and validity information for specific tests.
7. How to construct tables and graphs in order to synthesize and evaluate the collected information.

These writing assignments begin at the end of Chapter 2 and are intended to be done weekly, culminating in a draft of a term paper about a measurement-related topic. Two types of writing assignments are listed: One is suitable for a general measurement or assessment course, and the second focuses on measurement of change topics.

Also at the end of each chapter is a section of discussion questions, test questions, and clinically oriented exercises designed to encourage more active learning. Testing students' knowledge solidifies their understanding of the issues and problems of testing and measurement in general (Roediger & Karpicke, 2006). I have employed many of these exercises in my graduate testing class and found them to be an effective means of engaging students and helping them to learn the material through application.

I have taught this material in a beginning graduate-level course in educational and psychological measurement that typically enrolls 25–45 master's- and doctoral-level students. In a class of this size, the students' baseline grasp of the issues of psychological testing varies considerably. For that reason, I spend the first 3 weeks of the course reviewing a basic vocabulary of concepts that provides the students with a foundation for discussing the history, theory, and applications that follow. The review encompasses three major areas: basic measurement concepts (including reliability and validity), types of psychological measurements (e.g., self-reports, observational strategies, qualitative assessments), and test components (test construction, administration, scoring, and interpretation). As an adjunct to this book, I have put that vocabulary review into a Glossary that may be found at my website, *www.acsu.buffalo.edu/~stmeier.*

Acknowledgments

I wish to thank C. Deborah Laughton, Publisher, Methodology and Statistics, and Natalie Graham, Associate Editor, of The Guilford Press, for their persistence and help in bringing this book to life. I also give special thanks to Marietta Hoogs, the latest in a long line of graduate assistants who have provided help for my measurement research at the University at Buffalo. Thanks also to John Suler, Rider University; Dr. James W. Lichtenberg, Counseling Psychology, University of Kansas; and Dr. David A. Vermeersch, Psychology, Loma Linda University, who reviewed the manuscript and provided important feedback and support during this project.

SCOTT T. MEIER

Contents

CHAPTER 4   States, Traits, and Validity   89

MEASURING CHANGE IN COUNSELING AND PSYCHOTHERAPY

CHAPTER 1

Introduction and Rationale

Contemporary Psychological Testing

The contemporary status of educational and psychological testing is puzzling. On one hand, tests designed and employed to select individuals for appropriate placement into schools, jobs, and the military provide the best, most efficient methods available to obtain important, relevant information. In the context of counseling, Erford (2007) provided a succinct summary of testing's benefits:

> Assessment is the quickest way to understand students and clients. The better one understands clients or students, the better and faster one will be able to help them. Assessment saves the client time, money, and (most importantly) social and emotional pain. The more efficient a professional counselor becomes in knowing a student or client, the more effective and respected the counselor will become. (p. 2)

Similarly, Dahlstrom and others have observed that psychological tests have assisted in professional decisions about hundreds of thousands of "patients, clients, applicants, defendants, students, or employees in the United Sates and abroad" (Dahlstrom, 1993, p. 395).

On the other hand, critics of psychological testing report significant and extensive flaws. Perhaps the most telling and persistent criticism has to do with the lack of progress and innovation in testing. Martin (1988) maintained that "personality assessors are using the equivalent of the first designs

1

of the airplane flown by the Wright brothers" (p. 17). Sternberg and Williams (1998) pointed out that test publishers have not needed to innovate:

> No technology of which we are aware—computers, telecommunications, televisions, and so on—has shown the kind of ideational stagnation that has characterized the testing industry. Why? Because in other industries, those who do not innovate do not survive. In the testing industry, the opposite appears to be the case. Like *Rocky I, Rocky II, Rocky III*, and so on, the testing industry provides minor cosmetic successive variants of the same product where only the numbers after the names substantially change. These variants survive because psychologists buy the tests and then loyally defend them. (p. 577)

Interest in and knowledge of testing problems and issues remains largely relegated to a small, committed group of professionals. Put more frankly, most students and clinicians have little enthusiasm for learning about psychological measurement. Erford (2007) noted that "students new to the profession often show little excitement for a course in measurement or assessment" (p. 2) and tend to rate testing courses among the least interesting. As discussed further in Chapter 2, this situation is critical enough that Lambert (1991) has labeled it "a crisis in measurement literacy" (p. 24).

This tension between benefits and criticism of psychological testing may partially be explained by the first central theme of this book: *The history of science suggests that new types of measurement devices are needed to discover new phenomena as well as to deepen existing knowledge.* In other words, all measurement devices possess limitations that hinder a field's ability to conduct research and apply knowledge, and a natural step in the evolution of any scientific field is to develop innovative measures. Consequently, the second central theme of this book is that *problems with psychological testing will have significant implications for clinical practice and research.* Until the next generation of measures is developed, clinicians will conduct their work hindered by the limitations of their current formal and informal measurement and assessment procedures.

Contemporary Psychotherapy Research and Practice

These are strange times for researchers in academic psychology whose major areas are counseling, clinical, and school psychology. Researchers who obtain grant support and publish in the most prestigious journals have increasingly focused on narrow clinical populations in an attempt to develop *empirically validated or supported treatments* (ESTs). The EST approach essentially adopts the clinical trials procedure of evaluating drugs by using *randomly assigned* treatment and control groups to assess the efficacy of a particular treatment. ESTs make sense in that the advantages of randomization are significant for interpreting intervention studies, and the current political and grant-funding climate clearly favors more medically oriented approaches. Perhaps the major strength of the EST approach is that it provides a solid foundation for helping policy makers in the public and private sectors understand the efficacy of the examined psychotherapeutic method.

In practice, however, problems exist with ESTs. First, researchers can potentially manipulate the ease of finding statistically significant outcomes through the choice of outcome measures. As discussed later in this book, different sources of information about outcome provide consistently different reports about the amount of clinical progress evidenced by any group of clients. Second, almost any theoretically sound treatment will best a control group, but treatments seldom exhibit significant differences among themselves (e.g., Smith & Glass, 1977). Third, if there is any robust finding from the history of counseling and psychotherapy outcome research, it is that clients show a substantial range of responses to any intervention. Even with ESTs that demonstrate beneficial effects on average for a clinical group, some individuals will evidence no change, and some will worsen. This means that in actual practice, clinicians have no method for ascertaining whether a particular client will improve, remain unchanged, or worsen during the course of the prescribed EST.

In recent decades, counseling and psychotherapy researchers have been guided in their search for more specificity by Paul's (1967) question, "*What* treatment, by *whom*, is most effective for *this* individual with that specific problem, under *which* set of circumstances?" (p. 111). Similarly, Lambert, Garfield, and Bergin (2004) restated this question in terms of "whether we can isolate and identify the ingredients of practice" (p. 809). This approach, which focuses on identifying psychotherapeutic treatments that evidence efficacy with specific client populations, underlies the EST movement. As with any perspective on counseling research and practice, however, limitations exist. Kazdin (2000), for example, maintained that Paul's question "is not very feasible or useful in light of the extraordinary number of interventions, disorders, and moderators" (p. 214) that could potentially be examined in counseling research. Particularly with research conducted in field settings such as clinics, community agencies, schools, counseling centers, hospitals, and private practices, researchers face the daunting task of identifying and studying a potentially infinite number of factors that could influence outcomes.

One result of pursuing this research philosophy is that the existing literature exhibits a number of valid generalizations, but little in the way of specific guidance for practitioners. The major conclusions reached by counseling and psychotherapy researchers over the past half century are broad in scope: Most clients improve as a result of counseling and psychotherapy, the level of this improvement exceeds that seen in controls, the therapeutic alliance is associated with improvement, and when examined in large clinical samples, gains across counseling approaches appear to be roughly equivalent (Kazdin, 2000; Smith & Glass, 1977). More recent evidence also suggests that the severity of a client's problems and greater resistance by clients are associated with poorer outcomes (Norcross, 2004). Beyond these general findings, however, little consensus exists about such issues as how counseling works or what does change in clients as a result of psychotherapy. The field continues to generate a seemingly inexhaustible supply of interesting but disparate findings such as (1) the ability of different outcome measures to produce larger effects than those typically attributed to treatments (Lambert, Hatch, Kingston, & Edwards, 1986) or (2) that some clients exhibit large improvements on a measure of depression even before the identified intervention is implemented (Kelly, Roberts, & Ciesla, 2005). In essence, counseling and psychotherapy research might be considered *stuck*.

The broad findings of the outcome literature are important. They provide a credible basis for training students in psychotherapeutic techniques and help the field make a case with insurers, governments, and other funding agencies to pay for psychosocial interventions. But the types of questions that are most important at this point in time, what might be termed the interaction questions, seldom receive strong empirical answers. For example, it would be useful to know whether certain types of treatments for alcohol abuse work better with women than men, with younger versus older clients, with people of different cultures, and so on. But the field has not been able to produce very definite answers to these kinds of questions (e.g., Project Match Research Group, 1997).

The Implications of Research Stuckness for Clinical Practice

Without ongoing discoveries and the deepening of knowledge facilitated by measurement innovations, clinical practice will stagnate. In contemporary practice, what novice clinicians see as innovative treatment approaches are often previously developed methods that have been slightly modified or even forgotten. Clinical approaches and problems tend to cycle in and out of a field's awareness. This progression becomes apparent to clinicians as they gain experience: Ronnestad and Skovholt (2003) studied the development of counselors over the course of their careers and found that experienced therapists often came to the conclusion that "there is a sense that there is not and will not be any significant new knowledge in the field" (p. 26).

An equally serious problem, *treatment failure*, has been estimated to range between 10 and 50% of all clients (e.g., Persons & Mikami, 2002). In clinical practice, many therapists essentially ignore the issue of treatment failure except when it reaches the level of potential suicidal or homicidal behavior. The most likely explanation for this situation is that clinicians possess few systematic methods for identifying clients' lack of progress or preventing treatment failure, and most clinicians do not employ systematic methods for gauging treatment progress (Clement, 1994). In most cases, treatment failure simply consists of the client's dropping out of therapy after a few sessions.

In a few documented cases, however, treatment failures have had serious consequences. On October 24, 1995, PBS broadcast an episode of *Frontline* entitled "The Search for Satan." The story describes two young female patients, Pat and Mary, who were treated by a team of hospital-based mental health professionals who believed that these women had multiple personality disorder (MPD). The mental health professionals believed that the MPD resulted from ritual abuse that occurred during participation in a satanic cult.

With both Pat and Mary, however, a diagnosis of depression would have been much more parsimonious than MPD. At the time of her MPD diagnosis Mary had been experiencing panic attacks, weight loss, and difficulty concentrating. She had recently been attacked in a hallway at the school where she taught. Mary also had a history that indicated that she might be vulnerable to depression: She had been date-raped at age 19, became pregnant, and gave the child up for adoption. In addition, her husband suffered from alcoholism, and, after the birth of a later child, Mary had a hysterectomy and developed seizures. Mary began to see a therapist, but her seizures and blackouts led the therapist to refer her for evaluation for a dissociative disorder. Pat was also married, with two children. She had been depressed for 3 years following the difficult birth of one of her sons. Pat sought therapy and was diagnosed with MPD and referred to the same team of mental health professionals as Mary. Outside of the mental health professionals' interpretation of their symptoms, no evidence existed that Pat or Mary had participated in or been a victim of a satanic cult.

Mary reported that within the first 5 minutes of her referral interview, she was informed that she had multiple personality disorder. Mary was admitted into a hospital on the basis of the MPD diagnosis and began therapy sessions in which the focus included Mary's memories and knowledge about other possible cult members and cult activities. She received a variety of medications (including Prozac and a heart medication, Inderal) and was instructed to sever contact with family and friends outside the hospital. Mary reported that she was also told during treatment that she had murdered people and would go to prison. Mary's son was later admitted to the same unit with a MPD diagnosis, but Mary was not allowed to see him. Treatment of some MPD patients included restraints for 8–16 hours. Mary received 3 years of treatment in psychiatric wards and likened the experience to "going deeper and deeper and deeper into an abyss." Pat was also hospitalized for her MPD treatment. Because MPD was thought to have a genetic component, Pat and Mary both were told that they had to complete the treatment to break the cult cycle that would continue with their children. Both of Pat's children were also hospitalized with MPD and participated in therapy with their mother. The children were in therapy for about 3 years.

Mary worsened as her treatment continued. After several years, Mary was scheduled to be moved to a nursing home, but refused and discontinued treatment. She saw another therapist outside the hospital, who asked her if she simply wanted to stop thinking of herself as a person with MPD (as well as to stop the accompanying treatments). Mary indicated that she did not want to be a person with MPD, discontinued her medications, and physically regained her health. Pat also stopped medications and hypnosis, and her symptoms also disappeared. A court order was required to release Pat's sons from the hospital.

The consequences of mental health treatment were serious for Mary, Pat, and their families. Mary's husband filed for divorce, her son did not want to see her, and the state of Illinois listed her as a child abuser. In addition to enduring their treatments, all lost several years of their lives, including Pat's children who required remediation to resume normal schooling. Treatment for Pat and her children cost their insurer about $3 million; Mary's insurer paid about $2.5 million for her treatment.

In my measurement class I employ this episode as an example of hypothesis confirmation bias (HCB). As discussed in Chapter 3, HCB with mental health professionals occurs when a clinician prematurely decides on a diagnosis or hypothesis and then proceeds to ignore any subsequent information that disconfirms that diagnosis/hypothesis. For example, one of Pat's sons related a story of alleged satanic abuse when he described cutting open a stomach with a knife and watching the guts pop out. Even though Pat reported that the story was a fabrication based on a scene in a *Star Wars* movie, one mental health professional insisted it was true (independent of any other corroborating evidence) and even employed the story in court testimony to demonstrate the validity of the boy's abuse.

When graduate students see this broadcast, many come to the conclusion that the mental health professionals involved were quacks whose greed led them to abuse their clients. I do not believe this was the case. Instead, I would guess that these clinicians came to believe (and reinforced each other's belief) that they had discovered an important clinical problem. My best guess is that independent of interviews and interactions with clients, these clinicians had few means of (1) testing the belief that satanic ritual abuse, or some alternative process, was the cause of the clients' problems, or (2) obtaining outcome information that could provide useful feedback about Mary's or Pat's progress. This second point is particularly important in that it is in the processes of feedback where data resulting from clinical measurement can be put to use to inform decisions in clinical practice.

Although this example is one of the worst cases of negative client outcomes over the past 20 years of which I am aware, other problematic cases exist (e.g., Chafetz & Chafetz, 1994) and likely many others remain unreported. Equally troubling is the number of routine clinical failures that many clinicians appear to ignore (cf. Kendall, Kipnis, & Otto-Salaj, 1992, described in Chapter 6). Although better process and outcome measures, by themselves, will not eliminate treatment failures, the improved account-ability such measures offer should decrease their number.

Summary and Conclusions

Nunnally (1978) maintained that measurement is central to progress in social science research. Whereas counseling and psychotherapy researchers (and to a lesser extent, practitioners) have been very focused on outcomes, relatively little attention has been paid to issues concerning the measurement and assessment of said outcomes.

A major goal of this book is to help readers think about and learn how to create what might be termed *compassionate data*. Data, of course, are not compassionate per se, but their use can be. The objective is to generate and obtain data that enable mental health professionals to provide the best counseling and psychotherapy practices and outcomes possible with any particular individual. Professionals who employ process and outcome assessments are in the position of being more than data analysts. As demonstrated later in this book, data produced with such assessments can be a powerful tool in the decision-making process by providing important feedback to therapists and clients about clinical progress. To produce data that can be employed compassionately, mental health professionals need better testing and measurement methods. The development of improved tests falls primarily to researchers and test developers.

To provide a clearer picture of the current status of outcome assessment, and to offer motivation for innovation and change, I provide in the next chapter an account of the history of testing that focuses on the crucial role of traditional trait-based tests.

QUESTIONS AND EXERCISES

1. For 3 minutes, write down what you consider the major ideas of this section, chapter, or class. At the beginning of next week's class, share with the group.

2. In small groups or individually, consider this: Paul's (1967) question, "*What* treatment, by *whom*, is most effective for *this* individual with that specific problem, under *which* set of circumstances?" (p. 111, emphasis in original), has helped counseling and psychotherapy researchers conceptualize their research questions. Why do you think this question has been helpful to researchers? What alternative guiding questions can you create?

CHAPTER 2

A History of Traits

The Seeds of Conflict

Throughout psychology's history, financial support for scientific psychology has often been provided on the premise that discoveries and knowledge generation by scientists would ultimately improve the lives of individuals. Similarly, it is assumed that scientific methods created or evaluated the interventions practicing psychologists use (e.g., VanZandt, 1990). Dawis (1992) noted, for example, that early clinicians, armed with psychological tests, "had a technology for client assessment that had the decided appearance of professionalism ... [and] the scientific substance as well" (p. 11).

Most psychologists recognize the importance of meshing the two identities, as witnessed by the adoption by some specialties of a *scientist–practitioner training model* in which graduate psychology students learn both research and practice skills (Barlow, Hayes, & Nelson, 1984; Gelso, 1979). That integration, however, has been only moderately successful: Relatively few psychologists conduct research beyond that required in graduate school. Relatively few express interest in psychological science jobs at the beginning or end of the graduate school career, and few clinical practitioners base their work on current research information (Barlow, 1981; Herman, 1993; National Institute of Mental Health, 1976).

The struggle between those who wish to be scientific and those who wish to be socially relevant has had profound effects on the subject of this book, psychological measurement. *Measurement* is usually defined as the process of assigning numbers to objects according to agreed-upon rules (e.g., Stevens, 1951). The assignment process is the crucial aspect of the definition. Krantz, Luce, Suppes, and Tversky (1971) defined measurement as assigning numbers to objects "in such a way [that] the properties of the attributes are faithfully represented as numerical properties" (p. 1). In other words, data that result from the measurement process should reflect the characteristics inherent in the phenomenon of interest. *Psychological tests* are systematic procedures for observing behavior and describing it with a numerical scale or category system (Cronbach, 1970). *Psychological assessments* involve a human rater, as when a clinician takes the results of several tests and integrates them into a single set of conclusions. Psychological tests provide a method of describing a natural phenomenon, of transforming phenomena into data. The data resulting from any measurement procedure, however, reflect only some of the characteristics of the phenomena under examination (see Figure 2.1); in other words, *measurement error* is always present.

The Desire to Be Scientific

Although the American Psychological Association (APA) marked the 100th anniversary of its annual convention in 1992, some evidence suggests that the very first APA convention was organized to help psychologist Joseph Jastrow provide examples of psychological measurement for an exhibit at the 1893 World's Fair (Cronbach, 1992). In 1979 psychologists celebrated the 100th anniversary of the opening of Wundt's laboratory in Germany, an event often cited as the birth of scientific psychology. The youth of psychological science, just a century old, should be noted in any account of the history of psychological measurement.

Psychology came to be more formally recognized as a scientific discipline in the late 1800s, but events were taking place earlier in that century that shaped the early practices and procedures of scientific psychology. The most important events were related to developments in physiology, biology, and astronomy.

The Model of Physiology

In the 1800s, success in research and measurement of physiological processes provided examples of ideas and techniques that psychologists could

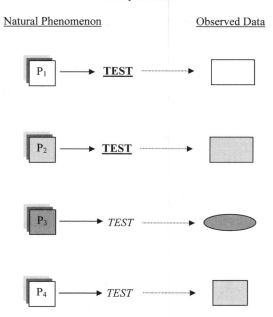

FIGURE 2.1. Transformation of characteristics of natural phenomenon into data. A measuring instrument is intended to produce data that reflect the characteristics of a natural phenomenon. Any test, however, will introduce some degree of error. In this illustration, tests measuring phenomena P_1 and P_2 produce data that largely reflect the important characteristics of the phenomenon. Other tests, as illustrated with phenomena P_3 and P_4, involve a more substantial distortion.

apply in their work. Wundt produced what some considered the first psychology book, *Physiological Psychology* (Heidbreder, 1933), describing how psychological experiments could be patterned after physiological ones: The scientist employs a controllable stimulus and records the objective responses of subjects. Similarly, Helmholtz provided practical demonstrations in his research on the eye and ear, showing that the experimental methods and measurement techniques of physiology and the natural sciences could be applied to psychological phenomena (Heidbreder, 1933).

Another early psychological researcher, Fechner, viewed studies of just noticeable differences—for example, distinguishing between objects of slightly different weights—as revealing a mathematical relationship between the physical objects themselves and a person's perception of those objects. A physicist and philosopher, Fechner sought to apply the methods of physical measurement to psychological phenomena (Falmagne, 1992). Fechner proposed that a person's ability to perceive a physical stimulus could be described by a logarithmic (curvilinear) function between the perceived sensation and measured stimulus value. With evidence of such a general relation (which he called Weber's law, after E. H. Weber, who provided the data used by Fechner), Fechner felt encouraged that psychological phenomena could be studied with the scientific method. As Heidbreder (1933) noted, "To Fechner's contemporaries, the remarkable feature of the psychophysical methods was the fact that they were quantitative. To measure mental processes was considered a startling innovation; to experiment with them in a manner that gave quantitative data marked the dawn of a new day" (p. 83).

As the methods and measurements of the physiological laboratory became available to psychologists, the phenomena studied with these tools—sensation and perception—appeared at that time to be likely candidates for the raw elements from which all important psychological entities were constructed. In the late 1800s, for example Galton suggested that sensory discrimination might be a sign of an individual's capacity for intelligent judgment. During the same period James McKeen Cattell employed tasks such as grip strength, detecting the smallest differences in weight between two objects, and reaction time to sound in an attempt to develop predictors of intelligence.

Biology and Individual Differences

Darwin's publication in 1859 of *The Origin of Species* provided another model for psychology. Two ideas seemed particularly relevant. First, individuals had to be considered in light of their ability to adapt themselves to their environment. Second, humans pass on to their descendants a genetic history. Interestingly, individual offspring display slight differences from their parents, differences that Darwin believed could be the source of materials for the processes of natural selection (Dawis, 1992).

Similarly, mental testers have a long history of seeing their work as having to do with the "selection" of individuals to fit the requirements of institutions. Cronbach (1957) put it this way:

> Institutions, by demanding adaptation, serve as instruments of natural selection among men....To Spencer, to Galton, and to their successors down to the present day, the successful are those who have the greatest adjustive capacity. The psychologist's job, in this tradition, is to facilitate or anticipate natural selection. He seeks only to reduce its cruelty and wastage by predicting who will survive in schools and other institutions as they are. He takes the system for granted and tries to identify who will fit into it. His devices have a conservative influence because

they identify persons who will succeed in the existing institution. By reducing failures, they remove a challenge which might otherwise force the institution to change. (p. 679)

Characteristic of a "helping" profession, psychological experimenters and intervenors tended to assist *individuals* in finding the best environmental fit and challenged institutions to adapt to individuals, rather than the other way round.

Darwin's cousin Francis Galton became interested in the role of heredity in intelligence and developed methods that inquired into personal and family history. Galton is often considered to be the first to introduce items that required *psychological ratings*. His measurement methods included tests of imagery in which individuals were asked to recall a previous experience in as much detail as possible. Galton also recognized differences between individuals in intelligence, an approach that required tests to quantify those differences and required statistical procedures such as standard scores and correlation of the quantitative data produced by the tests of differences. Interest in *individual differences* had also been fed by a controversy that ensued in astronomy in the years after 1796 (Rosenthal, 1976). The astronomer Nevil Maskelyne fired his assistant David Kinnebrook, whose timing of the transit of stars across a line in a telescope did not match those of the senior astronomer. It later became apparent that individual differences in reaction time explained the discrepancy, not the supposed incompetence of the junior astronomer. The idea that such individual differences were not restricted simply to reaction time was quickly accepted under the label of the personal equation.

Following the lead of scientists in other disciplines, Galton in the 1880s established a testing laboratory to assess individual differences (Danziger, 1990). Soon other laboratories appeared, with psychologists such as Joseph Jastrow, Axel Oehrn, Hugo Munsterberg, J. A. Gilbert, and James McKeen Cattell demonstrating new tests and collecting data (Boring, 1957). The American Psychological Association in the 1890s formed a national committee to further cooperation between laboratories. As Boring (1957) noted, testing was the natural development of the period. Psychologists began to recognize that different individuals could behave differently on the same tasks or in the same situations.

Thus, psychologists adopted some of the forms of the natural sciences. They emulated the physiologist's laboratory and experimental methods; they employed physical and physiological tests with which they presumably could measure psychological attributes. They adopted some of the then-current philosophical assumptions about the role of heredity, particularly about heredity's role in determining intelligence. They emphasized the quantification of individual differences in psychological measurement. With these imitations the field could act scientifically and appear scientific to psychologists and the lay public alike.

The Desire to Be Relevant

The Need for Classification

Around 1900, in response to the French government's need for a procedure to identify persons with mental retardation (Wolf, 1973), Alfred Binet developed a set of items that came to be called an intelligence test. Binet may be credited with setting in motion a series of events with profound repercussions for measurement methods.

Given the predominance of physiological measurements and experimental methods in psychology in Binet's time, it would seem natural to apply physiological methods to the problems posed by school selection. But Binet soon began to doubt the usefulness of such sensory–motor tests as reaction time as measures of intelligence (Freeman, 1955). Binet came to believe that intelligence was constructed not of simple elementary processes, but of the unified whole of mental processes. An experimental psychologist, Binet took the risk of abandoning the psychophysical tasks of the experimental laboratory. Fancher (1985) reported that Binet found that children's and adults' perceptual and sensory abilities were comparable, but that children were slower than adults on linguistic tasks such as assigning names to color perceptions. He also found that children could not define objects as adults could; they focused on the uses of the objects (e.g., a knife cuts meat) but had trouble with abstractions. Emphasizing the importance of tests that could differentiate adults from children, Binet concluded that more useful tests "required the application of higher and more complex faculties than simple acuity or reaction speed, such as sustained attention and the sophisticated use of language" (Fancher, 1985, p. 61).

The 1905 Binet–Simon test, although excluding tasks with direct schoolroom content (Dahlstrom, 1985), did include many practical, academic-like tasks, such as naming parts of the body and recalling pictures of familiar objects after they were displayed for 30 seconds (Freeman, 1955). Given that Binet's task was to determine students' likelihood of success in school, it is perhaps no surprise that these tests often resembled the criteria they were supposed to predict (Ceci, 1991; Frederiksen, 1986). More recent analyses of intelligence test items and school tasks suggests that students employ similar processes to solve both sets of problems (Snow & Lohman, 1984).

Stella Sharp in 1898 indicated that for the measurement of intelligence, Binet's approach was superior to Cattell's physiological measures because Binet's tests better predicted school achievement (Boring, 1957). Wissler's 1901 review of Cattell's testing with college students, for example, showed that reaction time correlated −.02 with class standing and .16 with a test of logical memory. In comparison, intelligence tests demonstrate much higher estimates of *reliability* (i.e., consistency of measurement) and *validity* (i.e., evidence that the test measures what it is supposed to measure) (Maloney & Ward, 1976; Murphy & Davidshofer, 1988). Cronbach and Meehl (1955) maintained that Binet's tests were also valued because they were correlated with schoolteachers' judgments of intelligence, thus providing a more objective confirmation of those judgments. Binet's tests became the prototype for all psychological tests (Dawis, 1992).

A critical problem remained, however, in that the nature of intelligence was not clearly understood. Fancher (1985) suggested that Binet believed that useful items required (1) the use of a variety of mental skills (e.g., memory, verbal fluency) and (2) practical judgment. But these observations constitute only the beginnings of a theory of intelligence. Moreover, Binet believed that intellectual levels could change and that certain instructional practices could improve those levels in children with retardation. Indeed, Fancher (1985) concluded:

> Binet differed further from Galton by conceptualizing intelligence as a fluid and highly individualized quality, shaped to a large extent by each person's environmental and cultural circumstances, and quantifiable only to a limited and tentative degree. The "intellectual level" yielded by one of Binet's tests was an estimate of a child's functioning in a particular society at a particular time; change in that level was to be naturally expected, as a function both of normal growth and of significantly altered circumstances. (p. 82)

Other societal needs led to the confirmation and extension of Binet's approach. The need to classify students, for example, was not limited to the realm of educational selection. Parsons began the vocational counseling movement with his 1909 publication, *Choosing a Vocation* (Shertzer & Stone, 1980). Parsons believed that students required systematic help in choosing a vocation. Parsons' approach assumed a matching model in which students' traits (i.e., abilities and interests) were compared with the requirements of potential vocations (Super, 1957). Such traits could be measured via intelligence tests and questionnaires such as Strong's Vocational Interest

Blank (Strong, 1943). And in World Wars I and II, the military required procedures for classifying the abilities of a large number of recruits to fit its occupations (Dawis, 1992). *Interviews* are the oldest form of psychological measurement, but they are time-consuming and inefficient with groups. Psychologists such as Otis responded by adapting the tasks and procedures of Binet and others so they could be administered to large groups of adults (Freeman, 1955; Murphy & Davidshofer, 1988). The resulting Army Alpha and Beta intelligence tests were designed to screen out the duller recruits and identify brighter ones for more responsible work (Boring, 1957). Similarly, Woodworth's Personal Data Sheet, the precursor to modern personality and clinical tests, was developed as a device to screen WWI recruits for their susceptibility to shell shock or war neurosis (Murphy & Davidshofer, 1988).

The Consequences of the Adoption of a Trait-Based Measurement Paradigm

As just described, the efforts of applied psychologists in first half of the 20th century were largely devoted to solving pressing social problems (Danziger, 1990). Breaking away from their origins in physiological and experimental methods, early measurement psychologists developed tests that met the selection purposes of the first half of the 20th century. Specifically, school and military administrators needed procedures for selecting and classifying large groups of individuals. The primary needs of those administrators were (1) efficiency, obtaining as much information about large sets of persons in as short a time as possible, and (2) control, obtaining sufficient predictability so as to assign individuals to appropriate school programs, jobs, and so forth. Because of these selection needs, tests were designed to be (1) measures of psychological traits present in all individuals, (2) as short as possible, (3) administered to large groups, and (4) evaluated primarily by their ability to predict future work- and school-related criteria. I refer to this perspective as the *trait-selection approach* to psychological measurement.

Traits are stable, enduring psychological characteristics thought to be passed on through heredity. Murphy and Davidshofer (1988) suggested that the concept of a trait has held several meanings. First, psychological traits are causes. Thus, persons who are introverted avoid extensive social interaction, that is, their introversion motivates them to avoid others. Historically, this is the most common meaning of traits. Second, traits function as convenient organizational schemes for perceiving and remembering similar information. Thus, individuals might tend to label certain behaviors (e.g., turning in a found wallet, paying all of the taxes you owe) as "honest" although their relatedness may only be illusory. Or the relation may be real: Individuals form concepts about how to act across situations that others perceive as traits (e.g., Stagner, 1984). Similarly, traits can be considered as expedient descriptive summaries of behavioral consistencies or act frequencies (Buss & Craik, 1983). The personality traits identified by factor analytic studies, for example, can be seen as "summarizing behavioral consistencies, rather than as underlying, fixed, causal entities" (Anastasi, 1985, p. 121). In this view, the causes of behavior remain unknown.

The trait assumption and methods employed to develop and evaluate trait-based tests shaped and continues to shape how psychologists think about measurement (Maloney & Ward, 1976; Martin, 1988). The trait assumption provided psychologists with the expectation that they would find consistency in all psychological phenomena. Most definitions of attitudes, for example, have assumed some consistency or persistence. Krech and Crutchfield (1948, cited in Scott, 1968) defined an attitude as "an enduring organization of motivational, emotional, perceptual, and cognitive processes with respect to some aspect of the individual's world" (p. 152). Similarly, Campbell (1950) wrote that "a social attitude is ... evidenced by consistency in response to social objects" (p. 31). Many contemporary psychologists continue to assume that they are measuring traits, as evidenced by the fact that psychologists observe and administer tests in their professional offices and assume that the results are generalizable beyond that particular situation (Martin, 1988).

Yet the trait-selection approach has not been able to explain a number of measurement-related inconsistencies. In addition, adoption of the trait-selection approach has had a number of unintended consequences. Both of these issues are explored in the rest of this chapter.

Loss of Experimental Methods Inhibits Recognition of Method Variance

Freeman (1955) noted that Binet's test development process could in some sense be seen as experimental: Binet selected test tasks on some basis and then tested their usefulness. But Binet demonstrated that one could predict school performance without resorting to traditional *experimental techniques* (i.e., involving manipulation of two or more independent variables). One consequence was an increase in mental testing, in the decades that followed, unconnected to traditional experimental inquiry. Aided by Fisher's developments in sampling theory, which allowed results to be generalized from samples to whole populations (Heppner, Kivlighan, & Wampold, 1999), experimenters in the early 1900s shifted their attention from measurement concerns to investigating the effects of educational and therapeutic treatments (Cronbach, 1957).

Thus began a split between experimental and psychometric traditions in psychology that continues through the present (Cronbach, 1957, 1975a). Experimentalists tend to treat individual differences as error, whereas test developers tend to ignore situational factors (Cronbach, 1957; Danziger, 1990). As Danziger (1990) wrote, "In the one case the idealization was that of a collective organism that exhibited only modifiability; in the other case it was that of a collective organism that exhibited only stable traits" (p. 87). Regarding treatments, experimentalists and correlationalists tend to be antagonistic: The former search for the best intervention to apply to all individuals, while the latter search for individuals who might best benefit from a single treatment (Cronbach, 1957). Throughout its history, experimental psychology has paid little attention to the construct validity of its dependent variables; in contrast, construct validity has increasingly become the focus of measurement validation efforts. The result of these differences is an incomplete description of psychological phenomena that hinders theory and measurement in experimental and measurement psychology.

Heidbreder (1933) maintained that without experimental methods, measurement psychologists are unable to study processes, that is, the factors that give rise to individuals' performance on psychological tests. Heidbreder (1933) defined a test as a device for

> revealing an individual's ability in a given performance, not for analyzing the process. It thus differs in intention from the typical experiment, which is directed toward finding out something not about the individual, but about the process that is being examined. (p. 108)

Danziger (1990) states that, in addition, "because the phenomena to be studied were not treated as processes to be analyzed, no special observational skill or experience was required" on the part of the person being observed (p. 92). Whether individuals were more or less able to understand psychological processes in themselves and others was not important.

The lack of experimental methods likely contributed to the failure to recognize, for many decades, a central conceptual problem that came to be known as method variance. *Method variance* refers to the empirical observation that a portion of every test score partially reflects the method used to obtain the data (Campbell & Fiske, 1959). In other words, scores on a test result from the method of measurement as well as the construct measured. For example, scores on a self-report measuring construct A will correlate, to some extent, with a second self-report measuring a different construct B simply because both tests are self-reports. Similarly, scores on a self-report measuring construct A will correlate less, to some extent, with an *interview* measuring construct A simply because each test represents a different method. Even slight differences within a general type of measurement can produce these effects. Meier (1984), for example, found that altering the response format on self-report measures, from true–false to Likert, could influence the resulting correlations among measures.

The Gain of Traits and Loss of Situations

Many psychologists interpreted Binet's results as evidence of an intelligence factor, which Spearman in the 1920s labeled *g*. Noting the intercorrelations of different components of intelligence tests, psychologists assumed that individuals applied *g* in all domains. Assumed to be a hereditary factor, *g* was thereby largely stable and immune to situational influences. It was a psychological trait. Thus, intelligence testing, which came to be the model and standard for all psychological testing, emphasized the importance of enduring psychological attributes over environmental influences.

Although research has provided support for the importance of heredity in intelligence and temperament, many psychologists believe that research and theory indicate that situational and environmental factors should also be considered (Sternberg, 1984). In the measurement area, this controversy has been described in terms of the consistency of behavior across situations. That is, if psychological phenomena are traits, then individuals who are honest, for example, should be honest across all of the situations they encounter. Yet behavioral psychologists maintain that environments and situations change behavior, influencing individuals to be honest in some situations and dishonest in others. A good example of a situational factor involves the possibility that *stereotype threat* can partially explain the persistent differences between white and black American students on intelligence and related academic tests (Estes, 1992). From a trait perspective, the higher scores of white students compared to blacks is a stable, inherited characteristic that cannot be significantly altered. The idea of stereotype threat, however, suggests that when black students perceive they are in an ability–testing situation, their performance is diminished by the increased pressure of the stereotype that blacks will perform poorly (Steele & Aronson, 1995).

Method variance and situational effects represent unexpected sources of inconsistency for the trait-selection measurement paradigm. Such effects are viewed as *error*, phenomena that affect scores on tests that are not intended to be reflected in those scores. As described below, psychologists and others developed methods to cope with error practically, but these methods have made relatively little contribution to understanding or diminishing error in measurement and assessment.

Handling Error with Classical Test Theory

Older sciences possess deterministic models in which one or more independent variables account for most of the variation in dependent variables (Lord & Novick, 1968). In a new science such as psychology, however, considerable uncertainty exists about the subject matter, prompting the use of probabilistic models and error terms. In other words, error and uncertainty exist in the descriptions developed by scientists in any new discipline. Factors other than one(s) proposed by the scientists to affect the phenomenon of interest will affect that phenomenon. As Loevinger (1957) stated, "When an item of behavior is viewed as an indication of a trait, all other traits and influences which determine it operate as errors" (p. 648). This is the foundation of the classical theory of psychological measurement: Test scores came to be conceptualized as a combination of true scores and error.

A *model* is a set of ideas designed to reflect one's current working knowledge of a phenomenon. It simplifies matters to describe the model in terms of a formula, as in the following:

$$Y = X - e$$

where Y is the score that reflects the test taker's true score on the phenomenon, X is the score the test taker actually received on a test, and e is error. Again, test developers employ the term *error* in a special way: They mean error to be unknown factors that influence test scores. Psychologists have proposed two types of error: *random* and *systematic*. Random errors are those that occur by chance; they appear to have no pattern or order. Systematic errors do possess some pattern or order. If students attempt to fake "good" on a survey of attitudes toward their instructor, for example, they are committing a systematic error. The resulting scores will be systematically distorted away from scores indicative of their true beliefs.

In contrast, early psychologists appeared to hold the following measurement model:

$$Y = X$$

where the observed score was assumed to be the true score. But Binet's test only moderately correlated with school performance, and so some notion of error had to be introduced to account for the discrepancy between these two indicators of intelligence. How could psychologists account for this error?

At least three possibilities existed. First, one could apply mathematical principles to cope with error. Second, one could require the testing psychologist to observe and perhaps interview the test taker to ascertain what factors besides the test stimuli affected the test score. Third, one could assume that most errors are systematic and establish a set of experiments to investigate the errors. As indicated below, psychologists largely chose the first two options and only recently have been pursuing the third.

Statistics Related to Measurement

Given the 20th century's military, educational, and occupational selection requirements—that tests be developed, administered, and scored as quickly and efficiently as possible—error is best dealt with using statistical procedures and principles. *Statistics* is a branch of mathematics whereby one describes populations numerically on the basis of partial samples and partial descriptions of the factors affecting the population. Interestingly, statistical research in the 18th century that investigated links between socioeconomic variables and social reform also spurred the development of trait ideas (Danziger, 1990). Crime rates, for example, appeared related to geographic locale, with the attendant environmental influences (e.g., poverty) readily recognized. To explain these statistical regularities, Quetelet conceived of the idea that individuals might possess propensities to commit acts such as homicide or suicide. Buckle argued that "group attributes were to be regarded as nothing but summations of individual attributes" (Danziger, 1990, p. 77). Propensities and attributes became traits, and the application of social statistics to individuals seemed a natural progression.

An important statistical procedure developed by Spearman and others in the early 1900s was the use of the *correlation coefficient*. A *correlation* summarizes the extent of any linear relationship between two variables. A correlation of .50 between a psychological test and a course grade, for example, indicates a moderate relation between the two. One could square the correlation to obtain an estimate of the variability in one score accounted for by the other. In this example, squaring .50 equals .25, indicating that 25% of the variance in the course grade can be accounted for by the psychological test. Seventy-five percent of the variance, however, is caused by error (i.e., unknown factors). Later, a related procedure, *factor analysis*, would become widely perceived by test developers as the procedure necessary to reveal the true nature of psychological phenomena hidden in test data (but see Lykken, 1971, for a strong demonstration of the limitations of factor analysis). Statistical techniques such as correlation coefficients and factor analysis could be employed during test construction to identify and eliminate test items and tasks that contained too much error (Coombs, Dawes, & Tversky, 1970).

Another important statistical procedure quickly utilized to handle error was *aggregation*. Psychologists such as Binet and Spearman recognized that error could be reduced through the use of large numbers of individuals and test items (Dawis, 1992). This was a result of the observation that in large samples, random measurement errors tend to balance each other out, thus increasing the ability to detect the trait in question. Thus, in a sample of 100, if one individual's intelligence test score was lowered because of fatigue, that error-filled score would not have much effect on the overall correlation between test score and job performance. Similarly, if an individual misread one item, that incorrect response would not have much effect on the reliability of a total score reflecting the sum of 100 items. Test construction became dependent on using large samples of individuals and initially large numbers of items.

The use of large samples to minimize measurement error, however, had several side effects (Danziger, 1990). It meant that research efforts with one or a few subjects were gradually abandoned. Such studies, particularly in the beginning of a research program, tend to provide qualitative insights into important issues, such as how the subject perceives and deals with experimental tasks and demands. Also, early experimental research, such as that conducted by Wundt, employed one of the members of the research team or another trained observer to function as subject. The assumption in these studies was that a naive observer could not provide reliable information. Naive observers, for example, might be more open to errors of interpretation of items or in the accurate recall of psychological data. Psychometric researchers, however, accepted naive observers. Danziger (1990) suggested that "the simple device of multiplying the number of subjects seems to have been resorted to as a compensation for their lack of skill and experience" (p. 78). Again, the assumption was that whatever errors the subject brought to the scale would be balanced or cancelled in the aggregation of many subjects' responses.

Gradually, an individual's score came to be seen as meaningful only in relation to others' scores. That is, tests became norm referenced, meaningful only in the context of the normal, bell-shaped distribution of many natural variables. As shown in Figure 2.2, such a graphic can illustrate the mean of the scores and contrast high and low scores with each other. Galton's scale of individual differences became the predominant basis for making sense of test data. This zeitgeist continues in contemporary discussions of psychological measurement. For example, Epstein (1983) stated that "it is meaningless to interpret the behavior of an individual without a frame of reference of others' behaviors" (p. 381), and Kleinmuntz (1967) maintained that "all meaning for a given score of a person derives from comparing his score with those of other persons" (p. 47). Large samples, then, were necessary both to cancel measurement errors and to scale individuals in relation to one another. No matter what the purpose of testing, psychologists came to pay attention to aggregated scores in aggregated individuals.

If you required many subjects, however, you also needed to assume that everyone in the sample possessed the characteristic. This is a *nomothetic* approach: Nomothetic measurements observe attributes of populations, whereas *idiographic* measures focus on characteristics of individuals. The traits of nomothetic measurement are assumed to be present in every person. A nomothetic theoretician would maintain that every person

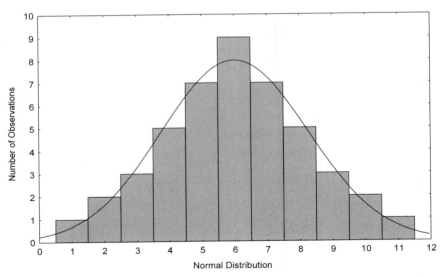

FIGURE 2.2. A normal distribution of scores. In a normal distribution, more scores cluster at middle values. The overall shape resembles a bell.

could be described as possessing some amount, for example, of the traits of neuroticism, extroversion, openness to experience, agreeableness, and conscientiousness (Goldberg, 1993; McCrae & Costa, 1985; Wiggins, 1982). Idiographic theorists believe that individuals possess unique characteristics that may be shared with all, some, or no other people. An idiographic account is concerned with how the characteristics of a person combine into a unified, unique personality (Allport, 1937). From an idiographic perspective, a particular person might be described as very neurotic and somewhat extroverted, but the dimensions of agreeable, open, and conscientious simply would not be meaningful to the study of this individual. From an idiographic perspective, error occurs when a score is assigned to an individual for a characteristic or situation that has no relevance for that individual.

Idiographic researchers study one or a few individuals, often over a long period. Nomothetic researchers study large groups, often on one occasion. Nomothetic researchers search for universal laws and believe that their research results apply to all persons, although such goals are also common to some idiographic researchers; for example, McArthur (1968) maintained that "we need to know many human natures before we can hope that Human Nature will be revealed to us" (p. 173). Both groups have tended to disparage each other. Allport (1937) quoted Meyer (1926): "A description of one individual without reference to others may be a piece of literature, a biography or novel. But science? No." (p. 271). Allport (1937) replied: "The person who is a unique and never-repeated phenomenon evades the traditional scientific approach at every step" (p. 5). Although nomothetic approaches dominate many areas of contemporary psychological measurement, it is not surprising that idiographic measurement has its strongest foothold in areas such as clinical assessment where psychologists tend to work with single persons.

The most prominent contemporary test theory is *item response theory* (IRT), an approach that essentially relies on statistical methods to handle testing issues. IRT assumes that responses to single test items are related to an underlying, unobservable trait. This relation, in cognitive ability items, can be described by a mathematical function, a monotonically increasing curve. Analyses based on this ideal curve have demonstrated considerable utility in test development and item analysis (Cronbach, 1991b). For example, two different *item characteristic curves* (ICCs) can be expected for discriminating and nondiscriminating verbal ability items. With a discriminating item, persons with good verbal skills should be more likely to correctly answer the question. A nondiscriminating item, however, would show no difference between persons of high and low verbal ability. Similarly, persons at the same ability level should provide different answers to items of different difficulty levels; for example, two persons of moderate ability should answer an easy item correctly and a difficult item incorrectly. Identification of poorly discriminating items allow their deletion at no loss of measurement precision. In addition, IRT analyses also permit the development of a calibrated item bank. From this bank may be drawn subsets of items that yield comparable latent trait scores, a useful benefit in many measurement applications.

Computer-adaptive tests (CAT) based on IRT has had commercial success with cognitive ability tests. With a CAT derived from an IRT model, an individual first completes a brief set of items. On the basis of those responses, the testing program selects more difficult or easier items to better fit the examinee's abilities. The program administers items with known difficulty and discrimination levels until the standard error of the examinee's ability score reaches a specified level or stops decreasing by a predetermined amount. A CAT produces an estimate of individuals' ability with fewer items, providing a more efficient measurement method, particularly for examinees of very low or high ability. CATs produce equal measurement precision as well as greater test security, a testing pace set for the examinee that may minimize frustration, and reduced time for test supervision (Hambleton, Swaminathan, & Rogers, 1991). All of these enhance the desired characteristics of trait-based tests.

Although IRT procedures have proven useful with trait-based tests, they are based on the assumption that tests measure a single or just a few underlying traits; most IRT applications have been focused on cognitive ability. Not surprisingly, IRT has provided little impetus for the study of other constructs, or for purposes other than selection. In addition, its emphasis on statistical methods has led to criticism about the difficulty of communicating IRT principles and results (Popham, 1993).

Assessment as a Complement to Measurement

Observing individuals during testing and conducting interviews (e.g., to determine history) were other methods of discovering factors that influenced test scores. The use of these methods was usually not an option for large-scale selection operations, but it might be feasible in clinical, educational, and occupational settings with smaller samples. Binet found it useful to think of the intelligence test as a clinical interview in which the examiner could get a sense of the methods and processes by which the examinee responded to items. Terman and Merrill (1937, cited in Murphy

& Davidshofer, 1988) suggested that Binet's intelligence test was "a method of standardized interview which is highly interesting to the subject and calls forth his natural responses to an extraordinary variety of situations" (p. 4). Certainly, including a task such as removing the wrapper from a piece of candy was highly interesting to the children taking Binet's tests (Dahlstrom, 1993). In contrast, educational testing before Binet was essentially an unstructured interview conducted between pupil and teacher (Thorndike & Hagen, 1961). Binet's method became an important demonstration of the benefits of combining psychological testing and clinical judgment. This combination is typically what psychologists mean when they employ the term *assessment*.

Since Binet's time it has been standard practice for psychologists who give psychological tests to interpret those results, when possible, in the context of the additional information they obtain from test takers. In a clinical context, this information includes a history of the presenting problems, family background and social supports, current medical problems, education, current employment, and financial resources. Martin (1988), however, suggested that test examiners must design their assessments to control unwanted factors in the information-gathering process. Ideally, assessors should use multiple settings, multiple sources, and multiple instruments to minimize error. Assessors must also pay attention to test taker characteristics that may influence scores, including motivation to respond accurately, age, ability to read, socioeconomic status, cultural and family values, and motor ability. When assessors cannot control for any of these factors, they must note alternate explanations in their test interpretations. In addition, contemporary psychologists face a new problem because of the increasing use of computers to administer tests and generate *automated interpretations*. Because such interpretations are typically based on evidence of varying reliability and validity estimates, it is the responsibility of the assessor to decide which statements in computer-generated reports are valid (cf. Eyde & Kowal, 1984).

It would be reasonable, consequently, to expect that clinical assessment would be more useful than testing alone. Surprisingly, adding clinicians' judgment to the mix often appears to hinder prediction of future events; that is, it is a source of error in such predictions. This is framed as an issue of *clinical versus statistical prediction*, as research has documented the problems that arise when it is the clinician (or employer, interviewer, and so forth) who combines test scores and other assessment information to make predictions about an individual's future behavior (Meehl, 1954, 1957, 1965; Wedding & Faust, 1989). Although more complicated than can be explained here, considerable evidence exists to suggest that test scores often make better predictors of future behavior or performance than clinical judgment (cf. Meier, 1994).

Deemphasizing Measurement Theory

Trait selection's emphasis on prediction as a key criterion for evaluating tests may also explain the relative dearth of measurement theories in psychology's first 50 years. From Binet onward, little agreement has been reached regarding explanations of the processes involved in psychological measurement. Substantial psychological theories have existed throughout psychology's history, of course, but they have not been applied to the issues of measuring psychological phenomena of interest. In addition, some early measurement psychologists clearly deemphasized theory. Gould (1981) reported that Spearman, for instance, suggested that psychologists forsake theory, instead taking psychology as the "barest empirical science. These he takes to be at bottom nothing but description and prediction. . . . The rest is mostly illumination by way of metaphor and similes" (p. 268). Similarly, Jessor and Hammond (1957) observed that "it is an artifact of tradition that theories have been utilized to derive experiments but not to derive tests" (p. 162).

Over time intelligence became defined as what was measured by intelligence tests, committing what Gould (1981) termed an *error of reification*. That is, mental testers came to believe that because the term *intelligence* was employed to label what intelligence tests supposedly measured, intelligence as a concept came to have an independent existence of its own. Nevertheless, it soon became apparent that no consensus could be reached about what constituted intelligence, and testers adopted a philosophy that one could value a procedure without understanding it (Cronbach, 1992). Freeman (1926, cited in Cronbach, 1992), for example, indicated that psychologists could measure intelligence even if they did not know what intelligence was. If the measurement procedure predicted something of interest, psychologists assumed that they would come to understand how it worked later. Decades later, psychologists may still avoid examining the meaning of what tests measure. Discussing personality measurement, Hogan and Nicholson (1988) indicated that the issue of what an item means to the respondent is irrelevant or misapplied to measurement. In support of this position they cited Meehl's (1954) argument that "item endorsements are interesting bits of verbal behavior whose nontest meanings remain to be determined" (p. 625). Epstein (1979) observed that "psychologists seem to take great pleasure in developing new scales (e.g., the nearly 500 Minnesota Multiphasic Personality Inventory [MMPI] scales), but little interest in determining what scores on them mean" (p. 381).

The issue of test meaning, however, has critical implications for validity. Martin (1988) noted that quite different societal and policy implications occur if one presents intelligence tests as partially flawed predictors of scholastic or occupational achievement as compared with tests of a person's stable capacity to learn. Martin (1988) suggested that if psychologists understand intelligence tests in terms of a stable capacity to learn, they will be inclined to use those scores in a policy of selection. However, if intelligence tests measure culture-specific cognitive skills, abilities, or aptitudes (cf. Gronlund, 1985, p. 296) that result at least partially from individuals' unique learning histories (as proposed by Thorndike cited by Dahlstrom, 1985), psychologists will develop intervention programs to improve those skills. Historically, psychologists have assumed that intellectual ability is indicated by scores on intelligence tests, regardless of test takers' cultural origins (Helms, 1992). Helms (1992) found that little research had been conducted to determine, for example, whether the ideas and concepts contained in intelligence test items are presented in language equally understood by all cultural groups. Helms maintained that good performance on such tests requires knowledge of white, rather than black, English language connotations and denotations. Given that few measurement theorists have paid attention to the processes involved in test response, it is not surprising that researchers have failed to investigate the test-taking processes and strategies of different cultural groups. But how many years of controversy in intelligence testing might have been avoided if the intellectual descendants of Binet had discussed their work in less general and more contextual terms?

Recent commentators continue to cite lack of theory as a major obstacle to developing better measurement and assessment instruments. Such observations are plentiful in the measurement and assessment literature:

> There are hundreds of psychological tests but no analysis in terms of basic explanatory principles, with no methodology for producing that connection. Personality theories arise either within naturalistic study—as in psychotherapy—or in the construction of psychometric instruments. (Staats, 1988, p. 4)

> Not only is there a need for more reliable and valid personality tests, but improvements in the theoretical bases of these instruments and in the criteria against which they are validated are necessary. . . . Many of these techniques represent relatively crude attempts to measure characteristics of human behavior. . . . It is generally recognized, however, that none of the available methods of assessing personality is completely satisfactory. The solution to the problem clearly lies in better research and development. (Aiken, 1989, p. 418)

Not only are new insights in short supply, but it is clear that not much thought of a theoretical nature has gone into the question [of psychological measurement]. Self-report personality research has had a strong emphasis on empiricism to the partial or total exclusion of theory. (Epstein, 1979, pp. 364, 377)

It is not the case, however, that the history of psychological measurement and assessment is devoid of attempts at theory development. By the middle of the 20th century, for example, evidence of more widespread interest in the processes of psychological measurement began to appear. The first technical recommendations for measurement produced by the APA were published in the mid-1950s. Cronbach and Meehl (1955) and Campbell and Fiske (1959) published their classic works on construct validity. Lord and Novick produced a major description of the concepts of item response theory in a 1968 publication, and Cronbach, Gleser, Nanda, and Rajaratnam described generalizability theory in a 1972 book. More recently, Wiley (1991) has proposed that instead of seeing test scores as reflecting a combination of true score and error score, one can see tests as reflecting *multiple validities,* two or more factors that influence test scores. One goal of any science—perhaps the major goal—is to increase the complexity of relevant theory by investigating errors, making them substantive factors in a theory (Kazdin, 1980). In other words, the statistician's error becomes the researcher's focus.

A relatively recent theoretical approach that focuses on understanding the multiple influences on test scores is *generalizability theory* (GT; Shavelson, Webb, & Rowley, 1989; Crocker & Algina, 1986; Brennan, 2005; Cronbach et al., 1972; Shavelson & Webb, 1991). GT approaches differ from classical test theory in several respects. First, the concept of reliability is replaced by *generalizability,* the ability to generalize a score from one testing context to others. GT recognizes that error is not always random; systematic error can be identified by examining variability of measurement data over conditions, called *facets.* GT suggests that multiple sources, including persons, content, occasions, and observers, can affect measurement devices; GT provides a theoretical and statistical framework for identifying and estimating the magnitude of those sources. Given this information, researchers can then compare the relative effects of different measurement conditions. By knowing the most important sources of measurement variability, they can design measurement devices and procedures to minimize undesired sources.

GT suggests that with any particular test, a universe of conditions exist that may affect test scores. Investigations of the relative effects of such conditions are called *G studies.* The results of G studies can then be used to design studies to identify sources of variability and error in situations where test scores will be employed to make real decisions about individuals.

These latter studies, termed *D studies*, can help modify some aspect of the testing conditions to provide the most precise data possible (e.g., standardize interviewer training, as noted in the previous example). Because of its potential applicability to investigating sources of error, GT would seem to have considerable potential for research focusing on theory development about psychological measurement and assessment.

Shavelson et al. (1989) described an application of GT in a study of disaster survivors' psychological impairment (Gleser, Green, & Winget, 1978). Two interviewers assessed 20 survivors; two raters then used the resulting interviews to determine survivors' impairment. Gleser et al. (1978) estimated variance components for the effects of survivors, raters, interviewers, and their interactions. Two components produced the largest variance: survivors (indicating individual differences between subjects) and the survivor-by-interviewer interaction (indicating measurement error, i.e., the interviewers produced inconsistent information from their interviews with different survivors). These results suggest that to improve the generalizability of measurement, the researchers should standardize the interviewers' procedures. Other potential sources of variation that might have been investigated include the different occasions of interviewing and the interview questions.

Loss of Precision

Although Binet thought that his tasks were more valid than physiological measures, he also believed that he had lost the precision of these laboratory methods (Freeman, 1955). *Precision* has been described as the degree of exactness with which a quantity is measured (Murphy, Hollon, Zitzewitz, & Smoot, 1986) or the ability of a measurement device to detect small differences (Babor, Brown, & Del Boca, 1990). Binet did sacrifice some precision. Although psychophysiological tasks such as reaction time could reliably detect small differences, Binet indicated that his intelligence tests would yield a classification or hierarchy that would suffice for practice. The practicing psychologist, then as now, needed a procedure that could produce gross, but reliable differences between subjects who were high, medium, or low in various cognitive abilities. With Binet's tasks, psychologists possessed a reasonable, data-based procedure for selection purposes.

Similarly, Stevens (1951) described the concept of *scale types*. *Nominal* scales are those that contain qualitative categories (e.g., red, blue, or green) but do not have information about differences in amount. *Ordinal* scales describe objects that differ from each other by some amount and that may be ranked in terms of that amount. *Interval* scales describe objects whose differences are marked by equal intervals, and *ratio* scales are interval scales that possess a zero point. Ordinal scales provide more precise information than nominal, interval more than ordinal, and so on. Given this background, I employ *precision* to refer to the ability of a measurement device to produce data that reflect the ordering, range, and distinctions of a phenomenon at a level sufficient for a particular purpose (cf. Nay, 1979).

Many psychological tests can successfully place individuals into broad, but distinct categories; a general consensus exists that psychological tests produce ordinal-level data. This presents problems for many purposes for which psychological tests might be employed. For example, suppose a hypothetical test classifies individuals as possessing low, medium, or high amounts of a psychological characteristic. Individuals who score at the top and bottom of that test (1) really differ by a substantial amount on the measured characteristic and (2) are likely to behave differently on some criterion that the test has been demonstrated to predict. More uncertain, however, is whether the test could distinguish between the people who score in the middle range and those in the extreme groups. For example, Kendall, Hollon, Beck, Hammen, and Ingram (1987) reviewed research with the Beck Depression Inventory (BDI) that found that more than 50% of individuals classified as depressed or not depressed change categories when retested, even when retesting occurs within only hours or days. If an insurer employed BDI scores to make decisions about when to terminate psychotherapy with depressed individuals, for example, we would have little confidence that a BDI classification of "nondepressed," after a period of treatment with any client, would remain stable for even a short period of time. Unfortunately, "one feature which all psychological tests share in common is their limited precision" (Murphy & Davidshofer, 1988, p. 2).

The important question about imprecision in psychological tests is, What causes it? I suggest that imprecision is caused by the presence of the aforementioned *multiple invalidities*. That is, because every psychological test is influenced by more than one factor, a score on a psychological test reflects multiple causes. When one or more influences facilitate the interpretation of test scores for a particular purpose, those influences can be termed *validities*. Other influences, however, that hinder the interpretation of test scores are *invalidities*. In the case of the BDI, for example, it may be that responses to many of its items are influenced by a person's transient moods. As a measure of the effects of counseling and psychotherapy, however, we might prefer a test of an emotional state that measures depression more reliably.

Limited precision is important because even a cursory review of the history of science supports the idea that new measurement techniques drive scientific development (Cone & Foster, 1991; Forbes & Dijksterhuis, 1963). As Tryon (1991) stated, "The history of science is largely coextensive with the history of measurement" (p. 1). Cone (1988) agreed: "It is certainly beyond argument that the building of all science rests on a foundation of accurate measurement" (p. 42). Meehl (1991) provided several examples: In chemistry, spectroscopy made possible knowledge about the composition of the stars; in biology, refinement of methods of measuring adenine and thymine along with advancements in X-ray technology made possible Watson and Crick's discovery of the structure of DNA. Philosophers of science note that scientific progress is not solely dependent on measurement advances, but new measurement techniques have allowed refined tests between rival theories and hypotheses (cf. Ellis, 1967). Continuous innovation in measurement theory and techniques seems to be important for progress in any science (Judson, 1980; Kuhn, 1970). Tryon (1991) indicated that this progress results from a measurement method's capacity to provide new data for ideas, extend human senses into new domains, and correct for limitations of human senses.

Dramatic examples of the link between measurement and scientific progress are particularly evident in astronomy. Galileo did not invent the telescope, but he employed it to observe Jupiter and its revolving moons, thus setting the stage for acceptance of a heliocentric view of the solar system. Galileo also encountered a validity problem familiar to measurement psychologists. Forbes and Dijksterhuis (1963) wrote that "no one yet understood the operation of the telescope and it is doubtful whether Galileo did so himself. In any case he made no attempt to prove that what he saw in his telescope really existed" (p. 210). Galileo could make basic observations and predictions with his telescope, but he could provide little evidence to verify the truthfulness of what he saw.

Progress in astronomical observation has been particularly rapid in the 20th century. As illustrated in the accompanying figures, instruments aboard NASA spacecrafts revolutionized astronomers' knowledge of the outer planets with such discoveries as volcanic eruptions on a moon of Jupiter, and the Hubble telescope aided similar discoveries of such esoteric objects as black holes. Figures 2.3, 2.4, 2.5, and 2.6 show the striking advances made in the observation of Saturn. The first photo displays drawings of Saturn created in the 17th century by early observers such as Galileo, who thought that the object(s) surrounding Saturn were ears. The second photo, made by an 100-inch telescope at the Mount Wilson Observatory in 1943, clearly shows several divisions of the ring. The third photo, made by the Voyager

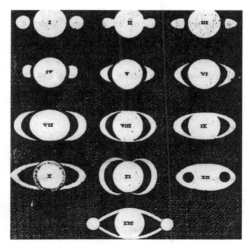

FIGURE 2.3. Early depictions of Saturn, around 1610–1644. From Alexander (1962). Copyright 1962 by Carnegie Observatories. Reprinted by permission.

spacecraft in 1981, displays considerably more detail; the fourth photo was made in 2004 and shows detail similar to that provided by Voyager. I would place psychological measurement's progress at the level of the 1943 photograph: We can observe basic surface structure, but very little detail.

What could account for the failure to produce more precise tests and the scientific progress that comes with them? Traditional views of the research process describe a cycle whereby theory produces inquiry and the resulting data refine and change theory. Platt (1977), for example, described the desired process as follows:

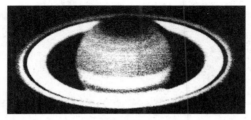

FIGURE 2.4. Saturn and ring system photographed in 1943 by 100-inch Hooker telescope, Mount Wilson Observatory. From Alexander (1962). Copyright 1962 by Carnegie Observatories. Reprinted by permission.

FIGURE 2.5. Voyager 2 photograph of Saturn ring system. Reprinted courtesy of the Jet Propulsion Laboratory, California Institute of Technology, Pasadena, CA. Reprinted by permission.

1. Formulate two or more competing hypotheses.
2. Devise a study that unambiguously contrasts those hypotheses.
3. Run a clean study (i.e., free of methodological explanations for the results).
4. Use the results to reject unsupported hypotheses.
5. Recycle the procedure.

FIGURE 2.6. Cassini 2005 photo of Saturn's moon Dione, with edge-on rings below.

This sequence of steps is designed to produce a conclusion with few or no alternative explanations. Research data, however, heavily depend on the quality or lack thereof of the measurement procedures used to procure it. If measurement problems are substantial, it is impossible to successfully complete Platt's component 3, run a clean study. Instead, problematic measurement presents a methodological alternative explanation. Meehl (1967), Kazdin (1980), and Dar (1987) all observed that when researchers fail to confirm expected relations in their work, they frequently dismiss the findings on the basis of scales' supposed low reliability or validity. Kazdin (1980) observed that "a common tactic among researchers is to lament the lack of sensitivity of a dependent measure as a possible explanation for the lack of findings" (p. 221). The investigator suspends judgment on experimental hypotheses because suspected measurement problems cause empirical results to be rejected; this stymies research progress. Lipsey (1990, 1998) presented a similar argument with the concept of *design sensitivity*, in which he suggested that problematic measurement methods can lower the power of research designs to detect effects.

The Wisdom and Tyranny of Tradition

As previously indicated, psychologists appear to ignore problems with a measurement procedure if the device fulfills a selection purpose. Psychologists have long employed intelligence tests because of the tests' predictive capacities, though we don't know precisely what they measure. The MMPI does not possess the predictive validity of intelligence tests, but MMPI proponents point to 10,000 published studies (Graham, 1990) as evidence that its effectiveness as a scale is well established.

In the context of continuing unresolved scientific questions, considerable safety exists in the use of a traditional test, particularly if no viable or distinct alternative exists. Surveys of clinicians find that the clinicians rely on traditional measures such as the MMPI and the clinical interview (Lubin, Larsen, & Matarazzo, 1984; May & Scott, 1989; Murphy & Davidshofer, 1988; Piotrowski & Lubin, 1990; Piotrowski & Keller, 1984, 1989). Researchers creating new tests often imitate previous measures. Developers of new intelligence tests, for example, have even borrowed the same items from previous tests. Jackson (1992) reported that Weschler used items from the Army Beta in the Weschler–Bellevue intelligence test. Hathaway (1972) noted that psychologists continue to employ 1940s technology in the use of the MMPI; it took nearly 50 years before a revision of the MMPI was accomplished. Similarly, Gynther and Green (1982) suggested that traditional self-report methodology had advanced no further since the scales of the 1940s and 1950s. Buros (1970) suggested that "it is sobering to think that our most widely used instruments in personality assessment were published 20, 30, 40 or even more years ago" (p. xxv).

Moderate success and a lack of alternatives may motivate psychologists to stick with traditional instruments. A side effect of this is that psychologists minimize the problems of the original devices and don't explore or experiment with new approaches that represent potential improvements. As Kaplan (1964) noted, "A conspicuously successful technique in some area of behavioral science is not only identified with 'scientific method,' but comes to be so mechanically applied that it undermines the very spirit of scientific inquiry" (p. 29). If problems do become so severe as to force an abandonment of a particular measurement procedure, psychologists have tended to recycle the procedure again at a later date. Interviews, for example, have been employed throughout psychology's history, but they fell into disfavor when research suggested that interview data could be influenced by numerous factors, such as interviewer race and gender (Murphy & Davidshofer, 1988), and that interviews were more reactive (i.e., transparent in intent) than questionnaires (Stone, 1978). Goldstein and Hersen (1990) observed, however, that "following a period when the use of the interview was eschewed by many psychologists, it has made a return. It would appear that the field is in a historical spiral, with various methods leaving and returning at different levels" (p. 4).

The Success and Failure of the Market

Any of these problems with the psychological measurement paradigm could have eventually derailed the enterprise. For example, if the field has no consensus about what intelligence tests measure—the most basic validity question one could ask—why do professionals continue to use them? A plausible answer is that despite their problems, psychological tests provide substantial benefits to society, that is, they continue to be socially relevant. A more complete answer, however, should also acknowledge the influence of the marketplace.

As a business student in my testing class pointed out, profit incentives, rather than scientific motives, appear to have driven much test development. By 1923 roughly half of the members of the APA were stockholders in a major test publisher, the Psychological Corporation (O'Muircheartaigh, 1997). Heidbreder in 1933 could distinguish between the traditional experimentalists, who preferred the elaborate apparatus of the laboratory, and the mental testers who were allied with applied psychologists working in industry, education, and clinics. Not only did experimental and psychometric work become separated, but psychological measurement became closely associated with applied psychology. This link continues today and can be seen in contemporary measurement textbooks that begin with a few chapters describing basic principles, followed by chapters describing specific tests in such areas as personnel psychology, counseling and clinical psychology, and educational and school psychology. From one perspective, the typical measurement and assessment text can be seen essentially as a catalogue of psychological tests that students will purchase and employ in their subsequent training experiences and careers.

Military, medical, educational, clinical, and business organizations were and continue to be the principal purchasers of psychological tests, and these groups remain primarily interested in the use of tests for selection and prediction. And the purchases are large: One estimate placed the value of the market for standardized educational achievement testing alone between $400 million and $700 million annually (Public Broadcasting System, 2005). That does not includes tests sold for other purposes, including personality assessment or assessment in business and industry. An advertisement in the American Psychological Association (1992) *Monitor* estimated that 20,000 psychological, behavioral, and cognitive measures are created annually. As Blaney (1992) noted, "this proliferation of scales probably arises in part from the fact that rewards—in citations and in dollars—may accrue from developing a scale or test which takes hold" (p. 55). Despite modest theoretical development or innovation, test publishers, test developers, and test users have done very well financially. Add the relative testing illiteracy of most mental health professionals (Lambert, 1991) to the typical consumer/client's near-ignorance of testing principles (cf. Paul, 2004), and a reasonable prediction is that the testing marketplace will continue to fail to produce significant innovation.

The introduction and growth of managed care and insurance companies in funding mental health services represents another failure of the market. Managed care organizations (MCOs) and other funding agencies in the 1990s initially pressed those who provide mental health services to provide evidence of effectiveness (Davis & Meier, 2001). The result was a renewed emphasis on measuring change, improving outcomes, and program evaluation, as managed care companies promised they would emphasize accountability and quality. For a variety of reasons, however, most managed care companies appear to have abandoned efforts to employ outcome data to increase quality and efficiency of clinical services (Davis & Meier, 2001).

Clement (1999) observed, "As I became involved with many MCOs, I was surprised by their apparent lack of interest in evaluating treatment outcomes" (pp. 91–92). Instead, many MCOs appear to focus on maximizing profits by denying services through utilization reviews that employ only rudimentary assessment instruments such as the Global Assessment of Functioning (GAF) scale.

Finally, researchers are just beginning to study whether the financial conflict of interest (FCOI) found in professions such as medicine also influence the actions of individuals involved in psychological testing. The basic premise of a FCOI is that an individual may have competing interests, as when an author of a published test may not wish to report information that questions the usefulness of that test. Truscott, Baumgart, and Rogers (2004) noted that recent reports in the medical and biotechnology fields show that FCOI can bias research, impede the dissemination of scientific information, and use publications in scientific journals to influence consumers. Truscott et al. (2004) summarized research, for example, that found researchers who conducted literature reviews about the effects of passive smoking and concluded that it was not harmful, were likely to have affiliations with tobacco companies. In their study, Truscott et al. investigated potential FCOI in assessment-related research published during 1997–2001 in six school psychology journals. They found evidence of FCOI in 26% of the assessment articles and also noted that researchers rarely acknowledged their financial interests in tests they investigated.

Summary and Implications

Decisions made early in the development of a scientific discipline influence subsequent trends and events (Danziger, 1990). The concept of a trait was the primary unit adopted by many early measurement psychologists. Although development and change were recognized, stable and enduring traits best fit early psychologists' assumptions about human nature and how they measured it. Consistency was understandable; inconsistency was error. Similarly, the testing paradigm focused on selection as the key purpose of measurement and assessment. In the early 20th century, psychological testing became a legitimate activity in the service of selection decisions for schools, the military, and business; contemporary commercial test publishing continues this approach. In many domains, psychological testing remains the best and fairest method for making decisions—regarding whom to hire, recruit, admit.

Classical test theory and its accompanying statistical emphasis provided a basic framework for understanding test scores as a combination of true score (of a trait) and error. More recently, item response theory (IRT), also trait focused and employing statistical concepts, has begun to succeed classical test theory. Test developers and psychometric researchers investigate relationships among constructs through correlational methods; experimental methods that might have been used to deepen theoretical understanding have been seen as irrelevant. Important problems such as method variance and state effects could be not be explained much beyond a descriptive level. Theoretical work aimed at better understanding of measurement processes in domains related to change resulting from psychosocial interventions was largely neglected or ignored.

Consequently, in areas as diverse as intelligence testing and the effectiveness of counseling and psychotherapy, crises and controversies stemming from measurement issues frequently occur. They may fade away, and then eventually reappear. Application of the trait selection paradigm to domains that are not trait-based or where the principal purpose is not selection often produces unexpected results. For example, psychotherapists frequently chose to measure therapy outcomes with traditional tests such as the MMPI that were not originally constructed for assessing change (Froyd, Lambert, & Froyd, 1996). Vermeersch et al. (2004) identified the MMPI as a example of an inappropriate outcome measure because "it is excessively long, very expensive, and contains many items that are not sensitive to change" (p. 38). As described in Chapter 1, researchers who have studied outcome measures' sensitivity to change have demonstrated that such tests differ considerably in their ability to detect the types and amount of change following therapy. Lambert et al. (1986) compared the Zung, Beck, and Hamilton depression scales as outcome measures of mental health interventions and concluded that "rating devices can by themselves produce differences larger than those ordinarily attributed to treatments" (p. 58). It is indeed a problem when the outcome measure itself can contribute to the estimate of the amount of change as much as or more than the intervention. In this context it is also not surprising that knowledge in the field about the efficacy and effectiveness of counseling and psychotherapy might be characterized as broad but not deep.

How then we can deepen and elaborate measurement and assessment theory and practices beyond trait conceptualizations employed for selection purposes? The aim of the next chapters in this book is to explore problems and potential explanations related to method variance and state effects. Better understanding of method variance and state effects offers the possibility of improving measurement and assessment of change.

General Measurement-Related Writing Assignment

Choose a theoretical construct you intend to measure (or are likely to measure) in the future. Conduct a brief literature review to find at least three sources who provide a theoretical (not operational) definition of that construct. In a table, report the author/year of each source (e.g., Davis, 2005) and the specific definition offered by that source. In the table underline all the important content domains specified by the definitions.

Change-Related Writing Assignment

Choose a theoretical construct you intend to measure (or are likely to measure) in the future for the purpose of assessing change. Conduct a brief literature review to find at least three sources who provide a theoretical (not operational) definition of that construct. In a table, report the author/year of each source (e.g., Davis, 2005) and the specific definition offered by that source. In the table underline all the important content domains specified by the definitions. Note whether any of the definitions address how the construct may be manifested differently as it changes.

QUESTIONS AND EXERCISES

1. For 3 minutes, write down what you consider the major ideas of this section, chapter, or class. At the beginning of next week's class, share with the group.

2. This chapter described a number of significant influences on psychological tests. Take 1 minute and write down what you consider the single most important factor that historically has influenced psychological tests. Then share the topic you chose with the instructor, who should create a list of student-nominated topics. Once the list is constructed, is there a consensus about a few important influences? Or does the class have very different ideas about what is most influential?

3. Write brief definitions for the following terms: *individual differences, intelligence, traits, error, method variance, correlation coefficient, nomothetic, idiographic, multiple validities,* and *precision.*

4. In small groups or individually, summarize the unintended consequences of the success of the trait-based selection paradigm in psychological testing.

5. In small groups or individually, consider this: Kuhn (1970) described the idea of a scientific paradigm in which a discipline essentially adopts a single, major ap-

proach to dealing with an issue or problem. If psychological testing has adopted the assumptions and methods of trait-based selection testing, what does that imply for other types of psychological tests that attempt to measure phenomena other than traits and for purposes other than selection? For example, how might clinical assessments or classroom tests be influenced by the prevailing paradigm? Report your ideas to the class as a whole.

CHAPTER 3

Reliability, Validity, and Systematic Errors

Introduction

Perhaps the most unexpected finding related to the measurement of psychological traits took many decades to recognize and formally address. *Method variance* refers to the fact that a portion of every test score can be attributed to the particular method employed to obtain or produce data (Campbell & Fiske, 1959). That is, scores on a test always reflect the method of measurement as well as the construct measured; it is interesting and troublesome that the method of measurement can sometimes exert a substantial influence. This chapter presents an overview and examples regarding the recognition and investigation of the effects of method variance and related issues. As described in the next section, the central theme of that history involves the evolution of thinking about test validity.

In testing related to counseling and psychotherapy, two methods are predominant: *self-reports* and *interviews*. The second half of the chapter illustrates how unwanted errors associated with these methods can influence test scores. To understand how method variance and other systematic errors can interfere with the interpretation of test scores, I begin by describing *reliability* and *validity estimates*, the key ideas employed in evaluating educational and psychological tests.

Thinking about Reliability and Validity

The classic definition of validity is that a valid test measures what it is supposed to measure. Cronbach (1992) reported that such a definition was officially noted in a 1921 publication by a group that became the American Educational Research Association (AERA). From this perspective, a test of honesty that actually measures honesty is valid; an honesty test which measures social desirability and honesty is less valid; an honesty test that measures only social desirability is invalid. Validity has been contrasted with reliability: *Reliability* is the consistency of scores on the same test, whereas *validity* is the consistency of scores between related tests (Campbell & Fiske, 1959). Similarly, Mischel (1968) defined reliability as agreement between tests under maximally similar conditions, and validity as agreement under maximally dissimilar conditions. It is important to recognize, however, that tests themselves do not possess reliability or validity. Rather, reliability and validity *estimates* are based on data provided by a sample of individuals with certain characteristics who complete the test under certain conditions. Consequently, reliability and validity estimates are not static, but assume a range of values that partially depend on variables other than the test itself.

Types of Validity

Validity during much of the 20th century was conceived of as the ability of a test to predict a criterion (Cronbach, 1957). Thus, *criterion validity* (or *predictive validity*, if the criterion is a future event) refers to validating a test by correlating its scores with those of a relevant criterion. For example, if you wish to predict who will succeed as a manager in a company, you need a test that correlates positively with indices of managerial success and negatively with indices of managerial failure. Similarly, if you develop a test to measure psychopathology, you could validate the test by comparing its scores with those of mental health professionals' ratings, or by comparing test scores of a group of persons with known psychopathology with those of a group of normal individuals. A second type of validity that historically has been influential is *face validity*, which concerns whether test content (items and instructions) appear to measure the subject of interest. For reasons explained below, face validity has never been a serious criterion for evaluating tests.

At least two factors influenced psychologists to refine their thinking about test validity. Before 1950, little consensus existed about a theory of validity (Cronbach & Meehl, 1955). Psychologists proposed numerous types of validity, such as intrinsic (Gulliksen, 1950), logical and empirical (Cronbach, 1949), factorial (Guilford, 1946), and face (Mosier, 1947), but it was difficult to know how to develop or recognize valid tests. Some structure was needed to organize and make sense of the diverse ways of thinking about validity.

Criterion validity itself also posed problems. First, a test that could predict managerial success was seen as having little generalizability to other nonmanagerial situations. Thus, data from this test would offer limited utility for formulating general scientific laws (Loevinger, 1957). In the clinical area, psychologists did not wish for their tests to be ultimately validated against criteria such as psychiatrists' ratings (Cronbach, 1992). Finally, criteria are also measurements that share many of the difficulties of predictors. These issues provided an impetus to develop other methods of test validation.

In response to the disorganization of validity concepts and the over-emphasis on criterion validity, the American Psychological Association (APA) published in 1954 its *Standards for Psychological Tests*. Those standards recognized four types of validity: *predictive, concurrent, content,* and *construct*. Concurrent validity was identical to predictive validity, except that with concurrent validity, predictor and criterion were measured at the same time. Later versions of the *Standards* (e.g., APA, 1985) combined predictive and concurrent validity into criterion validity.

Content validity and *construct validity* were concerned with whether a test measured what it was supposed to measure. Content validity focused on the content of the test items and their relation to the intended domain of the test. For a test to be valid in this sense, a test developer had to demonstrate that the content of a test's items was representative of the universe of relevant content. In achievement testing, for example, content validity results when test items (e.g., addition, subtraction) match the instructional topics (e.g., mathematics). Construct validity focused more on the abstract construct the test actually measured, regardless of test item content or other factors. For example, an honesty test might be composed of self-report items that apparently have little to do with honest behavior (e.g., "I always get up at 6:30 A.M.") but when aggregated are significantly correlated with honest behavior in some situations.

Initially, testers viewed content and construct validity as unrelated to the two other sorts of validity proposed in the APA document. Predictive and concurrent validity were evaluated by the validity of decisions based on tests. For example, if the criterion was first-year college GPA and Test A correlated with GPA at .40, it would possess greater predictive validity than a test that correlated at .30. Nevertheless, attempts to estimate the construct validity of Test A might well fail; that is, test developers might not understand what the test measured, even if it could predict GPA. As described in Chapter 2, much effort during the first 50 years of psychological measurement was devoted to finding tests that predicted socially relevant criteria.

Despite this initial split, the contemporary view places construct validity as the fundamental type of validity on which the other types depend (Anastasi, 1992; Kagan, 1988). As shown in Figure 3.1, predictive validity depends on construct validity because it is the psychological phenomena that both test and criterion measure that determine the relation between the two. I use the term *phenomena* deliberately to indicate that scores on any particular psychological test reflect multiple influences. More recent perspectives on validity recognize that tests possess multiple validities and invalidities (Meehl, 1991; Wiley, 1991). If one does not understand the multiple factors affecting test scores, then estimates of predictive validity are likely to be inconsistent because influences of scores on both predictor and criterion are not well understood.

The test developer must have knowledge of a test's validities and in-

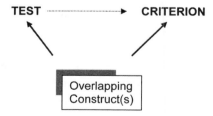

FIGURE 3.1. The strength of the relationship between a test and a criterion the test intends to predict depends on the extent to which the test and criterion share one or more constructs.

validities, in regard to a particular testing purpose, to understand how the predictor–criterion relation generalizes across situations. In addition, test developers concerned with predictive validity usually start the test development process with a large pool of items and determine which items (or aggregations of items) correlate with the criterion. Some of those correlations are likely to reflect actual predictor–criterion relations and some are likely to occur by chance. Indeed, if the initial estimate of predictive validity capitalizes on chance (which is likely to occur when the test developer uses the same individuals to evaluate test items and then correlates the resulting items with an external criterion), subsequent estimates are likely to be lower. This is the typical outcome of *cross validation* research, in which the psychometric properties of a scale found in one evaluation are checked in a second study.

Currently, definitions of construct validity focus less specifically on what a test measures and more on whether evidence exists to support that tests can be interpreted in terms of a certain use or purpose, that is, on the inferences drawn from test scores (American Educational Research Association, American Psychological Association, & National Council on Measurement in Education, 1999). In a counseling context, a clinician might be interested in screening clients at intake to identify those who might be more likely to drop out of therapy. If a test showed an ability to discriminate between future dropouts and continuers, that would provide evidence of predictive validity for this screening purpose (regardless of our knowledge of what the test actually measured). Note also that tests of predictive validity can be particularly useful in clinical contexts for avoiding hypothesis confirmation bias (Meier, 2003). By making a prediction about future events, we establish an explicit test for deciding whether to keep, modify, or abandon the explanation on which the prediction was based (Hill, 1991).

Constructs, Theories, and Valid Measurement

To understand construct validity, one must first understand the meaning of the term *construct*. Cronbach and Meehl (1955) defined a construct as an attribute of individuals evidenced by test performance. Murphy and David-shofer (1988, p. 98) defined constructs as "abstract summaries of some regularity in nature" indicated by observable events. Both of these definitions connect unobservable, latent constructs to observable events or behaviors.

Constructs are important in that they potentially allow generalizations beyond any specific situation at any particular point in time. They enable theorists to create scientific laws and to appropriately name phenomena. Cook and Campbell (1979) indicated that demonstrating the validity of constructs is crucial to all types of psychological research, both experimental and correlational. They wrote that "it should be clearly noted that construct validity concerns are not limited to cause and effect constructs. All aspects of the research require naming samples in generalizable terms, including samples of people and settings as well as samples of measures or manipulations" (p. 59).

Construct Explication

As indicated in Figure 3.2, some constructs may not be directly related to behaviors but rather to other constructs that are related to those behaviors. The process of describing the relations between abstract constructs and observable events is known as *construct explication*. Murphy and Davidshofer (1988) offered one description of this process:

1. Identify behaviors related to the constructs;
2. Identify related constructs;
3. Identify behaviors of these other constructs and see if they overlap with behaviors of original construct.

Suppose, for example, a research team develops a measure of depression. They might begin by reading the research literature and discovering that other researchers have proposed a number of behaviors thought to be

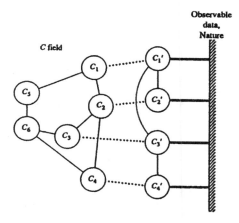

FIGURE 3.2. Relations between constructs and data. As Torgerson (1958) explained, constructs on the right lie close to real-world phenomena. Those on the left have no operational definition, but are connected to observable data via another set of constructs. From Torgerson (1958). Copyright 1958 by Social Science Research Council. Reprinted by permission.

associated with depression, such as disturbed sleep, loss of interest in usual activities, significant changes in weight, fatigue, and diminished cognitive abilities (American Psychiatric Association, 2000). Related constructs might include fear and anxiety, associated with such behaviors as excessive worry, irritability, trouble with concentration, and physical discomforts such as palpitations, sweating, and shaking (American Psychiatric Association, 2000). Given that the behaviors on the two lists are not especially alike, the researchers should be able to develop a depression scale that does not correlate with measures of fear or anxiety. If they employ depression and anxiety measures with a group of individuals and find low intercorrelations, they would have produced a useful start on construct explication as well as a *nomological net*, a description of relations between constructs and behaviors that constitute a theory (Cronbach & Meehl, 1955). If they find unexpectedly high correlations, however, a problem exists with the measurement devices or with the theory that suggests such construct–behavior links.

Nomological networks are desirable for constructs that theorists do not believe should be linked to one specific behavior. For a construct such as aggressiveness, theorists might not wish to define it solely as the occurrence, for example, of one person physically striking another. As Murphy and Davidshofer (1988) wrote,

> We cannot say precisely what aggressiveness is, but we can describe how an aggressive child might act and we can make reliable and meaningful statements about children's level of aggressiveness by observing their behavior. The more detail included in descriptions of the nomological network, the more precision there will be in describing constructs. (p. 101)

Few or no "incontrovertible indices" (Cone, 1988, p. 58) exist that enable us to operationally define psychological phenomena. Peterson (1968) stated that few "clear-cut types of behavior disorders … seem to occur in nature" (p. 5). Ordinarily, behavior is multiply determined and that means that scores on psychological measurements always reflect multiple validities and invalidities.

Multitrait–Multimethod Matrices: Investigating the Effects of Method Variance on Validity

If construct validity is the key type of validity, then evaluations of construct validity would seem to be central to understanding the psychometric properties of tests. Yet Murphy and Davidshofer (1988) observed that when assessing validity, test developers have no standards to compare tests against; it is for that reason that measurement psychologists seldom use the term *accuracy* when discussing tests. Instead, psychologists gather evidence from a variety of sources to demonstrate validity. Cronbach and Meehl (1955) suggested that construct validity could be investigated through studies of group differences, correlation matrices and factor analysis, the internal structure of tests (e.g., item intercorrelations), change over occasions, and studies of individuals' test-taking performance. Cronbach (1989) later amended that list to include the examination of items, internal correlations, score stability, protocol analysis of tests, varying test procedures experimentally, attempts to improve scores, correlation with practical criteria and other tests, and studies of group differences. Similarly, Murphy and Davidshofer (1988) wrote that laboratory and field experiments, questionnaires, and unobtrusive observations might provide construct validity data. Murphy and Davidshofer concluded that "it would be fair to say that any type of data or statistic might be useful in determining construct validity" (p. 103). Anastasi (1986) reached a similar conclusion: "Almost any information gathered in the process of developing or using a test is relevant to its validity" (p. 3).

Thus, a variety of criteria for evaluating the construct validity of any test were available. As described below, Campbell and Fiske (1959) offered one of the first well-organized approaches, and many of their basic approaches to evaluating validity remain in use today.

Campbell and Fiske

Campbell and Fiske (1959) culminated the efforts to describe test validity in the 1950s by providing a theoretical framework and pragmatic methods for evaluating the construct validity of a psychological test. First, they proposed that to be valid, a test of a particular construct should be more highly related to another test of the same construct (what is known as *convergent validity*) than to tests of other constructs or tests (i.e., *discriminant validity*). For example, if leadership and aggressiveness are conceptualized as two distinct traits, then two measures of leadership should correlate more highly with each other (convergent validity) than with any measure of aggressiveness (discriminant validity). Second, Campbell and Fiske (1959) observed that method variance is present in all psychological measures. As Cronbach (1957) put it, "Every score mixes general construct-relevance variance with variance specific to the particular measuring operation" (p. 676). Campbell and Fiske suggested that any test of a construct should be treated as a trait–method unit. Method and trait could be considered distinct influences. Thus, two measures of leadership should intercorrelate highly even if they are measured by different methods (e.g., self-report and ratings of observed behavior). Correlations of identical traits should be higher than any of the correlations between different traits measured via identical methods.

Criteria for Construct Validity

Using these principles, Campbell and Fiske proposed that construct validity be evaluated through the construction of a correlation matrix that displays correlations between tests of at least two different trait constructs and at least two different methods measuring those constructs. They employed the term *multitrait–multimethod matrices* (MTMMs) to describe such correlation tables. To clarify the convergent validity of a construct, a similar construct to the one in question should be included as well as a dissimilar construct. They also indicated that the methods employed to measure constructs are to be as different as possible so that there is no reason for believing that they share method variance. If such diversity is not possible, Campbell and Fiske (1959) suggested that "efforts should be made to obtain as much diversity as possible in terms of data-sources and classification processes" (p. 103).

Campbell and Fiske (1959) proposed specific criteria to demonstrate convergent and discriminant validity. First, reliability values of tests of the construct of interest should be high. Second, correlations between measures of the same trait should be substantial and significantly different from zero. These validity coefficients should indicate how the same trait is predictable by differing measurement methods. For discriminant validity, the first criterion indicates that the convergent validity value for a construct should be higher than the correlations between that construct and any other construct having neither trait nor method in common. Second, a construct should correlate more highly with independent measurements of the same trait than with measures of different traits that employ the same methodology. Third, the pattern of intercorrelations among constructs should be similar across the multitrait–multimethod matrix.

Campbell and Fiske's (1959) criteria appear to be relatively simple qualifications for psychological tests to meet. However, if shared method variance is substantial, correlations between different constructs measured similarly are likely to be high and is interpreted as evidence against construct validity. As Campbell and Fiske (1959) stated, "To the extent that irrelevant method variance contributes to the scores obtained, these scores are invalid" (p. 84). The critical question then becomes, To what extent does method variance influence psychological tests?

The answer in the literature seems to be: To a great extent. Campbell and Fiske (1959) reviewed several studies in which the highest correlations found in the MTMMs were those of different constructs measured by the same method. They concluded that their conditions for construct validity "are rarely met. Method or apparatus factors make very large contributions to psychological measurements" (p. 104). Among Campbell and Fiske's examples of the influence of method on measurement were Thorndike's (1920) halo effects, the finding of apparatus effects on research with laboratory animals, and Cronbach's (1946, 1950) response sets. Significant questions about construct validity remain even with intelligence tests and cognitive traits (e.g., Lohman, 1989). The lack of evidence for discriminant validity, coupled with the fact that scale developers infrequently perform rigorous evaluations of scales' divergent qualities, raises doubt about the foundations of many psychological research programs and practical applications.

Campbell and Fiske (1959) predicted that this problem would be resolved when measurement theorists described method variance more specifically in terms of explanatory constructs. They wrote that "it will then be recognized that measurement procedures usually involve several theoretical constructs in joint application" (p. 102). Understanding and controlling method variance to obtain a more valid score of the psychological construct of interest remains an important goal in psychological measurement. If test scores largely reflect measurement procedures, it becomes impossible to create constructs that generalize across methods. Although MTMMs and, more recently, *structural equation modeling* (SEM; see Heppner, Kivlighan, & Wampold, 1999) can provide an estimate of method effects, the major purposes of testing, such as theory building, selection, and measuring change, are typically hindered by method variance.

An MTMM Example

Clinicians and theorists have long wondered about the distinctness and overlap between the constructs of anxiety, depression, and stress (e.g., Moras, Di Nardo, & Barlow, 1992; Tellegen, 1985). These psychological phenomena are widespread in the population (American Psychiatric Association, 2000) and are believed related to other psychological traits and states (e.g., Zigler & Glick, 1988). Clinical lore and some empirical evidence indicates that persons experiencing high levels of stress are more likely to become physically ill (e.g., Cohen & Edwards, 1989; Martin, 1989), but depressed persons also seem more prone to illness (Anisman & Zacharko, 1992; Harris, 1991). Researchers in the area of stress and depression, however, tend to treat each area as relatively distinct.

Meier (1984) employed Campbell and Fiske's MTMM approach in a study of the construct validity of occupational stress. In addition to stress, measures of depression and personal orderliness (i.e., personal neatness, chosen as a discriminant construct) were selected. Because these constructs are primarily measured through self-reports, methods selected for this study were differences in self-report response mode. That is, measures of stress, depression, and orderliness were chosen by the formats of Likert scale, true–false response, and one-item simple self-ratings. Subjects were 320 university faculty members who spent at least 50% of their work time in teaching.

The resulting MTMM is displayed in Table 3.1. Given that Campbell and Fiske's (1959) approach is designed to test the validity of stable constructs, it follows that their first criterion for construct validity is that all scales be reliable. In Table 3.1, reliability values (coefficient alphas) are shown in bold along the diagonal; the values are plotted in Figure 3.3. Overall, these estimates, whose mean equals .77, are typical of psychological measures; the exceptions are the lower values for single-item self-ratings for depression and order (.57 and .60, respectively). The reliability estimates for self-ratings were obtained by correlating a self-rating of the construct with a rating of how the individual thought others saw him or her on the same construct. Figure 3.3 shows that reliability values for the Likert scale were generally higher than those for the true–false scales.

TABLE 3.1. Total Multitrait–Multimethod Matrix

Method	Likert			True–false			Self-ratings		
	1	2	3	1	2	3	1	2	3
Likert									
1. Stress	**88**								
2. Depression	57	**88**							
3. Order	−18	−13	**87**						
True–false									
1. Stress	61	65	−09	**76**					
2. Depression	57	67	−13	69	**80**				
3. Order	−17	−17	74	−14	−23	**86**			
Self-ratings									
1. Stress	65	53	−14	63	59	−12	**73**		
2. Depression	55	62	−12	54	63	−13	60	**57**	
3. Order	−14	−23	70	−12	−20	73	−10	−13	**60**

Note. Decimal points are omitted. Reliability values are in **bold** and underlined numbers are convergent validity estimates.

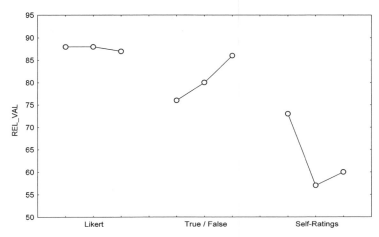

FIGURE 3.3. Plot of reliability values by self-report response mode. Reliability values are highest for the multi-item Likert and true–false scales. Likert scales' reliability values are slightly higher than true–false scales, possibly a result of the greater range of values present in Likert ratings.

Also shown in Table 3.1 are the underlined convergent validity estimates. Campbell and Fiske (1959) suggest that different measures of the same trait should correlate highly. The three stress intercorrelations of .61, .65, and .63 meet this criterion.

Table 3.2 is a deconstructed version of Table 3.1 showing the appropriate correlations for Campbell and Fiske's (1959) first discriminant validity criterion: Each convergent validity coefficient underlined should be higher than the correlations between that variable and any other variable having neither trait nor method in common. The correlation values are plotted in Figure 3.4. Eleven of 12 comparisons meet this criterion. Only the .65 correlation between Stress/True–false and the depression/Likert scales exceeds the corresponding Stress/True–false and Stress/Likert correlation of .61. The Stress/Depression correlations, however, fall very close in value to the convergent validity correlations for the Stress measures.

Table 3.3 displays the relevant correlations for the second discriminant criterion. Each convergent validity coefficient underlined should be higher than the correlations between that variable and different traits that employ the same method. Ten of 12 comparisons meet the criterion. The .69 correlation between Stress/True–false and Depression/True–false scales exceeds the .61 correlation between the Stress/True–false and Stress/Likert scales and the .65 correlation between Stress/True–false and Stress/Self-rating. As

TABLE 3.2. First Discriminant Validity Criterion

Method	Likert			True–false			Self-ratings		
	1	2	3	1	2	3	1	2	3
Likert									
1. Stress									
2. Depression									
3. Order									
True–false									
1. Stress	<u>61</u>	65	−09						
2. Depression	57								
3. Order	−17								
Self-ratings									
1. Stress	<u>65</u>	53	−14	<u>63</u>	59	−12			
2. Depression	55			54					
3. Order	−14			−12					

shown in Figure 3.5, overall the convergent validity and the Stress/Depression correlations are very similar in magnitude.

In sum, the measures of occupational stress appear reliable, intercorrelate highly, but also overlap with measures of depression. Meier (1984) noted that measures of stress meet approximately the same number of validity and reliability criteria when applied to the measures of order and

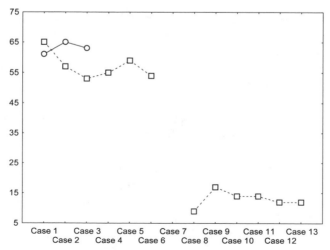

FIGURE 3.4. Convergent validity and first discriminant validity criterion. Correlations are absolute values of correlations displayed in Table 3.2.

TABLE 3.3. Second Discriminant Validity Criterion

Method	Likert			True–false			Self-ratings		
	1	2	3	1	2	3	1	2	3
Likert									
1. Stress									
2. Depression	57								
3. Order	−18								
True–false									
1. Stress	61								
2. Depression				69					
3. Order				−14					
Self-ratings									
1. Stress	65			63					
2. Depression							60		
3. Order							−10		

depression. Meier (1984) concluded that to the extent that depression and order have gained acceptance as constructs, occupational stress merits similar regard.

Given the relatively weak support for construct validity found in Meier (1984), Meier (1991) conducted a second validity study in which 129 college students completed measures of occupational stress, depression, and

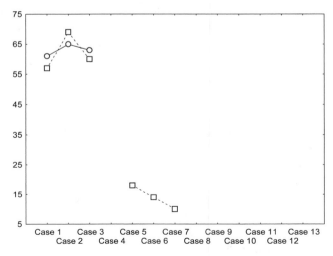

FIGURE 3.5. Convergent validity and second discriminant validity criterion. Correlations are absolute values of correlations displayed in Table 3.3.

physical illness. Stress and depression measures were again highly correlated with each other (*r*'s near .60), and both correlated with a measure of physical symptoms (*r*'s near .30). In a hierarchical multiple regression analysis with symptoms as the dependent measure, gender and stress accounted for a significant amount of the variance (adjusted *r* square = .17). Depression accounted for no additional variance, suggesting that it had no discriminant validity from occupational stress. These findings echoed the conclusions of Schroeder and Costa (1984; see also Watson & Pennebaker, 1989), who suggested that previously found relations between stress and illness are largely a result of neurotic responding by subjects to self-report measures. In other words, neurotic subjects (i.e., persons prone to negative mood states) were more likely to agree with items assessing stress, depression, and illness regardless of the actual occurrence of the thoughts, behaviors, or feelings measured by the different scales.

Problems with Campbell and Fiske's Approach

Although Campbell and Fiske (1959) proposed a useful approach to construct validity, critics have noted difficulties. As indicated in the stress–depression example, considerable ambiguity can exist in the application of Campbell and Fiske's criteria. No specific level exists for determining when differences between correlations are sufficient to proclaim that a test construct possesses adequate convergent or discriminant validity (e.g., Jackson, 1975). One could perform a *z* test to determine if correlations significantly differed, but most multitrait–multimethod researchers choose not to, presumably because of the triviality of the results. In addition, researchers select the constructs and methods employed to demonstrate similarity to and differences from the construct in question. Selection of similar methods (as in Meier, 1984) or similar constructs makes tests of discriminant validity more difficult. The reverse can be true: Researchers can choose dissimilar methods and constructs to make Campbell and Fiske's criteria easier to attain. Given the history of observational bias in all sciences and the variety of methods for assessing construct validity, it is not surprising to find that developers of tests and constructs frequently interpret results as supportive of construct validity. However, critics of the same tests and constructs often interpret similar or identical validity data in the opposite direction. In any event, much is left to the judgment of researchers. Evaluations of construct validity are hindered by a lack of consensus about acceptable procedures for evaluating discriminant validity (Burisch, 1984).

Campbell and Fiske's methods have also been criticized for the use of observed instead of latent variables (Kenny & Kashy, 1992). Latent variables produced by statistical techniques such as factor analysis presumably should be closer to true values than the untransformed observed scores. The predominant solution adopted by researchers to this problem has been the use of confirmatory factor analysis (CFA; Joreskog, 1974; Kenny & Kashy, 1992; Schmitt & Stults, 1986). In CFA researchers specify in advance which measures of a trait should load on a single trait factor and which measures assessed by a particular method should load on a single method factor. Yet issues remain about the use of particular analytic procedures (Kenny & Kashy, 1992; Millsap, 1990), leaving questions about CFA's usefulness for determining construct validity.

The Factor Analytic Approach to Construct Validity

The method for ascertaining construct validity most closely aligned with the trait-selection paradigm is *factor analysis*. Test developers assume that scores on any large number of items or tests reflect a smaller number of more basic factors or traits. *Factor analysis* refers to a set of statistical procedures employed to examine the correlations among test items and produce an estimate of a smaller number of factors that account for those relations. Thus, a *factor* found in a factor analysis consists of a group of highly intercorrelated variables (Vogt, 1993). These factors are assumed to be *latent*, that is, underlying the actual item responses.

Two basic types of factor analysis are commonly employed: *exploratory* and *confirmatory*. In exploratory factor analysis little or no knowledge is available about the number and type of factors underlying a set of data. Test developers typically employ exploratory factor analysis when evaluating a new set of items during the test construction process. With confirmatory factor analysis, knowledge of expected factors is available (e.g., from theory or a previous exploratory factor analysis) and employed to compare factors found in a new data set. A good way to begin learning about factor analytic techniques and their output is through manuals or websites provided by software companies like SPSS and SAS.

For many, if not most, test developers, exploratory factor analysis has become the default method for determining the construct validity of a test. That is, the test developer creates dozens or hundreds of items, with those items subsequently completed by hundreds or thousands of respondents, and then the developer subjects the resulting responses to some type of factor analysis. The resulting factors are then interpreted by the test developer in terms related to the construct of interest.

Serious interpretive problems can occur with factor analysis. Golden, Sawicki, and Franzen (1984) maintained that test developers must employ a theory to select items that will be subjected to factor analysis "since the resulting factors can only be interpreted accurately within the context of a theoretical base" (p. 27). Nevertheless, many, if not most, test developers base their item selection only loosely on theory, often because a rough theoretical base is all that exists in many educational and psychological domains. In his book *The Mismeasure of Man*, Gould (1981) similarly criticized the use of factor analysis in the creation of intelligence tests. Gould indicated that many social scientists have reified intelligence, treating it as a physical or biological entity instead of a construct. Gould maintained that "such a claim can never arise from the mathematics alone, only from additional knowledge of the physical nature of the measures themselves" (p. 250), and suggested that no such evidence exists in the case of intelligence. He concluded that "the history of factor analysis is strewn with the wreckage of misguided attempts at reification" (p. 268).

Understanding the theory related to test scores employed in a factor analysis extends to understanding methodological issues, including method variance, that may influence item responses. A good example of such a problem can be found with a test called the Counseling Self-Estimate Inventory (COSE; Larson et al., 1992; for a similar example, see Rodebaugh, Woods, & Heimberg, 2007). To construct the test, 213 counseling students completed an initial pool of items, whose scores were then factor analyzed and grouped into scales on the basis of the factor analytic results. As shown in Table 3.4, the first two identified factors were a 12-item scale and a 10-item scale. The table contains a brief version of each item's content along with the *factor loadings* for each item. Factor loadings are the correlations between each item (or variable, using a more generic term) and the factors found in the factor analysis. Test developers inspect such a table to (1) identify one or more sets of items that load on the identified factors, (2) set a cutoff point on the factor loadings (.40 employed with the COSE) to decide which items belong to the identified factor, and (3) name the factor based on the content of the identified items. Larson et al. (1992) labeled Factor I items as *microskills* (i.e., a set of basic counselor skills recognized primarily by counselor educators) and Factor II items as *process* (i.e., what the client and counselor do and experience in session, a factor recognized by clinicians).

The problem is that the *microskills* items are all positively worded,

TABLE 3.4. Factor Loadings for COSE Brief Item Content of Positively Worded Microskills Scale and Negatively Worded Process Scale

Brief item content (item #)	Factor	
	I	II
Microskills Scale		
Counselor interpretation easy to understand (32)	**.64**	.40
Counselor interpretation consistent with client statements (25)	**.59**	.21
Counselor interpretation concise (11)	**.58**	.35
Counselor interpretation effective (21)	**.57**	.07
Counselor response is of an appropriate length (15)	**.56**	.33
Counselor can conceptualize client problems (58)	**.54**	.38
Appropriate responses to clients (10)	**.53**	.28
Counselor content consistent with client statements (17)	**.53**	.23
Client sees counselor as competent (20)	**.51**	.36
Active listening responses concise (6)	**.50**	.23
Counselor ends session appropriately (9)	**.47**	−.05
Counselor can assess client's readiness to change (60)	**.41**	.12
Process Scale		
Counselor interpretation may not help client specify problem (56)	.14	**.58**
Inappropriate responses to clients (16)	.15	**.56**
Counselor responses ineffective (43)	.12	**.55**
Counselor may not understand nonverbals (38)	.13	**.54**
Counselor responses are too deliberate (34)	.29	**.52**
Counselor inappropriately confronts (42)	.10	**.52**
Counselor assessments inaccurate (41)	.04	**.50**
Counselor cannot set concrete goals (59)	.20	**.47**
Counselor unable to maintain energy (27)	.28	**.43**
Counselor wording may be confusing (12)	.22	**.43**

Note. Factor loadings above .40 are in bold. Data from Larson et al. (1992).

whereas the *process* items are all negatively worded. That is, the content of the each scale is confounded with positive or negative item wording that may promote *acquiescence* (i.e., agreement) or *criticalness* (i.e., disagreement) response biases. Indeed, examination of Table 3.4 indicates that the content of the two scales evidences considerable overlap, and it seems plausible that the factor analytic results indicate that test takers primarily responded to the positive or negative wording of the items. This problem with the COSE is discussed further in Chapter 5.

Other criticisms of factor analyses suggest that test developers should not rely on factor analysis alone as the key method for examining construct validity. Some research suggests, for example, that factor analysis may fail to reveal the actual structure of the psychological phenomenon under study;

Lykken (1971) noted that in the few cases where the structure of the phenomena is already known, factor analysis of relevant data did not provide
a convincing fit. Similarly, factor analyses with varimax rotation tend to
produce a single major factor (Golden et al., 1984). Given that theories and
observations of most psychological phenomena indicate the presence of
multiple domains or components, factor analytic results suggesting a single
major element do not match expectations about what should be found.
Finally, Kline (1998) noted that many factor analyses are technically flawed,
leading to results "of little scientific value" (p. 51). This may be another way
of saying that experts may disagree about the exact steps needed in any
particular factor analysis. Kline (1998), for example, wrote that "if there has
been adequate sampling of subjects and variables and there is a large sample
of subjects, relative to the number of variables and factors, and if the correct
number of factors, as selected by the Scree or Velicer tests or by statistical
tests after maximum likelihood analysis, if Direct Oblimin rotation is used,
then it is likely that simple-structure, replicable factors will be obtained"
(p. 64).

History of Self-Report and Interview Errors

Human judgment ratings (HJRs) are qualitative or quantitative assessments
made by individuals, about themselves or others, along a psychological dimension. HJRs consist of two types: *self-reports* and *other ratings*. Self-reports
are judgments made by individuals about a psychological attribute (e.g.,
rate your current job satisfaction). Other ratings occur when one person
rates another on a psychosocial dimension, as when a manager interviews
prospective employees and rates their interpersonal skills.

As previously noted, the use of large samples in psychological research
meant that one no longer needed to assume, as was the case in early experimental work, that the person who made the report was a psychological
expert. In the large sample paradigm, as long as the person provided data
of some validity, errors would cancel in the aggregation. With both self
and other ratings, Danziger (1990) observed that "during the early period
of personality psychology, and to a considerable extent thereafter, it was
simply assumed that personality ratings were an unproblematic product of
attributes of the task, not attributes of the rater" (p. 160). Test items were
assumed to be face valid across individuals and individuals were assumed to
be able to respond in a valid manner to those items.

Given this background, it should be no surprise that self-reports and ratings by others constitute the methods most frequently employed throughout the history of psychological measurement. With the exception of a few areas such as behavioral assessment, most contemporary psychologists continue to rely on self-reports. Kagan (1988), for example, cited research indicating that most personality research during the 1980s was based on self-report questionnaires. Noting that self-reports have been employed in alcohol research since the beginning of the 20th century, Babor, Stephens, and Marlatt (1987) observed that the use of verbal reports remains "the procedure of choice for obtaining research data about patient characteristics and the effectiveness of alcoholism treatment" (p. 412). If self-reports are assumed to be credible and valid in some sense, their widespread use is inevitable, given their ease of development, administration, and scoring. Indeed, investigators are continually tempted to create new instruments in their research areas. Hartman (1984) noted that "if a behavior has been studied by two investigators, the chances are very good that at least two different self-report questionnaires are available for assessing the behavior" (p. 133).

Self-Reports

Despite the widespread use of self-reports, psychologists often adopt one of the following dichotomous beliefs: (1) Because individuals can self-report, self-reports must be valid, or (2) because self-reports can be distorted by test takers, self-reports are useless. The first position represents that taken by most early measurement psychologists. In contrast, self-report critics espousing the second position have pointed to studies comparing self-reports to what the critics see as a more objective criterion, that is, overt behavior. Psychologists have consistently found discrepancies between self-reports of psychological phenomena and overt behavior indicative of or related to the phenomena (e.g., Doleys, Meredith, Poire, Campbell, & Cook 1977; Dunning, Heath, & Suls, 2004; Schroeder & Rakos, 1978). Dunning et al. (2004) noted that "a wealth of evidence suggests that people make substantial errors when they evaluate their abilities, attributes, and future behavior" (p. 78). Kagan (1988) summarized another variation on this perspective:

> A serious limitation of self-report information is that each person has only a limited awareness of his or her moods, motives, and bases for behavior, and it is not obvious that only conscious intentions and moods make up the main basis for variation in behavior. ... Less conscious indexes, including facial expressions, voice quality, and physiological reactions, occasionally have a stronger relation to a set of theoretically predicted behaviors than do self-reports. The reader will remember that when a large number of investigations were derived from psychoanalytic the-

ory, the concept of unconscious ideas was prominent and self-report was treated as replete with error. (p. 617)

Evidence of problems with self-reports remains plentiful throughout the testing literature. Consider these examples of inconsistency in self-reports:

1. When the choice "To think for themselves" is offered on a list of alternatives, 61.5% of individuals choose this as "the most important thing for children to prepare them for life." In an open format, however, only 4.6% offer this choice (Schuman & Presser, 1981).
2. When asked to rate their success in life, 13% report high success when the scale ranges from 0 to 10. When the scale ranges from −5 to +5, 34% do so (Schwarz, Knauper, Hippler, Noelle-Neumann, & Clark, 1991).
3. The correlation between items measuring marital satisfaction and life satisfaction ranges from .18 to .67, depending on question order and introduction (Schwarz, Strack, & Mai, 1991b).
4. Individuals change their responses to test items when the items are rephrased from positive ("Do you feel the world is a good place to live in?") to negative ("Do you wish that you had never been born?") (Hazlett-Stevens, Ullman, & Craske, 2004; Ong, 1965).
5. Retesting in as short a period as 1 day can result in substantial changes in test scores (Hough, Eaton, Dunnette, Kamp, & McCloy, 1990; Dahlstrom, 1969).

Similarly, Bailey and Bhagat (1987) reviewed research indicating that the act of completing questionnaires and interviews can create or alter the level of held beliefs and attitudes. Bridge et al. (1977), for example, randomly assigned individuals to distinct groups of subjects, who were questioned regarding their opinions about cancer and crime, respectively. Respondents repeated the survey several weeks later. Although the initial survey did not find differences in attitudes toward cancer and crime between the two groups, Bridge et al. (1977) found that individuals initially questioned about cancer, as compared with in dividuals questioned about crime, increased their assessment of the importance of good health on retest. Bailey and Bhagat (1987) also cited a study by Kraut and McConahay (1973) that found that prospective voters, randomly sampled for a preelection interview, showed a significantly higher turnout (48%) than the noninterviewed population (21%). All of these are examples of serious violations of the measurement field's expectations about the consistency of behavior and suggest that effects other than traits are influencing responses to self-report questions.

Interviews and Observational Methods

In the history of psychological testing, the most commonly employed method of gathering information has been the interview. Studies show that more than 95% of all employers use interviews and that most see the interview as the most influential part of the hiring process (Guion, 1976; Miner & Miner, 1979; Murphy & Davidshofer, 1988). An interview can include both self-reports and ratings by others, and the latter are the focus of this section.

The greatest advantage and disadvantage of interviews is their face validity. That is, the data produced in an interview appear credible to the interviewer and the interviewee. Fremer (1992, p. 4) quoted Thorndike (1969):

> The teacher who is most critical of standardized testing is often endowed with unlimited faith in the accuracy of his own judgments. He knows! It is vitally important that we do not, in identifying the shortcomings of test data, manage at the same time to build up the teacher's view that his own judgment is infallible.

One may substitute clinician, employment interviewer, or any other rater role for teacher in the quote above. It is often difficult for interviewers to believe that the information they gather from interviewees may somehow be invalid.

Employment and clinical interviews are two of the most researched types of measurement and assessment methodologies. Interviews are often conducted in industrial/organizational (I/O) settings for the purpose of personnel selection. Similar ratings are also employed for measuring job performance and leadership evaluation.

Like self-reports, ratings by others can produce problematic information. For example, Murphy and Davidshofer's (1988) review of the research literature examining the effectiveness of the employment interview suggested that little empirical basis exists for its popularity. Interviews have often been found to be unreliable; that is, interviewers exhibit little consistency in their judgments of applicants. Interviews also appear problematic in that many systematic sources of error, including the applicant's gender, age, ethnicity, and physical attractiveness, affect interview outcome. Little evidence exists to suggest that the interview adds to the effectiveness of selection tests for making good hiring decisions. Schwarz and Oyserman (2001) noted that when compared to self-reports, "others' behaviors are even more poorly represented in memory, unless they were extreme and memorable" (p. 144). Research results suggest that employment decisions are best made on the basis of data from tests alone rather than tests and interviews.

Why do employment interviewing practices persist in the face of this evidence? Murphy and Davidshofer (1988) offered two reasons. Like therapists, interviewers rarely receive systematic feedback about the validity of their decisions and so may be likely to overestimate their judgments' effectiveness. Also, interviewers may feel more confident in their ability to conduct an interview than to employ more difficult techniques such as psychological tests.

Murphy and Davidshofer (1988) noted that clinical and employment interviews are fairly similar. Both are usually less structured than tests and are often intended to obtain information unavailable from tests. During both types of interviews, interviewers pay attention to the interviewees' answers as well as their behavior. Like employers, clinicians rely heavily on interviews and place more weight on interview data than on data from other sources. Consequently, clinical interviews should also evidence considerable problems (Garb, 1992, 1998).

Measurement Error

Error refers to one or more factors that influence measurement in unintended ways, ways that test developers do not recognize or understand. Error interferes with the purpose of testing, making it more difficult to interpret data as intended. Random errors are those that occur unpredictably, whereas systematic errors occur in some regular manner and may accumulate, as does a trait, with aggregation of items and persons. Historically, test theorists and developers have assumed that all errors in measurement operate as random errors rather than systematic errors. That is, at the scale of the individual, errors might be systematic—one person may distort responses because of fatigue, another because of poor comprehension—but in large groups such a assemblage of errors will behave as if they were random (Murphy & Davidshofer, 1988).

Psychologists have sought to identify systematic errors in the measurement process in the hope that such errors can be identified, controlled, or removed. I discuss these errors below in terms of individuals' response patterns that appear biased from the perspective of the test developer or administrator.

Systematic Errors Associated with Self-Reports

Dissimulation and Malingering

Dissimulation refers to faking "good" or "bad" on test items (Murphy & Davidshofer, 1988), and *malingering* occurs when individuals simulate or exaggerate psychological conditions (Smith & Burger, 1993). Given that many test items and tasks are transparent in their intent to detect such phenomena as psychopathology or dishonesty, test takers may be motivated to generate distorted answers that suit their purposes rather than reflect valid or retrieved information. For example, prejudiced individuals may report to an opinion poll interview that they would vote for an African American or female presidential candidate when in fact they would not. Similarly, individuals who wish to receive disability payments may exaggerate their complaints and symptoms. Dahlstrom (1985) noted that as early as the 1930s investigators were able to demonstrate the ease of faking answers on psychological tests. Terman and Miles (1936), for example, found that the most discriminating items on a scale designed to show personality differences between men and women were also the most susceptible to change under explicit instructions to fake test answers in a masculine or feminine direction.

During the test construction process, test developers attempt to identify and reject items that may be easily faked. Developers have created scales to detect malingering (e.g., Beaber, Marston, Michelli, & Mills, 1985; Rogers, Bagby, & Dickens, 1992; Schretlen, 1986; Smith & Burger, 1993), as well as tests that include special items designed to detect dissimulation. Psychiatric patients, for example, appear less able to provide normal responses when item subtlety increases (Martin, 1988). Martin (1988) reviewed the best-known MMPI scales designed to identify distorted responding, including the (1) Lie scale, items in which the respondent may claim great virtue, (2) F scale, infrequently answered responses that may indicate a tendency to fake illness, and (3) K scale, subtle items intended to assess defensiveness and willingness to discuss oneself. A weighted derivation of the K scale is added to other MMPI clinical scales to correct for the generation of defensive responses. The problem with identifying items sensitive to dissimulation is that such items may also be sensitive to other factors. The F and Fb scales of the Minnesota Multiphasic Personality Inventory-2 (MMPI-2), consisting of items reflecting clinically aberrant and statistically rare responses, are also affected by symptom exaggeration, psychosis, and random responding (Berry et al., 1992). The Variable Response Inconsistency (VRIN) scale (Tellegen, 1988) is composed of statistically and semantically rare item pairs and appears to be able to separate random responders from other groups (Wetter, Baer, Berry, Smith & Larsen, 1992).

SOCIAL DESIRABILITY

Social desirability refers to a tendency to respond with answers that the respondent believes are most socially acceptable or makes the respondent look good (Edwards, 1953; Nunnally, 1967). Social desirability, then, is a type of *response set*, an orientation toward responding to give a particular impression (as compared with *response styles*, whereby the individual responds in a particular direction, as when answering "True" to all items). Paulhus (1991) noted that psychometricians have been aware of social desirability effects since at least the 1930s (e.g., Bernreuter, 1933; Vernon, 1934). Social desirability researchers maintain that it is a separate trait that varies among individuals (i.e., individuals have different needs for approval) and that it is social desirability (SD) that most personality tests actually measure. Edwards (1970), for example, summarized research demonstrating strong correlations between the probability of personality item endorsement (contained in tests such as the MMPI) and those items' social desirability value. Errors associated with self-reports of SD behaviors can include refusal to answer questions as well as underreporting or overreporting of incidence and/or frequency of behaviors (Catania, Gibson, Chitwood, & Coates, 1990). In the area of computer-based interviews, for example, researchers take an increase in frequency of self-reports of undesirable behaviors as reflective of more honest response (Brown & Vanable, 2005).

Despite an acknowledgment of the potential effects of social desirability, no consensus has been reached about how to think about the construct. Dahlstrom (1969) suggested that social desirability may simply be another component of, instead of substitute for, factors such as neuroticism that are measured by scales such as the MMPI. Social desirability, then, becomes not so much an error that must be eliminated or controlled but another type of psychological trait. Similarly, Martin (1988) suggested that socially desirable responses may not be invalid, because most people do behave in a socially desirable manner. That is, individuals do attempt to manage the impressions they make on other people (Messick, 1991), and a social desirability component is also present in the criteria predicted by psychological tests. Social desirability effects continue to be documented with self-reports (Baer & Miller, 2002; Cash, Grant, Shovlin, & Lewis, 1992; Stice et al., 2004). Stice, Fisher, and Lowe (2004), for example, found low correlations between dietary restraint scales (i.e., self-report measures of efforts to restrain food intake) and actual calorie intake observed unobtrusively. This result calls into question the previously accepted finding that dieting may be related to the onset of certain eating disorders.

Problems such as social desirability bias may have persisted partially because of the dominating assumptions of selection testing. For example, McCrae and Costa (1983) wrote,

> As an item or scale characteristic, therefore, SD [social desirability] is a potentially serious problem in situations in which information is required about the absolute level of a response. For most psychological applications, however, absolute levels of scale scores are meaningless or difficult to interpret. Instead, normative information is used to compare the score of one individual to those of other persons from populations of interest. If the scores of all individuals are uniformly inflated or decreased by SD, it will make no difference in interpreting scores, since rank order and position in a distribution are unaffected. (p. 883)

Two problems exist with this argument. First, for many testing purposes, including selection, the absolute level of response is important. Second, we would not expect scores in a group of individuals to be uniformly affected by SD, because people vary in how much they distort their views according to social desirability.

In psychotherapy outcome research, it is quite plausible that social desirability effects would influence the mean of individuals' scores on such negative constructs as stress, anxiety, depression, and drug abuse. As shown in Figure 3.6, at intake clients might underreport scores on a socially undesirable construct such as anxiety; the resulting scores would display a range restriction or floor effect (a). Many psychological interventions, however, teach clients to recognize and accept the experience of some amounts of anxiety as normal. If this education was the primary intervention effect—thereby reducing the socially undesirable perception of anxiety—posttest scores in the intervention condition might demonstrate a greater range as well as an increase in mean anxiety level from pretest to posttest (b). The pre–post data might lead to an erroneous conclusion that the intervention caused an increase in anxiety.

To the extent that social desirability moves test scores toward the floor or ceiling of scale values and restricts the range of scores, interpretation of subsequent analyses becomes problematic. As discussed in Chapter 2, theoretical advances require increasingly precise measurement procedures that demonstrate the smallest distinctions (and therefore, greatest range) possible; to the extent that social desirability reduces such distinctions, measurements cannot reflect the full characteristics of the phenomenon. The usefulness of

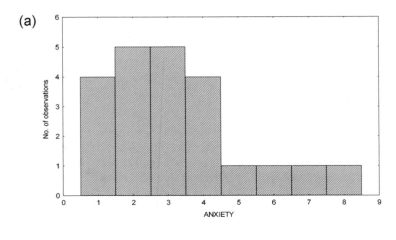

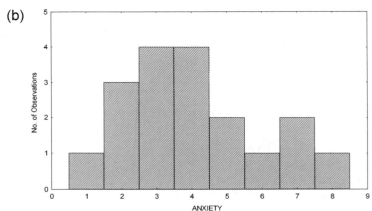

FIGURE 3.6. Social desirability effects on anxiety scores. (a) Pretest scores on a measure of anxiety might underrepresent actual levels of anxiety because of social desirability. (b) If the major effect of psychotherapy was to normalize the experience of anxiety, scores after the intervention might reflect actual anxiety but make it appear that the intervention increased anxiety scores.

selection testing depends on concurrent and predictive validity coefficients, correlations that will be attenuated or shrunk when range restriction occurs. For example, an employment test might actually correlate .70 with job performance, but range restriction in the test (and, possibly, the criterion) would shrink the found correlation to .35. Statistical corrections for attenuation have been developed, but the transformed correlation can overestimate the actual relation (Murphy & Davidshofer, 1988).

Schwarz and Oyserman (2001) suggested that social desirability effects are more often observed in interviews than in self-reports because of the latter's greater confidentiality. The interviewer's gender, age, or race may motivate a respondent to provide more socially desirable answers (Schwarz, 1997). The content of questions can also affect responses: Hser, Anglin, and Chou (1992), for instance, found that reports from male addicts showed greater inconsistency between two interviews for more socially undesirable behaviors, such as narcotics use, than for socially desirable behaviors, such as employment.

Barlow (1977) provided a clinical example of socially desirable responding. He described a patient who came to psychotherapy with problems of anxiety and depression, which the patient indicated were associated with social situations. Over a 1-year period the patient made progress in a treatment emphasizing the learning of social skills, but still complained of anxiety and depression. Finally, the patient blurted out that the real cause of the discomfort was the strong feelings of homosexual attraction he experienced in some social situations. When asked why he did not report this previously, Barlow (1977) wrote, "he simply said that he had wanted to report these attractions all year but was unable to bring himself to do so" (p. 287). Although homosexuality may be less of a taboo subject than it was for many people in the 1970s, issues surrounding such sensitive topics as sexuality and substance abuse remain subject to social desirability errors. It is common for clients to withhold sensitive information from therapists until they establish a working alliance.

Systematic Errors Associated with Ratings by Others

Raters can make errors, that is, they may be influenced by factors other than those intended for the rating process. As with self-reports, evidence that raters provide difficult-to-interpret information is also plentiful. Research comparing multiple raters of the same target often reveals at least some degree of inconsistency (Achenbach, 2006; Lambert & Hill, 1994). Botwin and Buss (1989; also see Cheek, 1982, and Quarm, 1981) instructed 59 couples to rate self and other behaviors along 22 personality dimensions such as responsible, secure, and extroverted. The self–other correlations of these sets of ratings ranged from .14 (secure) to .64 (emotional instability), with a mean of .43. Christensen, Margolin, and Sullaway (1992) found considerable differences in mothers' and fathers' reporting on the Child Behavior Checklist about their children ages 3–13. Mothers reported more negative behaviors than did fathers, and parents disagreed about the occurrence of a behavior twice as often as they agreed. Christensen et al. (1992) found more consistency with behaviors described as more disturbed, overt, and specific. Powell and Vacha-Haase (1994) reported that children experience difficulty in accurately reporting their behavior, and Kazdin (1988) noted low correlations between parent and child reports. Finally, Dix (1993) found that parents who were experiencing a negative emotional state (because of divorce) were more likely to see their children's age-appropriate behavior as maladjusted.

Similarly, Heppner et al.'s (1992) review of process research—which examines factors relating to client change from the perspective of the client, counselor, and outside observers—revealed inconsistencies across multiple sources. Tichenor and Hill (1989), for example, found near zero correlations among ratings by clients, counselors, and observers on different process measures. Other researchers have found that different types of observers assess different constructs, all of which relate to psychotherapy outcome (Heppner et al., 1992; Horvath & Greenberg, 1989; Marmar, Marziali, Horowitz, & Weiss, 1986). Studies of ratings by counselors in training, peer observers, and supervisors display similar inconsistency (Fuqua, Johnson, Newman, Anderson, & Gade, 1984; Fuqua, Newman, Scott, & Gade, 1986). Like Christensen et al. (1992), Heppner et al. (1992) suggested that agreement among observers should increase with more overt and concrete behaviors.

Murphy and Davidshofer (1988) identified several types of systematic rater errors, including *halo* and *leniency* errors. More recently, researchers have focused on a related phenomenon, the *hypothesis confirmation bias* (HCB). Each is described below.

Halo Errors

Among the first rater errors to be studied (e.g., Thorndike, 1920; cf. Cooper, 1981), halo errors are those in which a rater's overall impressions about the ratee influence ratings about specific aspects of the person. In other words, a rater holds a stereotype about a ratee, and that global impression hinders a more precise or valid rating in specific domains. As shown in Figure 3.7, if a supervisor believes a particular employee is "good," then that supervisor may rate all instances of the employee's performance as high, regardless of the actual performance. The rating process is influenced by the supervisor's beliefs, instead of data observed, stored, and retrieved from memory about specific behaviors. Nisbett and Wilson (1977) also distinguished between (1) halo errors that cause global ratings even when specific information is held by the rater and (2) errors made when only ambiguous data are available.

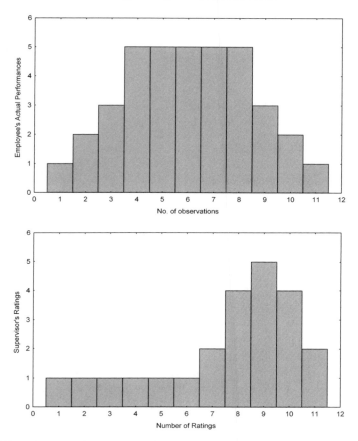

FIGURE 3.7. Halo error. The top graph displays hypothetical data indicating that a particular employee's performances range from poor to good, with all performances roughly resembling a normal curve. The bottom graph displays ratings by the same employee's supervisor, indicating that the supervisor rates most performances as good despite the actual range of quality. Because the supervisor's ratings consistently exceed the employee's actual performances, the supervisor displays a halo error.

Leniency and Criticalness Errors

In this class of errors, the rater is under- or overestimating the performance of the ratee. Leniency errors might be detected by data whose mean deviates considerably from the midpoint on a scale or a data distribution that is positively or negatively skewed (Murphy & Davidshofer, 1988; Saal, Downey, & Lahey, 1980). Leniency errors may be a cause of ceiling or floor effects (Kazdin, 1980). In a ceiling effect, all ratings cluster near the top of the scale; with a floor effect, they cluster at the bottom. When an intervention is implemented, ceiling and floor effects can hinder the detection of the intervention's impact. Suppose a researcher designs a pretest–posttest study examining the effects of a stress reduction program on air traffic controllers (whose actual stress levels approximate a normal distribution). As shown in Figure 3.8, an observer's biased judgments of controllers' stress might significantly underestimate those levels at pretest. How could a decrease resulting from the intervention be detected at posttest?

Hypothesis Confirmation Errors

Hypothesis confirmation bias (HCB) refers to the tendency to pay attention to information that confirms initial expectations and beliefs, and to ignore other, disconfirming information. Considerable evidence, for example, suggests that researchers (1) find what they expect or wish to find in experimental data and that (2) those expectations may be communicated to subjects (Rosenthal, 1976). Rosenthal (1976) documented numerous cases throughout the sciences in which data refuting accepted ideas were ignored or rejected. He noted that Newton did not see the absorption lines in the solar spectrum produced by a prism because he did not expect them to find them there. Similarly, Blondlot's 1903 discovery of N-rays, which appeared to intensify reflected light, was confirmed by other scientists, only to be later discounted as observer error. Observers' expectations have also led to faulty counts of blood cells by laboratory technicians and mistaken associations between cancer and cherry angioma, a skin condition.

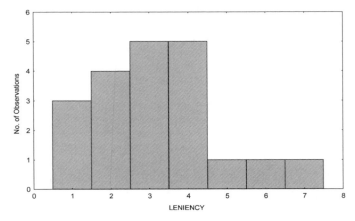

FIGURE 3.8. Leniency error. Leniency errors can cause a floor effect in scores.

Clinicians, like laypersons, researchers, and employment interviewers, may inappropriately crystallize their early impressions of other people (Darley & Fazio, 1980; Hoshmand, 1994; Jones, Rock, Shaver, Goethals, & Ward, 1968). Murphy and Davidshofer (1988) observed that "there is a pervasive tendency to overestimate the accuracy of one's judgments, and clinicians do not seem to be immune from this tendency" (p. 374). Citing Meehl (1973), Meier (2003) noted that in case conferences, clinicians commonly decide on a diagnosis and course of treatment within 5–10 minutes of a client description. To the extent that clinical hypotheses are misleading or incorrect, clinicians are likely to ignore important information contrary to their initial impression. Yet HCB appears limited to personal beliefs and expectations: Haverkamp (1993) found that clinicians were more likely to employ confirmatory biases when they self-generated a hypothesis about a client than when a hypothesis was provided via a client's statement of the problem.

Meier (2003) illustrated the HCB by first observing that for any phenomenon, two or more possible explanations exist. As shown in Figure 3.9, for any particular explanation evidence exists that may confirm or disconfirm that explanation. An observer will choose a single explanation, if the HCB occurs, and attend only to the confirming evidence. Figure 3.9 shows

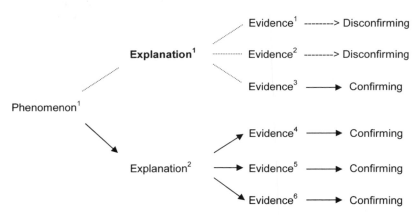

FIGURE 3.9. How HCB influences judgment. In this illustration, two explanations are apparent for a phenomenon. We collect three pieces of evidence per explanation to test each explanation. For Explanation[1], two pieces of evidence appear to disconfirm the explanation. Three pieces of evidence are collected for the second explanation, and all three support the explanation. Which is the best explanation? If a person has previously decided that Explanation[1] is best, the HCB predicts he or she will ignore the disconfirming evidence and pay attention only to confirming information.

that for the first explanation, two of three pieces of available evidence appear to disconfirm the explanation. All three pieces of evidence for the second explanation support Explanation[2]. A choice between the two explanations, consequently, would seem straightforward. A person who has decided before the evidence is collected that Explanation[1] is true, however, will be more likely to ignore or discount the two pieces of disconfirming evidence. In fact, a person convinced that the first explanation is true may pay no attention to any evidence regarding the second explanation.

Applying this logic to clinical situations, Meier (2003) proposed that clinicians' theories and beliefs can prevent them from noticing and thinking about relevant clinical information that could potentially be useful for modifying and improving counseling interventions (Hoshmand, 1994). HCB is also a potential explanation for Bickman et al.'s (2000) finding that most clinicians do not have alternative treatment plans for failing clients: These clinicians appear unaware that they can conceive of other ways of thinking about failing clients.

Causes of Inconsistency

Investigations of systematic errors in self-ratings and interviews have identified a large number of potential causes of inconsistency in human judgment ratings. Table 3.5 displays just a brief sample of proposed causes, culled from lists provided by three researchers. What these lists and the testing literature lack is a coherent theory for organizing these elements.

In the next sections I classify and describe potential causes for self-report errors in three categories. *Cognition* refers to an individual's thoughts,

TABLE 3.5. A Partial List of Causes of Measurement and Assessment Errors

Thorndike (1949; in Murphy & Davidshofer, 1988)	Paul (1986)	Nelson (1977a)
Test-taking skills	Carelessness	Motivation
Ability to comprehend instructions and items	Fatigue	Valence
Response sets	Boredom	Instructions
Health	Information overload	Type of behavior
Fatigue	Emotional strain	Timing
Motivation	Attention shifts	Schedule of self-monitoring
Stress	Equipment failure	Type of recording device
Set for a particular test	Variations in lighting and temperature	Number of behaviors concurrently monitored
Examiner characteristics	External distractions	

expectations, and beliefs; *affective and motivational influences* refers to a person's experienced and expressed feelings; and *environmental and cultural influences* refers to factors in an individual's environment that influence behaviors. Although other classification systems have and could be proposed to explain sources of inconsistency, these categories are familiar to persons who conduct counseling and psychotherapy.

Cognitive Influences

Cognition refers to how individuals think about and process information. Cognitive psychology's rise as an important paradigm has led many measurement psychologists to consider the role of cognitive factors in the testing process. That research has led to an expansion of the complexity of the cognitive processes people employ when answering questions. As Schwarz and Oyserman (2001) noted, "even apparently simple behavioral questions pose complex cognitive tasks," with the consequence that "self-reports can be a highly unreliable source of data" (p. 128).

Many contemporary descriptions of the item response process rely heavily on cognitive models (e.g., Babor et al., 1990; Biemer, Groves, Lyberg, Mathiowetz, & Sudman, 1991). Theorists usually include the following stages in the item response process:

1. Individuals, over time, notice their behavior or the behavior of others.
2. They store that information in memory, where it is subject to some degree of decay.
3. Individuals are presented with an item or task that they attempt to comprehend and then relate to information in memory.
4. Individuals retrieve the information and employ it in response to the item or task.

Schwarz and Oyserman (2001) provided a more detailed explication of this typical self-report process, maintaining that with each question or item respondents must:

1. Understand the question.
2. Identify the behavior of interest.
3. Retrieve relevant instances of the behavior from memory.
4. Correctly identify the relevant reference period requested by test instructions (e.g., "last week" or "in general").

5. Search that reference period to retrieve all occurrences of the behavior in question.
6. Correctly date the retrieved occurrences so that they fit within the reference period.
7. Correctly add up all the retrieved occurrences.
8. Translate this information into the response categories provided (e.g., "many," "few," "none").
9. Honestly provide the result of the recall effort.

To provide an example of how error can affect self-reports, I describe below three issues that predominantly affect the first step ("Understand the question").

Item Comprehension Problems

The issue of how respondents construe the meaning of test items extends beyond simple distortion. As Kagan (1988) noted, every question forces the respondent to decide on the meaning of the terms, and "the investigator cannot assume similar meanings" (p. 617). But that is a nomothetic assumption shared by many test developers. Walsh and Betz (1985; see also Wiggins, 1973) stated that "it is assumed (at least to some extent) that each item on a test and all the words in that item have some similar meaning for different people" (p. 17). In fact, research suggests that respondents attempt to create a pragmatic meaning for each question (Schwarz, 1997), and Kuncel (1973) found evidence that some test takers modify the meaning of test items to make the items easier to answer.

The problem becomes more complex when respondents differ by culture, gender, age, or other salient characteristics (Johnson, Hickson, Fetter, & Reichenbach, 1987). Johnson et al. (1997) indicated that survey developers may assume that concepts and language are equally understood by all respondents, regardless of culture, and that this error may be referred to as a *category fallacy*. *Etic concepts* are those ideas thought to be universally understood, whereas *emic concepts* are culture specific. When test developers treat emic concepts as etic, they become *pseudoetic* and result in a category fallacy. In support of this conceptualization are research results showing that respondents process and provide more complex information when completing questions in their native language (Church, Katigbak, & Castaneda, 1988; Marin, Triandis, Betancourt, & Kashima, 1983).

To the extent that respondents find ambiguous such test elements as items, instructions, and format (Blaney, 1992), they may be expected to respond inconsistently. For example, what do people do when asked a question for which they are uncertain about the answer? MacGregor, Lichtenstein, and Slovic (1988; see also Bradburn, Rips, & Shevell, 1987; Sudman, Bradburn, & Schwarz, 1996) suggest that the simplest strategy to pursue, when estimating an uncertain quantity, is to intuitively produce a number based on whatever information comes to mind. Although inexpensive, simple, and often approximately correct, research has shown that such intuitive judgments can be associated with systematic biases (MacGregor et al., 1988). MacGregor et al. note that such judgments tend to remain close to an initial value (Tversky & Kahneman, 1974) and may be influenced by recency effects (i.e., remembering the most recent information only).

Some evidence suggests that many items on psychological tests engender subtle differences among respondents in comprehension and recall of information (cf. Baker & Brandon, 1990; Watson, 1988). Such individual differences in item processing are likely to be compounded by the ambiguity found in self-report scales. Gynther and Green (1982) suggested that many self-report items are "stated in such a general fashion that test takers can only respond on the basis of their implicit personality theories rather than how they actually behave and feel in specific situations" (p. 358). Helfrich (1986) found that item understanding may be influenced by item ambiguity as well as the presence of negatives in the item, passive voice, and respondent age. Angleitner, John, and Lohr (1986) reviewed research that found (1) a negative correlation between item length and test–retest consistency and (2) a negative correlation between ratings of item comprehensibility and the number of letters and sentence clauses in items. They also found that (3) according to subject ratings of scales such as the MMPI and 16 Personality Factors, 25% of the items were ambiguous and 50% difficult to understand, and (4) in one study, almost 20% of subjects changed their item responses over a 2-week test–retest interval. Angleitner et al. (1986) concluded that "one cannot help but be impressed by the degree of response inconsistency elicited by most personality questionnaire items" (p. 97). And unlike interviews, self-report questionnaires do not provide additional explanations that might clarify test-related ambiguities (Schwarz, 1997).

Test Cues

Schwarz (1999) noted that research evidence indicates that when asked to report information, respondents do not retrieve all the applicable knowledge. Instead, they tend to recall information that is chronically accessible, that is, information that comes to mind whenever the person thinks about it. However, some information is temporarily accessible, that is, it comes to mind when a context or situation prompts the person to recall it. One of those contexts is the content of preceding items. If teens answer a series of questions focused on gang fights and stealing, the subsequent question "Do you fight with your siblings?" is more likely to be interpreted as a request for information about physical fighting than about verbal arguing. Similarly, when respondents can view all items in a test, they tend to more frequently endorse earlier items than later ones (Schwarz & Oyserman, 2001). Finally, Schwarz and Oyserman (2001) cited Parducci's (1965) *range-frequency theory*, which indicates that individuals may base their self-reports on the range of behaviors they are asked to rate. That is, individuals examine the behaviors in a list, rank them from highest to lowest in frequency, and then respond to the whole list on the basis of this scaling. With a sufficiently large range, individuals may try to use all categories of the rating scale equally often.

Schwarz and Oyserman (2001) noted that the frequency scales and reference periods respondents employ to answer questions can lead to different answers because the scales and periods themselves help people to interpret the meaning of the items. Response formats with low-frequency answers (e.g., event occurs once a year) may be interpreted as seeking reports of rare events, whereas high-frequency formats (e.g., event occurs daily) imply minor events. Similarly, the form of the question can influence responses: *Closed questions* (to which the respondent can answer in one or a few words or phrases) produce different reports than *open questions* (to which the respondent can answer in one or more sentences).

Schwarz (1999) also described *assimilation effects* (where positive association encourages positive judgments) and *contrast effects* (where comparisons against a standard are made). Regarding contrast effects, Schwarz (1999) provided the example of the popular U.S. secretary of state Colin Powell. When respondents were asked if they knew which political party he joined, they tended to subsequently rate the Republican party more positively (i.e., an assimilation effect). When they were asked to rate former U.S. senator Bob Dole (an unsuccessful presidential candidate) with Powell, Dole's ratings decreased compared to ratings independent of Powell (contrast effect). Similarly, Strack, Schwarz, and Gschneidinger (1985) instructed respondents to recall three positive or negative events. Those who reported positive events subsequently indicated higher life satisfaction than those who reported negative events.

Self-reports typically require test takers to respond to true–false formats or multipoint Likert scales. Response formats can potentially provide information to the test taker about how to respond (Schwarz, 1999). Among the important response dimensions is the number of response alternatives. A test such as the MMPI offers two possibilities to the test taker (true or false) and an additional category to the test scorer (items left blank). Because Likert scales theoretically should increase the variability of responding, most contemporary tests employ such scales, using between five and nine possible responses (cf. Dawis, 1987; Murphy & Davidshofer, 1988). Increasing the number of response alternatives, however, may increase the cognitive processing required of the respondent. Two likely results of such increased demand are (1) a lengthening of item completion times and total test times when large numbers of items are involved (cf. Lohman, 1989) and (2) an increased likelihood of unmotivated or unskilled respondents generating, as opposed to retrieving, responses.

Concreteness or ambiguity is another dimension along which rating scales can be described. Thus, rating scales may be anchored simply by two global descriptors (e.g., poor or excellent), or they may include a number of explicit behavioral descriptions. As an example of the latter, to receive a rating of 1 on a dimension of promptness, an employee must always meet the required deadline. Considerable ambiguity seems to exist in the content and format of most rating scales (Murphy & Davidshofer, 1988). Schwarz (1999) also observed that respondents may use response formats as guides to answer ambiguous questions. Questions that request frequency responses can provide such information. Responses that include only low-frequency categories (e.g., "less than once a year" to "more than once a month") may lead the respondents to conclude that the questioner is seeking information about relatively rare events. For example, respondents reporting on the frequency of irritating experiences with a low-frequency scale believe that the question refers to major annoyances, whereas respondents with a high-frequency response format believe the question concerns minor annoyances (Schwarz, Strack, Muller, & Chassein, 1988).

Similarly, the numbers on the response formats may provide clues that the respondents employ to answer questions. Schwarz, Knauper, Hippler, Noelle-Neumann, and Clark (1991a) asked individuals to rate their success in life on 11-point scales (with identical descriptors) that ranged from 0 to 10 or −5 to 5 (see below).

	Not at all successful						Extremely successful				
Unipolar:	0	1	2	3	4	5	6	7	8	9	10
Bipolar:	−5	−4	−3	−2	−1	0	1	2	3	4	5

Thirty-four percent provided a value between −5 and 0 on the 5–5 scale, whereas only 13% endorsed equivalent values between 0 and 5 on the 0–10 scale. Further investigation indicated that respondents interpreted a scale value of 0 (on the 0-10 scale) as reflecting an absence of achievements. When the 0 was the midpoint on the −5–5 scale, 0 and below was interpreted to mean the presence of explicit failures. Schwarz (1999) concluded that

> A format that ranges from negative to positive numbers conveys that the research-er has a bipolar dimension in mind, where the two poles refer to the presence of opposite attributes. In contrast, a format that uses only positive numbers conveys that the researcher has a unipolar dimension in mind, referring to different degrees of the same attribute. (p. 96)

Respondents also tend to assume that midrange values reflect average behaviors, and that the extremes of the scale reflect extremes of the phenomenon in question (Schwarz, 1999). The range of the response format has been shown to alter reports about television viewing, psychological symptoms, sexual behaviors, and consumer behaviors (Schwarz, 1999), with the effect strongest for ambiguous questions. The type of scale can also influence subsequent judgments. Schwarz (1990) indicated that when a frequency scale implies that the respondent's behavior is above or below the average, subsequent reports of satisfaction can be influenced in predictable directions.

Some surveys provide respondents with open response formats, as compared with the closed formats described above. With open formats respondents are likely to omit information they believe is obvious to the as-sessor. Schwarz (1999) noted research by Schuman and Presser (1981) that found that when the choice "To think for themselves" is offered on a list of alternatives, 61.5% of individuals choose this as "the most important thing for children to prepare them for life." In an open format, however, 4.6% offer this choice.

Low Cognitive Ability

Stone, Stone, and Gueutal (1990) noted that test researchers rarely study the ability of test takers to understand test instructions, item content, or response alternatives. They proposed that if respondents lack the cognitive ability to read and interpret questionnaires, their motivation and ability to complete a questionnaire will be impaired. Stone et al. (1990) suggested that such effects could be detected by comparing the psychometric properties of questionnaires completed by groups with different levels of cognitive ability.

Stone et al. (1990) employed the Wonderlic Personnel Test to classify 347 Army Reserve members into low, medium, and high cognitive ability groups. Subjects also completed an additional 203 items in a test battery of 27 measures that included the Job Diagnostic Survey, which contains scales to measure such constructs as task identity, autonomy, extrinsic feedback, satisfaction with job duties, and organizational commitment. Stone et al. found significant differences in coefficient alpha for 14 of the 27 constructs. In 12 of those cases, alpha rankings were as predicted, from lowest to highest reliability estimates matching low to high cognitive ability. Stone et al. also found (1) a significant correlation ($r = -.23$) between cognitive ability and the number of missing questionnaire responses and (2) that the scales most adversely affected by low cognitive ability were composed of only three or four items. Finally, Stone et al. noted that estimates place one-third of the U.S. workforce as functionally illiterate and that job titles may provide rough estimates of cognitive ability.

Berk and Fekken (1990) reported a similar finding about the relation between cognitive ability and scale properties. They investigated a person reliability index, a measure of the stability of an individual's test responses, computed with the scales of the Jackson Vocational Interest Survey. This index, which results from producing two scores per scale (each based on half of the items) and then correlating scores across pairs of scales, was significantly correlated across two administrations of the scale ($r = .60$). This result indicates that the person index can function as a reliable measure of whether a profile will remain stable over a brief time period. Interestingly, a measure of verbal ability was significantly correlated ($r = .28$) with a measure of scale stability, suggesting that subjects who were more verbally skilled had more stable scores.

Affective and Motivational Influences

Individuals' affective characteristics and states also influence the testing process. Given the widespread use of psychological tests for selection decisions, it would seem apparent that considerable emotion could result from an individual's perceptions of testing consequences. High-stakes tests can help decide whether a person obtains a particular job, is admitted to a desired school, or avoids an unwanted intervention. Cronbach (1984) noted that

> Draftees have been known to report impressive arrays of emotional symptoms, hoping for discharge. In an ordinary clinical test, exaggerating symptoms may be a gambit to enlist sympathy and attention. An unsuccessful student may prefer to

have the tester believe that his troubles are caused by an emotional disturbance rather than to be thought of as stupid or lazy. (p. 471)

In addition, when tests become the vehicle to create a label or diagnosis that becomes known to test takers and other decision makers, their consequences can have effects that last long beyond any immediate decision. Such labeling can potentially influence individuals' self-concepts and behavior across a range of situations; for example, a student who is placed in a remedial class on the basis of a test may overgeneralize a lack of skill to other content areas (cf. Fairbanks, 1992). This type of effect is one reason psychologists have increased their attention to ethical issues in testing. For example, Messick (1989a, 1989b, 1980) discusses test validity in terms of the function of testing (interpretation and use) as well as the justification for testing (appraisal of evidence and consequence).

Test Anxiety

Test anxiety refers to the emotional experience of individuals who anticipate negative consequences following from test performance (Gregory, 1992). While noting that past research has shown that test anxiety negatively affects test performance (e.g., Hembree, 1988), Gregory (1992) also questioned whether poor performance precedes and causes the anxiety. For example, Paulman and Kennelly (1984) found that test anxious students had ineffective test-taking strategies, and Naveh-Benjamin, McKeachie, and Lin (1987) found that many test anxious students also possessed poor study habits.

Gregory (1992) cited studies indicating that test anxious individuals appear to possess a threshold that once crossed, results in severe performance drops. For example, Sarason (1961, 1972) found no difference in performance on a memorization task between high- and low-anxiety individuals when the task was presented as neutral and nonthreatening. When the task was presented as an intelligence test, however, the highly anxious students' performance declined significantly. Similarly, Siegman (1956) found that highly anxious individuals performed worse on timed, as opposed to untimed subtests of the Weschler Adult Intelligence Scale (WAIS). The results may be explained by the *cue utilization hypothesis* (Easterbrook, 1959), which indicates that emotional arousal alters individuals' ability to attend to environmental cues. As arousal increases, attention is narrowed to task-relevant stimuli; however, once arousal crosses a threshold, individuals lose their capacity to effectively process cues related to the task.

For individuals who perceive a topic or test situation as anxiety producing, completing the test quickly constitutes escape (negative reinforcement). Gentile (1990; see also Geen, 1987) argues that this is widespread in academic tasks, and it is likely to occur in clinical assessment as well. Similarly, Cronbach (1946) noticed that some students may speed through a test, giving the appearance of random responding.

Negative Emotional States

The emotional states that individuals bring to the testing situation can influence test response. Brody and Forehand (1986) found that depressed mothers were more likely than mothers with low depression to interpret their children's noncompliant behavior as indicative of maladjustment. Neufeld (1977) observed that psychologists may avoid testing persons with schizophrenia and some depressed persons because these individuals are presumed to be unable to make valid judgments about their psychological attributes. Contrada and Krantz (1987) reported data indicating that illness and accompanying treatment can affect self-reports. Perceptual and cognitive distortions that may interfere with performance on measurement tasks are also apparent in such clinical phenomena as eating disorders, stress, anxiety, and depression (Halmi, Sunday, Puglisi, & Marchi, 1989; Meier, 1991).

Some authors have proposed an association between affective disorders and test response style. Freeman (1955), for example, suggested that (1) obsessive–compulsive persons provide test responses that are too detailed, but also full of uncertainty and doubt; (2) anxious persons have difficulty finding appropriate words or blurt out inappropriate replies; and (3) psychotic individuals demonstrate disorganized thinking and bizarre content in their responses.

Schwarz (1999) reported on research that indicates that individuals report more intense emotions retrospectively than concurrently (e.g., Parkinson, Briner, Reynolds, & Totterdell, 1995). This may be due to the reference period employed by respondents. Schwarz noted that concurrent reports typically refer to 1 day or so, whereas retrospective reports request information about longer periods. Respondents may infer that with the briefer period the questioner is interested in more frequent events, and that the longer period asks for more infrequent (and possibly, intense) events. It is also possible that with more time, respondents feel more comfortable holding the intense emotions in consciousness.

Fatigue and boredom are psychological states whose effects are presumed to be an interaction between the test taker and test characteristics. Given that traditional personality and cognitive ability tests can require several hours of effort, it is not surprising that some respondents report fatigue and negative thoughts at the end of tests (cf. Galassi, Frierson, & Sharer, 1981). Fatigue effects have been observed, for example, in surveys of magazine readership, crime reports, and symptom lists (Sudman & Bradburn, 1982). In general, humans attempt to minimize their cognitive processing load (e.g., Fisher & Lipson, 1985). Sudman and Bradburn (1982) noted that questionnaire respondents who become aware that "yes" answers are followed by lengthy follow-up questions may quickly learn to answer "no." Similarly, questions may vary in the amount of detail they request respondents to recall (e.g., current salary versus current interest on savings). As Biemer et al. (1991) noted, when questions become too difficult for respondents, they may prematurely terminate their cognitive processing. Whereas rapport with interviewers may help motivate respondents to expend more effort, no such support is present with self-reports (Schwarz, 1997).

Environmental and Cultural Influences

The testing environment can also influence test takers' responses. Potential factors include the presence or absence of an observer, the test taker's and test administrator's gender and race, the physical characteristics of the testing room (e.g., temperature and lighting), and the use of testing apparatus such as pencils or computer keyboards (which may pose difficulties, for example, for persons with physical disabilities). Probably the most studied problem involves the presence of behavioral observers.

Reactivity

Although the term has been employed in the literature with different meanings, I define *reactivity* as the possible distortion in test scores that may result from individuals' awareness that they are being observed by other persons for the purpose of measurement (Kazdin, 1980). The assumption is that as a result of noticing that testing is occurring, or becoming aware of the purpose of testing, individuals may respond differently than they would in unobserved situations. Hartman (1984) reviewed research that found that children's reactivity is influenced by such observer attributes as gender, age, and activity level, whereas adults are influenced by observers' tact and appearance. Other research shows that respondents will pay attention to different aspects of a research situation, depending on their knowledge of the researcher's interests (Norenzayan & Schwarz, 1999).

Reactivity has also been described in terms of the transparency of testing or research. The purpose of test items, for example, can be described as more or less obvious to test takers. The potential importance of reactivity can be illustrated by results reported in Smith and Glass's (1977) meta-analysis of psychotherapy outcome research. Smith and Glass calculated correlations between the amount of psychotherapy gain and such variables as client intelligence, therapist experience, and the reactivity of outcome measures. To gauge reactivity, Smith and Glass rated the transparency of each measure— how obviously the testing procedure was intended to measure something expected to be changed by therapy—employed in the 375 psychotherapy studies they examined. Of all factors examined, reactivity correlated highest with psychotherapy gain at .30. This means that studies that employed the most transparent measures demonstrated the greatest therapeutic gain, leaving open an important alternative methodological explanation for study results.

Stereotype Threat

Related to the idea of reactivity is *stereotype threat*, which occurs when members of a group produce less than optimal performance on a test because of group members' perceptions and reactions to a negative stereotype about the group (Beilock & McConnell, 2004; Steele & Aronson, 1995). The seminal study of stereotype threat was performed by Steele and Aronson (1995), investigating African American students who perceived stereotype threats that indicated they would do more poorly on tests of intelligence. Steele and Aronson (1995) found that in a testing situation in which African American students were led to believe that the test was diagnostic of intellectual ability, they underperformed on difficult Graduate Record Examination (GRE) items in relation to white students. In a testing situation in which the task was presented as unrelated to ability, no difference was found between African American and white students' performances.

Similar to results found with test anxiety (Gregory, 1992) cited earlier, the effects of stereotype threat may be related to the threat's impact on individuals' working memory. Beilock and Carr (2005), for example, presented participants easier or more difficult math problems in high- and low-pressure situations. They defined working memory as "a short-term memory system that maintains, in an active state, a limited amount of information with immediate relevance to the task at hand while preventing distractions from the environment and irrelevant thoughts" (Beilock & Carr, 2005,

p. 101). Beilock and Carr found that people with higher working memory, but not individuals with lower working memory, evidenced a significant decline on high-demand problems in high pressure situations. Referring to high-stakes testing situations, Beilock and Carr (2005, p. 104) suggested that "the individuals most likely to fail under pressure are those who, in the absence of pressure, have the highest capacity for success." Extrapolating this finding to stereotype threat, it may be likely that individuals with the largest working memory capacity may show the largest decrements in performance when they perceive stereotype threat.

Summary and Implications

Although discussions of test validity clearly changed through the first 50 years of the 20th century, initial ideas about validity focused almost exclusively on measures of traits employed for selection purposes. This narrow focus likely hindered, and continues to hinder, the development of new thinking about validity. Similarly, Campbell and Fiske's (1959) work on convergent and discriminant validity may be seen as both a culmination of ideas about trait testing and setting the stage for further progress. Campbell and Fiske's multitrait–multimethod approach allowed a descriptive examination of the effects of method variance, although it did not provide a very thorough explanation of the phenomenon or a specific method to produce such an explanation. Campbell and Fiske's approach and later derivatives focus primarily on traits, leaving open the question of how to assess the construct validity of measures of psychological states.

Method variance is a ubiquitous phenomenon that may partially account for the difficulties test developers encounter when attempting to produce evidence of discriminant validity. Shared method variance on self-reports, for example, may artificially inflate correlations between measures of theoretically dissimilar constructs. Method variance has been proposed as a major culprit in such construct validity problems, but often left unaddressed is the question of why method variance exists in the first place. Although test developers historically were primarily interested in knowing the amount and type of the construct being measured, independent of the effects of method, such a goal seems unreachable without a better theoretical understanding of the causes and processes of method variance.

Recall the Sternberg and Williams (1998, p. 577) quote in Chapter 1: "No technology of which we are aware—computers, telecommunications, televisions, and so on—has shown the kind of ideational stagnation that has characterized the testing industry." Regarding self-reports and interviews, the field continues to deal with many of the same problems that became apparent over the past 100 years. The trait-based paradigm is useful for selection purposes but cannot adequately account for other influences on human behavior, in general, and test-taking behavior in particular. Errors associated with interviews and self-reports continue to hinder the profession's ability to produce data that can be of help to clients, and our ability to cope with such errors depends on the development of better theories related to systematic errors.

The historical evidence suggests that the field has largely failed to evolve in terms of deepening our understanding of method variance and errors associated with self-reports and interviews. What is needed is a method of summing up and integrating knowledge about systematic errors, a theory that would guide and stimulate research in preparation for developing methods of understanding, minimizing, and perhaps controlling factors that cause measurement error. Chapter 5 offers an outline of such a theory, setting the stage for improving construct explication in measurement and assessment.

When creating and evaluating tests, psychologists should draw from substantive theory about the construct in question as well as from measurement theory. Given that construct explication is the process of connecting theory to observable events, any test's construct validity results from proper construct explication. Evidence of problems with construct validity with any particular test presents potentially valuable feedback about how to modify and improve the construct explication process. Construct explication should be an iterative process in which theory is employed to create a measurement procedure, which in turn is employed to produce data, which is then employed to refine the theory and the procedure. These principles equally apply to clinical measurement. If tests employed to measure change in counseling and psychotherapy have not been well explicated, we will not understand important influences on test scores and subsequently will be restricted in our ability to use those scores to help clients. To begin this process, the next chapter describes how conceptualizations about psychological *states* might affect measurement procedures, particularly clinical assessment.

General Measurement-Related Writing Assignment

For the construct chosen, write a sentence or two explaining the likely purpose(s) for which you will measure. For example, you might wish to use a measure of academic achievement to screen for admission to graduate school. Then write a sentence or two describing the likely sample(s) for which you will employ the measurement. For example, you might wish to examine the predictive validity of a measure with students of color.

Change-Related Writing Assignment

Write a paragraph describing the likely sample(s) for which you will employ the change-related measurement. For example, you might wish to see if psychotherapy was successful with a group of depressed college students. As best you can, describe the demographic characteristics of intended samples, including gender (e.g., 75% women, 25% men), race/ethnicity, and age. Do you expect any of these characteristics to influence the degree of change?

QUESTIONS AND EXERCISES

1. For 3 minutes, write down what you consider the major ideas of this section, chapter, or class. At the beginning of next week's class, share with the group.

2. Write brief definitions for some or all of the following terms: *Reliability, validity, construct, construct validity, predictive validity, nomological net, multitrait–multimethod matrix, self-reports, ratings by others, malingering, social desirability, halo errors, hypothesis confirmation bias, reactivity,* and *stereotype threat.*

3. In small groups or individually, answer this question: What are the major advantages and disadvantages of using factor analysis as a method to evaluate test validity?

4. In small groups or individually, list the major advantages and disadvantages of using self-reports as a testing method.

CHAPTER 4

States, Traits, and Validity

Introduction

What exists beyond traits, those stable, enduring psychological characteristics? The logical opposite is *states*, transitory psychological phenomena that result from developmental or situational causes. Spielberger (1991) credited Cattell and Scheier (1961) with introducing the state–trait distinction. Even theorists interested in measuring traits acknowledge the presence of state effects in psychological testing. Lord and Novick (1968), for example, observe that in mental testing "we can perhaps repeat a measurement once or twice, but if we attempt further repetitions, the examinee's response changes substantially because of fatigue or practice effects" (p. 13). Similarly, Matarazzo suggested that the Minnesota Multiphasic Personality Inventory (MMPI) measures states, not traits, and that the test "reflects how you're feeling today, or how you want to present yourself that day" (Bales, 1990, p. 7). Dahlstrom (1969) likewise indicated that MMPI scales' reliability should not be assessed through test–retest methods because "there is scarcely any scale on the MMPI for which this general assumption [of temporal stability] is tenable for any period of time longer than a day or two" (p. 27). Even intelligence may possess state properties: IQ test scores have been shown to be affected by amount of schooling (Ceci, 1991; see also Bandura, 1991, and Frederiksen, 1986). Retest of intelligence scores at 1-year intervals show high stability but decrease substantially when the retest interval lengthens beyond that period (Humphreys, 1992).

Although trait conceptions have historically dominated measurement, psychologists have always recognized states and struggled to integrate them into measurement theory and practice. Loevinger (1957), for example, reviewed Fiske and Rice's (1955) theory for explaining intraindividual response variation. Fiske and Rice suggested that individuals will change their response to an item because:

1. Something changes within the individual (e.g., the individual matures),
2. The order of item presentation changes, or
3. The stimulus situation changes.

Fatigue, for example, is a physiological variable that might produce inconsistent responding on psychological tests. When the SAT was recently revised to include a written component, for example, anecdotal reports suggested that increased fatigue might be causing a decrease in average SAT scores. Fiske and Rice (1955) suggested that variability due to an influence such as fatigue is systematic, although Loevinger (1957) noted that this belief differs with the classical test theory assumption that such errors are random. Loevinger also reviewed studies that demonstrated, over retesting, improvements in personality functioning and intelligence. Such improvements, Loevinger suggested, are a function of practice effects and learning. In other words, psychological phenomena also demonstrate state effects.

In this chapter I discuss state effects resulting from situational or environmental influences. In these instances, scientific disagreement about trait conceptualizations led to the development of theories about the effects of situations and environments, as well as ways of measuring those effects.

History

Watson in the early 1900s focused on behavior, not internal psychological constructs like traits. Behaviorists maintained that a psychological phenomenon was not real unless it could be directly observed. Given such assumptions, there was little need for measurement concepts: Whatever could be operationally defined (in the laboratory) or observed (in the clinic), existed. The psychological phenomena of interest to the mental testers, however, were almost always assumed to be unobservable: Traits were *latent*. No single behavior could constitute intelligence, for example, but intelligence formed an abstract, useful construct that could explain clusters of behavior. Intelligence itself was not directly observable, and to this day the most advanced theories of mental testing discuss intelligence in terms of latent traits.

Traditional psychological measurement versus behavioral assessment is one of many historical controversies found in psychology (Staats, 1983). Proponents of these two approaches tend to be interested in traits or behavior (Fiske, 1979). In one world sits traditional measurement, with its emphasis on traits, "real, relatively stable differences between individuals in behavior, interests, preferences, perceptions, and beliefs" (Murphy & Davidshofer, 1988, p. 17). In another is behavioral assessment, with its emphasis on psychological states as influenced by the environment. Rarely do the ideas of these approaches mix.

Some initial integration of the two positions has occurred (e.g., Silva, 1993), but the process remains incomplete. Behavioral assessors, for example, have more recently observed that fear is a construct. That is, no single index of fear exists, but the construct of fear may be useful for certain purposes. In the clinic, many effective behavioral techniques have been developed to alleviate patients' fears. In the course of applying those techniques, however, assessors have observed a *desynchrony* between different indices of fear. At the conclusion of treatment, it is possible for a person who is snake phobic, for example, to be able to approach a snake and verbally report no fear, but still have an accelerated heart rate. Unless each phenomenon is defined by its measurement mode, theorists must resort to the use of a construct to make sense of this situation. Rachman and Hodgson (1974) cited Lang's (1968) definition of fear as a construct composed of "loosely coupled components" (Rachman & Hodgson, 1974, p. 311) that may covary or vary independently. Because of such cases and concepts, some behavioral assessors have become interested in applying traditional measurement concepts in their domain (e.g., Hartman, 1984).

Traits are assumed to be stable across situations. Use of the term *trait* implies that enough cross-situational stability occurs so that "useful statements about individual behavior can be made without having to specify the eliciting situations" (Epstein, 1979, p. 1122). Similarly, Campbell and Fiske (1959) stated that "any conceptual formulation of trait will usually include implicitly the proposition that this trait is a response tendency which can be observed under more than one experimental condition" (p. 100). Persons described as honest, for example, are expected to display honest behavior regardless of the situations in which they find themselves. Figure 4.1 displays examples of cross-situational consistency and inconsistency. For example, individuals who score low on a test of honesty may behave dishonestly in classrooms (C) and stores (S), whereas more honest individuals

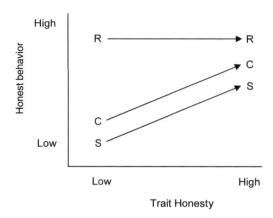

FIGURE 4.1. Cross-situational consistency and inconsistency. Do honest people behave honestly in all situations? R refers to a religious setting such as a church or temple; C refers to a classroom setting; and S refers to a store. As an example of cross-situational inconsistency, even persons with low trait honesty may behave honestly in a religious setting.

behave honestly in those settings. In religious situations (R), however, both high- and low-honesty individuals may behave honestly. Honest behavior in this example is both situation specific and cross-situationally consistent.

Continued faith in trait measurement has been maintained at least partially by its success. For example, most measurement in vocational psychology is guided by trait-and-factor theory. The tests employed by vocational psychologists typically measure occupational interests, also assumed to be stable. Test takers' interest scores are compared with the scores of successful workers in all occupations to determine the best fit. The theory of work adjustment (Dawis & Lofquist, 1984; Lofquist & Dawis, 1969) proposes that to maximize worker satisfaction and production, individuals' abilities and needs must be matched with job requirements and reinforcers. Abilities, needs, job requirements, and reinforcers are assumed to be relatively stable. Yet vocational counselors have also been influenced by a developmental concept, that of *vocational self-concept crystallization* (Barrett & Tinsley, 1977). Developmental theorists have suggested that vocational identities—individuals' beliefs about their abilities and needs—tend to grow and shift until the time when they crystallize, thought to be around age 18. That is, one's vocational identity becomes a trait, presumably stable for the remainder of one's life. A similar idea, the *differentiation hypothesis* (Anastasi, 1985), has been proposed to account for the emergence in individuals of group factors of intelligence (i.e., more specific abilities such as verbal or spatial ability).

As noted previously, traits were first employed with the concept of intelligence, a phenomenon assumed to be transmitted through heredity and largely immune to environmental influences. Although measures of intelligence predicted school performance better than physiological measures, scores based on the performance of these mental tasks still fell considerably short of the mark of total prediction. If intelligence tasks fail, where is the next logical place to look for variables to assist in prediction? Personality and temperament were psychologists' answer to that question.

The Controversy of Mischel and Peterson: The Benefits of Conflict

Developers of personality and temperament tests closely copied the assumptions and procedures of intelligence tests (Danziger, 1990). With both intelligence and personality tests, scaling involved aggregation; that is, a total score was obtained by adding the total number of correctly performed tasks or endorsed items. Most important, personality, like intelligence, was assumed to be consistent across persons and independent of environments. Yet trait-based tests do not produce entirely consistent scores. Loevinger (1957) wrote that "circumstances contrive to keep behavior largely unpredictable, however constant its propensities" (pp. 688–689). The importance of environment was emphasized in 1968 with the publication of Mischel's *Personality and Assessment* and Peterson's *Clinical Study of Social Behavior*. These books ignited a controversy between measurement and personality theorists that continues to smolder.

Mischel (1968) contended that personality constructs were unstable, that is, that the influence of traits was relatively small compared with the influence of situations or environments. He reviewed findings of measurement studies and proceeded to criticize personality psychologists for failing to account for environmental factors when measuring traits: "What people do in all situations and on all tests can be affected, often quite readily, by many stimulus conditions and can be modified substantially by numerous environmental manipulations" (p. 10). Mischel favored measuring behavior in specific situations as opposed to measuring signs of underlying mental processes that could presumably predict future behavior. Mischel believed that new theories needed to be developed that could account for human adaptability, perception, cognition, self-regulation, and self-modification.

Peterson (1968) sounded a similar theme when he stated that because of the influence of situations on behavior, research had "suggested very strongly that traditional conceptions of personality as internal behavior dispositions were inadequate and insufficient" (p. 23). Peterson reviewed studies supporting this position in a number of areas, including research documenting the effects of examiners on the behavior of individuals taking *projective devices* (i.e., psychological tests that present ambiguous stimuli). Whether Rorschach examiners were friendly or distant, Peterson noted, influenced the number and types of responses produced by examinees. Discussing personality assessment in the context of clinical applications, Peterson (1968) concluded that because "strong positive evidence for validity and utility is nowhere to be seen ... it looks as if entirely new approaches to the clinical study of behavior will have to be developed" (p. 3).

Mischel's and Peterson's publications prompted many psychologists to reexamine trait-based measurement approaches. The violation of the expectation of personality consistency produced three major responses. Traditional theorists sought out more evidence for the consistency of traits. In contrast, some psychologists came to reject intrapsychic traits entirely. Most mainstream psychologists did not follow this extreme direction, however, preferring to search for explanations in the interaction between psychological traits and environments. Each position is described more fully below.

The Rejection of Traits: Behavioral Assessment

Behaviorists emphasized the dominance of environmental reinforcement in shaping an individual's behavior, be it motor or verbal. In contrast to traditional psychological measurement, behavioral assessors are interested in measuring individuals' past learning histories and current environmental influences (Nelson & Hayes, 1986). Behavioral assessors observe behavior in natural or contrived settings and attend to stimuli, behavioral responses, and the consequences of those responses.

The processes, assumptions, and procedures of behavioral assessment differ from those of traditional measurement. Hartman (1984) emphasized that behavioral assessment is direct, repeated, and idiographic. Assessment is direct in that the assessor measures observable behavior. Any observed behavior is considered to be a sample of potential behavior, as opposed to a sign of an underlying, unobservable trait (cf. Goodenough, 1950, cited in Cronbach & Meehl, 1955). Behavior is measured repeatedly for the purpose of demonstrating relative stability before intervention, and change after intervention, thus demonstrating that the intervention is the cause of the behavioral change. Assessment may consist of continuous recording of behavior (when only a few behaviors occur) or some type of strategic sampling with many behaviors.

Behavioral psychologists assess idiographic variables, that is, those unique to the individual in question. Cone (1988) argued that nomothetic, trait-based measurements produce data remote from single cases. He suggested that idiographic instruments would be more sensitive to individual behavior change. In this context, idiographic measures are *criterion referenced* (i.e., scores are compared with some absolute measure of behavior), whereas nomothetic are *norm referenced* (i.e., scores are compared among individuals). Norm-referenced tests are constructed to maximize variability among individuals (Swezey, 1981). However, items that measure behaviors infrequently performed by the population are unlikely to be included in norm-referenced tests. Jackson (1970), for example, suggested that items checked by less than 20% of the test development sample be dropped because they will not contribute to total score variability. Yet those infrequent, idiographically relevant items may be the very ones of interest to therapists and theorists.

In traditional psychological measurement, anyone can be a self- or other observer if enough measurements are gathered to decrease measurement error. In contrast, behavioral assessment involves trained observers. Described further in Chapter 5, training consists of learning the contents of an observation manual (containing definitions of relevant behavior and scoring procedures), conducting analogue observations, on-site practice, retraining, and debriefing (Hartman, 1984; Nay, 1979; Paul, 1986). Hartman (1984) noted that research has indicated that more accurate observational skills have been associated with older persons, women, and greater levels of social skills, intelligence, motivation, and attention to detail.

Behavioral assessors traditionally have expressed ambivalence about the utility of psychometric analyses. More recently, however, behavioral assessors have begun to attend to validity estimates of constructs such as anxiety and fear that are likely to be manifested with more than one behavior. Whether measures of eye contact, voice volume, and facial expression all relate to a client's complaint about shyness (Kazdin, 1985), for example, can be framed as a question of construct validity. Yet Cone (1988) stated that

> Construct validity will be of no concern to behavioral assessors, in one sense since constructs are not the subject of interest, behavior is; in another sense, behavior can be seen as a construct itself, in which case the instrument will have construct validity to the extent that it "makes sense" in terms of the behavior as the client and the assessor understand it. (p. 59)

Cone (1988) also questioned the importance of discriminant validity, saying that it "is not relevant to an assessment enterprise that is built on the accuracy of its instruments. By definition, an accurate instrument taps the behavior of interest and not something else" (p. 61).

Cone (1988) and Pervin (1984) indicated that additional theoretical and psychometric criteria need to be established for behavioral assessment. For example, Cone (1988) proposed that a behavioral measure, to be considered accurate, must be able to (1) detect the occurrence of a behavior; (2) detect a behavior's repeated occurrence; (3) detect its occurrence in more than one setting; and (4) have parallel forms that allow detection of covariation to demonstrate that the behavior can be detected independent of any particular method. Cone also observed that no guidelines currently exist for selecting dimensions relevant to particular clients or for developing instruments to assess these dimensions; interestingly, both of these criteria are strengths of nomothetic approaches (cf. Buss & Craik, 1985). Cone proposed that such guidelines include (1) determining the environmental context of the problem; (2) determining how other people cope with the problem in that environment; and (3) constructing a template of effective behaviors to match against the clients' current repertoire. Such a template could be used to guide therapy and as a gauge of therapy's effectiveness.

Reinforcing the Trait Argument

Some contemporary psychologists consider the attack to be repulsed and the battle won (e.g., Block, 1977; Epstein, 1990; Goldberg, 1993). For example, Anastasi (1985) stated that "the long-standing controversy between situational specificity and personality traits has been largely resolved" (p. 134). Anastasi's solution was to redefine traits as repositories of behavioral consistencies. Traits so defined are not causes, but simply convenient descriptions of psychological regularities that occur and may be influenced by environmental contexts.

On the basis of studies employing a variety of research methodologies and samples, personality researchers have become increasingly confident that long-term stability of personality traits exists. West and Graziano (1989) concluded that research studies have demonstrated substantial long-term stability of personality in children and adults. They also noted, however, that stability declines across longer measurement intervals, is lower in children, and depends on the particular traits measured. Moreover, predictions of personality from one time point to another account for only about 25% of the variance, leaving considerable room for environmental and person–environment influences. Examining the stability of vocational interests,

Swanson and Hansen (1988; see also Campbell, 1971) found similar results: Although individual variability and environmental influences existed, trait stability could be demonstrated over time. Similarly, Staw and Ross (1985) studied 5,000 middle-aged men and found that job satisfaction remained stable even when employees changed jobs and occupations. In a laboratory study with 140 undergraduates, Funder and Colvin (1991) found behavioral consistency across laboratory and real-life settings, although consistency varied by type of behavior.

Epstein (1979, 1980) proposed that trait inconsistency results from insufficient aggregation of measurement observations. For example, one can aggregate 30 test items into a total score, and this total score is likely to predict criteria better than any one of the individual items. Similarly, one can aggregate scores across different measurement occasions. Although acknowledging evidence that behavior changes as a result of situational variables, Epstein (1979) reviewed research that found that aggregating psychological measurements results in a substantial increase in validity coefficients. In terms of classical test theory, aggregation works because behavioral consistencies accumulate over multiple measurements, but random errors do not (Rushton, Jackson, & Paunonen, 1981). Epstein (1979) also conducted a series of studies that found that through aggregation, intercorrelations of measures of behavior, self-reports, and ratings by others could exceed the typical .30 ceiling.

Most contemporary psychologists view the scores produced on intelligence tests as stable and as indicative of latent traits that operate across environments. Schmidt and Hunter's (1977) work on validity generalization, for example, indicates that for general classes of occupational groups, tests of cognitive abilities may be valid across a wide variety of situations. Their research demonstrated that a significant portion of the variability among validity coefficients reported in the literature results from methodological problems such as small sample size, criterion unreliability, and scale range restrictions. When these sources of error are removed, cognitive tests have relatively stable validity within occupational groups. This work complements the position of Mischel (1968), who found that cross-situational consistency existed for behavioral correlates of cognitive abilities. However, validity generalization proponents' claim of negligible variation over situations has not been universally accepted (Tenopyr, 1992; also see Cronbach's, 1991b, analysis of Hedges's, 1987, data).

Much of the contemporary work on traits focuses on the *Big Five*. Given the desire for a taxonomy of important traits, personality psychologists have reached a consensus about what are termed the Big Five factors (Cattell, 1946; Goldberg, 1990; Digman, 1990; McCrae & Costa, 1989; Norman, 1963; Tupes & Christal, 1961; Wiggins & Pincus, 1989). These orthogonal or independent factors—neuroticism, extraversion, openness to experience, agreeableness, and conscientiousness—have been proposed as nomothetic structures to guide the measurement of personality and inter-personal behavior. Factor analyses of trait descriptors, produced by different methods (e.g., self-report and ratings by others) and with different samples (including cross-cultural), have resulted in the identification of five factors (Botwin & Buss, 1989; John, Angleitner, & Ostendorf, 1988; McCrae & Costa, 1985, 1987). Two major components of the circumplex model (i.e., circular relations among factors) of interpersonal behavior, dominance and nurturance, have also been connected to the Big Five factors of extroversion and agreeableness (Trapnell & Wiggins, 1990).

A significant issue for clinicians is whether the Big Five provides useful information. Paul (2004) quotes McAdams as criticizing the Big Five for simply describing "the psychology of the stranger." That is, the Big Five represents relatively shallow information that individuals quickly glean when they meet a stranger, not the in-depth knowledge learned about a coworker, friend, or family member. Empirical results also provide some ambiguity about the Big Five model (Botwin & Buss, 1989; Block, 1995; Briggs, 1992). Botwin and Buss (1989), for example, instructed 59 couples to report information about the self and partner regarding previously performed behaviors corresponding to the five-factor model. Factor analyses of self and partner data yielded similar results, but Botwin and Buss concluded that the re-sulting factors, labeled responsible-stable, insecure, antagonistic-boorish, so-ciable, and culture, departed substantially from the five-factor model. When ratings data were adjusted for the frequency level of the behaviors, however, the resulting factors closely matched the five-factor model.

Person–Environment Interactions

The importance of *person–environment interactions* has been recognized for some time (Kantor, 1924; Lewin, 1935; Murray, 1938, cited in McFall & McDonel, 1986). In person–environment interactions, a person's behavior and the environment in which that behavior occurs are viewed as a feed-back loop in which each influences the other (Magnusson & Endler, 1977). Instead of focusing on persons or situations, behavior must be measured in context, as a process that occurs in a steady stream. Bowers (1973) noted that from an interactionist perspective, individuals influence their environ-ments as much as their environments influence them. To a significant extent, people create their own environments to inhabit (Wachtel, 1973; Bandura, 1986).

Bowers (1973) approached interaction from the perspective of Piaget's concepts of assimilation and accommodation. Individuals assimilate observations from the environment into preexisting cognitive schemas. At the same time, those schemas are modified to accommodate new information in the environment. Bowers (1973) stated that "the situation is a function of the observer in the sense that the observer's cognitive schemas filter and organize the environment in a fashion that makes it impossible ever to completely separate the environment from the person observing it" (p. 328).

Most interactionists assume that cognition mediates the perception of the environment. This is important because it means that behavior that appears inconsistent may actually be indicative of a single construct. For example, Magnusson and Endler (1977) observed that anxiety may motivate a person to speak excessively in one situation and withdraw in another. The behaviors differ, but the causal construct (anxiety) is the same across situations. As shown in Figure 4.2, the relation between behavior and construct may also be nonlinear. Thus, anxiety may motivate an individual to increase the amount of talking until it reaches a threshold where the individual begins to decrease speech and finally withdraws.

Magnusson and Endler (1977) discussed this type of consistency using the term *coherence*. They suggest that coherent behavior can be understood in terms of the interaction between an individual's perception of a situation and the individual's disposition to react in a consistent manner to such perceived situations. The factors that influence this interaction, such as intelligence, skills, learning history, interests, attitudes, needs, and values, may be quite stable within individuals. As shown in Figure 4.3, individuals C and D, who score highly on a test of honesty, may show more honest behavior across two situations than individuals A and B, who obtain low

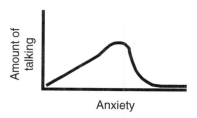

FIGURE 4.2. Nonlinear relation between speech and anxiety. Anxiety may cause an increase in the amount an individual talks until a threshold is reached. Then the individual talks less and finally withdraws.

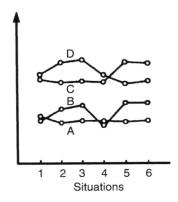

Situations

FIGURE 4.3. Situations' effect on the consistency of behavior. Two individuals (C and D) who score highly on a test of honesty may show more honest behavior across two situations than two individuals who obtain low scores (A and B). However, C and D may also display differences between themselves in honest behavior across situations even though their mean behavior score is the same across situations. From Magnusson and Endler (1977). Copyright 1977 by the Copyright Clearance Center. Reprinted by permission.

scores. However, C and D may also display differences between themselves in honest behavior across situations—perhaps because of slight differences in their perceptions of those situations—even though their mean behavior score is the same across situations. From the perspective of the individual, the behavior appears coherent. From the perspective of the observer who looks only at group differences, the behavior appears consistent. From the perspective of the observer who looks at individuals across situations, the behavior appears inconsistent.

Appropriate techniques for measuring and analyzing the processes suggested by interactionist theory remain in dispute (Golding, 1975; McFall & McDonel, 1986; Walsh & Betz, 1985). For example, McFall and McDonel (1986) maintained that (1) analysis of variance (ANOVA) procedures that examine statistical interactions fail to investigate the theoretically central question of how person–situation variables interact over time; (2) investigators can easily manipulate experiments to show the relative importance of person, situation, or interaction factors; and (3) problems of scale remain, that is, no framework exists for how to determine the meaning of different units or chunks of the person–situation process. Bowers (1973) suggested that a rigid adherence to research methodologies has obscured the interactionist perspective. Experimental methods help investigators primarily to understand the influence of situations, and correlational methods may assist in the understanding of person differences.

Aptitude-by-Treatment Interactions

Treatments can be conceptualized as types of situations (Cronbach, 1975b; Cronbach & Snow, 1977). In a study in which an experimental group is contrasted with a control group, both groups are experiencing different types of situations. Persons can also be conceptualized as having aptitudes, that is, individual characteristics that affect their response to treatments (Cronbach, 1975b). As shown in Figures 4.4 and 4.5, in an aptitude-by-treatment interactions (ATI) study researchers attempt to identify important individual differences that would facilitate or hinder the usefulness of various treatments (Snow, 1991). From a commonsense perspective, ATIs should be plentiful in the real world. From the perspective of selection, intervention, and theoretical research, finding ATIs would seem to be of the utmost importance.

ATIs were Cronbach's answer to the problem of unifying correlational and experimental psychology (Snow & Wiley, 1991). Cronbach (1957, 1975b) noted that the battle over the relative dominance of traits versus environment was maintained by ignoring the possibilities of interactions. For example, Cronbach (1975b) reported a study by Domino (1971) that

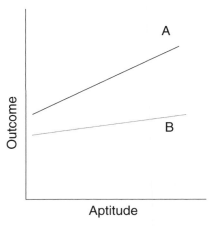

FIGURE 4.4. Aptitude-by-treatment interaction—1. In an ATI, the aptitude of subjects interacts with treatments to produce differing outcomes. Here individuals high on an aptitude enjoy a much better outcome when completing Treatment A than Treatment B. From Cronbach (1957). Copyright 1957 by the American Psychological Association. Reprinted with permission.

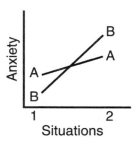

FIGURE 4.5. Aptitude-by-treatment interaction—2. Here A refers to a group of individuals with high anxiety and B to a group with low anxiety. Situation 2 causes an increase in anxiety for both groups, but the change is disproportionately larger for group B. Note that treatments and situations can be considered interchangeable in this graphic.

investigated the effects of an interaction between learning environment and student learning style on course performance. Domino hypothesized that students who learn best by setting their own assignments and tasks (independent learners) might show the best outcomes in a class when paired with teachers who provided considerable independence. Similarly, students who learn best when provided with assignments by the teacher (achievement through conformity) might perform better when paired with instructors who pressed for conformity (e.g., teachers who stress that students meet the teacher's requirements). Domino did find empirical support for this interaction.

Cronbach (1975b) and others (cf. Fiske, 1979; McFall & McDonel, 1986; Scriven, 1969), however, largely abandoned the search for general laws via ATIs in favor of local, descriptive observations. Cronbach (1975b) noted that results supporting ATIs are inconsistent, often disappearing when attempts to replicate occur. He saw time and history as the major culprits: Many psychological phenomena change over time, frustrating attempts to fix them as general laws. Cronbach (1975b) indicated that trait conceptions do not hold to the extent necessary to demonstrate consistent ATIs. This may also be interpreted as support for the position that situations have stronger effects than traits or trait–situation interactions.

Approaches such as ATIs and person–environment interaction theories have had relatively little impact on psychological measurement. The problem, Walsh and Betz (1985) believe, "is one of measuring and describing the multidirectional transactions. Currently this is a measurement task that has been very difficult to operationalize and make real" (p. 13). Measurement error is a plausible explanation for the failure to find person–environment interactions (Cronbach, 1991b); imprecise measurement leads to a loss of statistical power that obscures interactions. And because of cost and the fact that investigators have yet to settle on a taxonomy for situations (McFall & McDonel, 1986), person–environment approaches have yet to command the attention given to traditional measurement.

Environmental Assessment

Instead of searching for stability in individuals, another group of theorists and researchers seek to find consistency in environments and situations. Attempts to categorize and measure environments form the essence of this measurement approach (Conyne & Clack, 1981; Walsh, 1973). One of the major tasks of environmental assessment is an analysis of environment types, and many classifications systems have been proposed to accomplish this task (cf. Goodstein, 1978; Huebner, 1979; Steele, 1973). Conyne and Clack (1981) proposed that an environment consists of physical, social, institutional, and ecological–climate components that shape and are shaped by people. Moos (1973) classified human environments into ecology, behavior setting, organizational structure, inhabitants' behavior and characteristics, psychosocial climate, and functional reinforcements (i.e., environmental stimuli).

Many vocational psychologists hold similar assumptions about the relative stability of work environments. An occupational setting may attract certain types of individuals on the basis of the setting's fit with the needs and abilities of the worker. Holland (1959, 1985) proposed one of the best-known and well-researched occupational classifications. He suggested that work environments may be classified as involving one or more of the following dimensions:

1. *Realistic* environments, where work entails mechanical skill, physical strength, motor coordination, and concrete problems
2. *Investigative* environments, with an emphasis on research activities, scientific accomplishments, mathematics ability, and abstract problems
3. *Artistic* environments, involving artistic activities and competencies, and an emphasis on expressive, original, and independent behavior
4. *Social* environments, where work involves social interactions, liking others, cooperation, and help giving
5. *Enterprising* environments, involving selling and leading activities, self-confidence, aggressiveness, and status
6. *Conventional* environments, involving recording and organizing records and data, conformity, and dependability

Holland (1985) believed, however, that individuals' characteristics may change the climate of the work setting. The most important variable in this regard is the extent to which individuals' needs and abilities are congruent with the work environments in which individuals find themselves. Very incongruent individuals leave environments, whereas moderately incongruent individuals will change, moving toward the dominant persons in the environment.

Most person–work environment fit theories suggest that the degree to which individuals fit their work environment determines their level of productivity and job satisfaction. Thus, Realistic individuals working in Realistic occupations will be most productive and satisfied, as will Investigative individuals in Investigative occupations, and so on. Holland's theory also provides for similarity of occupational types (e.g., Investigative and Artistic occupations are more similar than Investigative and Conventional occupations) so that different fits may be rank ordered in terms of their degree of expected productivity and satisfaction.

A crucial question in environmental assessment is whether to classify environments or perceptions of environments. The person who initially developed the idea of person–environment interaction, Kurt Lewin, continued a Gestalt perspective in which behavior was believed to occur in the context of an individual's total perceptual field of an environment (Lewin, 1951). That is, people are surrounded by a self-generated psychological environment and a nonpsychological environment. As in other person–environment theories, cognition has been proposed as a significant mediator of how environmental events are perceived, understood, and transformed by individuals (Conyne & Clack, 1981; Bandura, 1986). From this perspective, an understanding of how an individual thinks about a situation is necessary for a person–environment analysis. For example, McCall (1991) observed that after completing a Marine Corps confidence course, recruits may view the course as a confidence builder or as intimidating. Some theorists had hoped that cognition might prove to be stable across situations, but research results have not been supportive. For example, attributional style—characteristic ways individuals explain and interpret life events (Fiske & Taylor, 1984)—appears to possess little consistency across situations (Bagby, Atkinson, Dickens, & Gavin, 1990; Cutrona, Russell, & Jones, 1984).

What kinds of measurements are undertaken in environmental assessment? Conyne and Clack (1981) provided several examples. *Cognitive maps* are spatial representations of individuals' psychological environments. Conyne and Clack described a researcher who instructed students to plot where in their neighborhoods they felt high and low stress. The resulting map helped to explain truancy by showing that a city school bus route stopped at many high-stress areas where students were afraid of being physically attacked. However, many environmental assessment procedures consist only of self-report questionnaires that ask respondents to rate environments along different theoretical dimensions. In Moos's (1979a, 1979b) social climate scales, for example, individuals rate such environments as their college residence hall, classroom, family, and work along such dimensions as relationships, personal growth, and system maintenance and change. Similarly, vocational psychologists measure environments by assessing (via self-reports) the interests and abilities of persons successful in specific occupations.

Moderators of Cross-Situational Consistency

Moderator variables are those that change the nature of the relation between two other variables. For example, one may propose that Investigative individuals would be most productive and satisfied in an academic or scientific environment as compared to other occupational situations. However, one might find that other variables, such as ethnicity or gender, affect that relation. Female and male academics might produce equal number of publications, but women might also experience less job satisfaction if they are paid less.

A variety of potential moderating variables have been proposed and investigated related to cross-situational consistency. Research has suggested differences in consistency by response mode and by levels of aggregated measures (Diener & Larsen, 1984; Epstein, 1983; Mischel & Peake, 1982; Rushton, Brainerd, & Pressley, 1983). For example, Violato and Travis (1988) found that male elementary school students demonstrated more cross-situational consistency on the variable of behavioral persistence. Similarly, Connell and Thompson (1986) found infants' emotional reactions were more consistent across time than their social behavior. Variables such as age (Stattin, 1984), gender (Forzi, 1984), socioeconomic status, and cognitive abilities (Violato & Travis, 1988) have also been found to moderate cross-situational consistency.

Bem and Allen (1974; also see Diener & Larsen, 1984; Lanning, 1988; Zuckerman et al., 1988) suggested that individuals themselves are moderators of cross-situational consistency. That is, some persons may act consistently across situations, and others may not; cross-situational consistency could be considered an individual difference variable. Thus, in person A, the trait of honesty is manifested across all situations; with person B, honesty occurs only at church; and person C exhibits little honesty in any situation. Investigators who conduct studies averaging these individuals would find no support for cross-situational positions, but a disaggregation of the data might demonstrate such consistency for pairings of similar individuals such as A and C. Bem and Allen (1974) found that students' ratings of their cross-situational consistencies often did match their behaviors in different situations. For example, students who said they were friendly across situations did show more consistency. However, more recent research has provided mixed support for this position. Chaplin and Goldberg (1984) failed to replicate Bem and Allen's results, and Greaner and Penner (1982) found a low reliability estimate for the one-item consistency measure previously employed by Bem and Allen.

Summary and Integration

Tryon (1991) suggested one possible resolution to the state–trait dilemma. First, evidence for situational specificity simply requires demonstration of different levels of behavior in one situation as compared with another. As shown in Figure 4.6, individuals may demonstrate, in general, more anxiety in two testing situations (situations 2 and 4) than in two lectures (situations 1 and 3). Arguments for traits, Tryon indicated, involve persons maintaining their rank on a construct within the distribution of behavior. If Persons A, B, C, and D rank first, second, third, and fourth in the amount of anxiety they display at a lecture, and then maintain that ranking in other settings, trait arguments will be upheld even if overall levels of anxiety change. Tryon (1991) believed that it is possible to hold both the situational specificity and trait positions inasmuch as "activity is both very different across situations yet predictable from situation to situation" (p. 14). He concluded:

> Situational differences are so large that they stand out immediately. Person consistency is more subtle and requires aggregation to reach substantial effect size. The Spearman–Brown prophecy formula indicates that either effect size can be made arbitrarily large depending upon the level of aggregation chosen. The implication for research and clinical practice is that one should choose the level of aggregation that provides the necessary effect size to achieve the stated purpose of the empirical inquiry at hand. (p. 14)

From a historical viewpoint, the trait–state debate led to useful research and theoretical development suggesting that psychological phenomena

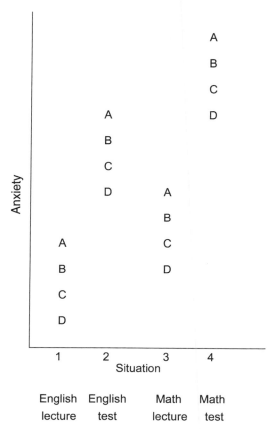

FIGURE 4.6. Coexistence of situational specificity and trait consistency. A, B, C, and D refer to four persons who are taking an English and a math class. Situations 1 and 3 are lecture periods for the English and math classes; situations 2 and 4 are the testing periods those classes. Groups of individuals will show different average levels of anxiety between the lecture and testing situations, thus supporting situational specificity. However, individuals' levels of anxiety could remain in the same rank order across situations, thus supporting trait concepts.

can demonstrate both trait and state characteristics. In other words, psychological phenomena are likely to demonstrate some stability (that is, to be a reflection of psychological traits) as well as change (that is, to be influenced by environmental and developmental factors). Goldberg's (1993) question, "Do traits exist?" may be rephrased as Cone's (1991), "What levels of aggregation of tests and criteria are needed to demonstrate trait properties?" To demonstrate trait consistency, it appears necessary to aggregate items, persons, and occasions of measurement. In addition, some people and dimensions appear more stable than others (Bem & Allen, 1974; Martin, 1988). Overall, test scores should evidence greater validity if the test developer and test user consider and employ appropriate measurement procedures in light of both the trait and state properties of the construct as well as the intended purpose of testing.

For purposes of measuring process and outcome in counseling and psychotherapy, the influence of states, environments, and situations has two implications. First, psychotherapy itself can be considered a social situation that impacts clients' thoughts, feelings, and behaviors. The most basic question about psychotherapy's impact, then, is what changes and what remains stable after a period of therapy? Surprisingly, relatively little is known about what changes as a result of counseling and psychotherapy. Weisz, Huey, and Weersing (1998), for example, noted that "the lack of specificity regarding which elements of the treatment are producing which aspects of client change has led to calls for a more fine-grained analysis of the processes of child psychotherapy that influence treatment outcome" (p. 65). Second, test takers experience the process of completing a psychological test as a situation, and their perceptions of the testing situation can have unintended effects on test scores. Researchers and theorists have focused primarily on effects that result from differences in testing method (e.g., being observed versus completing a self-report). Clients who know they are being observed during a role play related to social anxiety, for example, may produce different behavior than the behavior described in the self-reports they provide about their socially anxious behavior. But the testing situation comprises more than just the type of testing method, and the field possesses relatively little knowledge about the kinds or size of the effects produced by other aspects of test taking.

General Measurement-Related Writing Assignment

Choose at least three tests to measure your construct of interest. For the three measures you chose, conduct a brief literature review (searching sources such as *PsycINFO*, *Tests in Print*, *Mental Measurements Yearbooks*, and *Test Critiques*, or test manuals for published tests) and find at least one source for each measure who reports the purpose(s) for which the test was employed. In a table, report the author/year of the source as well as the type of purpose. In many cases, sources will not explicitly report the purpose(s) for which the test may be appropriately used, and you may need to infer this.

Change-Related Writing Assignment

Choose at least three tests to measure your change-related construct. For each of the three measures you chose, conduct a brief literature review (searching sources such as *PsycINFO*, *Tests in Print*, *Mental Measurements Yearbooks*, and *Test Critiques*, or test manuals for published tests) and find at least one source who reported the use of one of the tests for measuring change and summarize that report in a paragraph. If you can find no report of a particular measure being used to assess change, describe other uses for which it has been employed.

QUESTIONS AND EXERCISES

1. For 3 minutes, write down what you consider the major ideas of this section, chapter, or class. At the beginning of next week's class, share with the group.

2. Write brief definitions for the following terms: *states, behavioral assessment, Big Five, aptitude-by-treatment interactions, cross-situational consistency,* and *situational specificity.*

3. What are the major differences between trait-based measurement and behavior assessment?

4. Suppose you are a faculty member who directs a graduate program in a counseling field. You decide that you will develop a test that will help you select the best graduate students from the pool of applicants. Divide students into small groups and assign each group the task of developing a selection test based on the assumptions of one of the following philosophies: Behavioral assessment, traits, person–environment interactions, aptitude-by-treatment interactions (ATIs), or environmental assessment. Once complete, share your testing method(s) with the class as a whole and discuss how they differ and overlap.

CHAPTER 5

Context Effects and Validity

Introduction

How can the testing field develop a better theoretical understanding of the long list of measurement problems? Danziger (1990) suggested that during the historical development of psychology, certain methods became the only acceptable alternatives available to investigators. The decision to employ these methods, Danziger noted, was not necessarily rational and was certainly influenced by political forces within the testing profession and economic forces in the testing marketplace. As seen from the historical review provided in previous chapters, selection purposes have driven thinking about psychological measurement and assessment. One can frame the purpose of tests in terms of cost-effective decision making for selection, but such a perspective can also obscure and complicate the use of tests for other purposes. A basic theme of this book is that the adoption of selection-focused, trait-based testing as an implicit paradigm for educational and psychological testing has had a host of unintended consequences.

One of the major consequences is the confusion that results from the frequent manifestation of inconsistency where the trait-based paradigm predicts consistency. As noted in Chapter 4, situations and environments have been shown to produce strong effects on human behavior when trait theory indicates they should not. Chapter 3 describes examples of inconsistency

110

discussed in the testing literature in terms of systematic errors in self-reports and ratings by others. The measurement literature can be summarized as a catalogue of an expanding list of errors and associated microexplanations. Discussing decades of research on error with surveys, O'Muircheartaigh (1997) summarized:

> No clear pattern was found to explain the many and various effects that were demonstrated to exist. The lack of a clear theoretical framework made it difficult to classify effects in any parsimonious way and hindered attempts to formulate a general theory of survey methods. (p. 12)

The measurement field enjoys many empirical demonstrations of error but would clearly benefit from a more comprehensive theory to explain them.

Understanding Inconsistency:
Clues from Psychophysics Measurement

A reasonable explanation for the lack of a measurement theory that can handle problems such as systematic errors and method variance is the relative youthfulness of psychological science. Although test developers and administrators may have been primarily interested in mapping key traits of interest, the administration and completion of most psychological tests often evoke errors involving an interaction of person, test, and situational characteristics. What might be helpful at this point in time is an examination of a testing domain where such parameters are simplified. Such an area has existed for more than 100 years: psychophysics.

Gracely and Naliboff (1996) described the two central measurement tasks in psychophysics as *sensory detection* (whereby a judgment is made about whether a stimulus is present, such as the presence of a light or a tone), detection of *pain thresholds* (where a sensation is always present), or some combination of the two. Thus, psychophysical judgments involve a response criterion that results in the detection of a stimulus or the labeling of a stimulus as painful (Gracely & Naliboff, 1996). In comparison to the more complex rating tasks seen with self-reports and ratings by others with psychological constructs, these psychophysical judgments present a simpler phenomenon for study of measurement issues.

Much of the more recent work of psychologists who study perception and sensation may be characterized as attempting to understand and cope with methodological factors that interfere in the study of how people perceive and report sensations. Researchers typically conceptualize errors in psychophysical studies as occurring when individuals use some characteristic other than an internal response criterion as an artificial gauge for reporting a stimulus detection or threshold.

In the *method of constant stimuli*, an experimenter randomly presents a range of stimulus intensities around the expected detection threshold; the method can be employed to detect sensations as well as when sensations become painful. The threshold is defined as the point where the stimulus is detected 50% of the time. Gracely and Naliboff (1996) reported that research with this method, however, indicates that the "transition between no sensation, nonpainful sensation and pain sensation . . . [is] not distinct and vary over trials" (p. 244). In the *staircase threshold method* for determining pain threshold, a series of stimuli are presented, and the subject describes each as not painful or as producing mild pain. If the stimulus is perceived as not painful, its intensity is increased; if painful, then intensity is decreased. Gracely and Naliboff (1996, p. 248) noted, however, that the experimental subject can easily detect the relation between the response and the increase or decrease in the stimulus intensity, leading to error in persons who may wish to minimize (or maximize) the pain stimuli or who are very anxious about pain.

Gracely and Naliboff (1996) also described pain measurement issues in clinical settings where a patient reports on a single, relatively stable pain sensation. Self-report items might look like these:

	True	*False*			
My tooth hurts.	1	0			

or:

	Not at all		*Somewhat*		*Very much*	
Rate the degree to	1	2	3	4	5	6
which your tooth hurts.						

This measurement situation is comparable to a test with a single item: In general, tests with more items evidence better reliability and validity estimates because responses to single items contain more random error. When multiple items are aggregated into a single total score, random error is balanced and effectively reduced.

The Limitations of Psychophysical Measurement

Gracely and Naliboff (1996) observed that psychophysical methods require responses to dozens of stimuli and thus (1) reduce error variance and (2) allow for the evaluation of measurement consistency. On the basis of this insight, they developed a Descriptor Differential Scale (DDS) in which a person compares a single pain sensation to 12 separate quantified descriptors on a +10 to −10 scale. Presented in random order, the descriptors might include "faint," "extremely intense," and "mild" (Gracely & Kwilosz, 1988); an example is presented later in this chapter. In a study with 91 dental patients, Gracely and Kwilosz found that the DDS exhibited adequate psychometric properties (e.g., 1-hour test–retest reliability equaled .71). Gracely and Naliboff (1996) noted additional advantages for this approach, including:

1. The pattern of item responses can be examined in groups to determine if the descriptor values are consistent (e.g., do all patients provide ratings that indicate that the pain sensation descriptor "mild" is greater than the descriptor "faint"?).
2. Consistency can be examined in individual responses to identify persons who are not attending to the task or not able to perform the task.
3. Multiple items mean alternate forms can be created.
4. Paper or computer forms can be created so that items are presented randomly, thus reducing order effects.
5. The inclusion of a verbal descriptor with the rating scale forces a response on the basis of the descriptor's meaning, not only on the basis of a spatial location on the rating scale (where research suggests that people tend to space their responses out evenly across the scale format).
6. As is generally true with aggregation, the use of multiple items reduces random error.

Nevertheless, Gracely and Naliboff (1996) noted that such *bounded scales* (i.e., that have clear end points, such as the DDS and the two "tooth hurts" items shown above) will be susceptible to rating biases related to stimulus range, frequency of presentation, and a tendency to spread out responses. Particularly with patients with chronic pain, moving from a single pain rating to multiple assessments may introduce motivational and fatigue effects. Other errors in psychophysical procedures relate to subjects' goals (such as wishing to minimize pain or discomfort, or attempting to manipulate the experimenter's perception of them), perception of side effects related to the delivery of a stimulus, and emotional factors such as anxiety and depression (Gracely & Naliboff, 1996).

Another example of a problem with a bounded scale was provided by

Bartoshuk, Fast, and Snyder's (2005) work on supertasters. They noted that recent psychophysical research has found that the number of fungiform papillae on the tongue is associated with taste capacity. Individuals with many of these papillae are supertasters, individuals very sensitive to some types of tastes. Bartoshuk (2000) described research that found that ceiling effects on some types of rating scales can skew data produced by supertasters and make comparisons with groups of individuals with regular taste abilities problematic. As shown in Figure 5.1, when supertasters must use a bounded category scale that includes "very strong" as the most intense sensation, their most intense ratings of substances such as salt and a bitter-tasting chemical named PROP cluster against the top of the scale, resulting in a proportional reduction of ratings of weaker stimuli (Bartoshuk, 2000). Using the same categorical scale, regular tasters may rate some stimuli as more intense than supertasters did, although in fact supertasters had to have experienced the

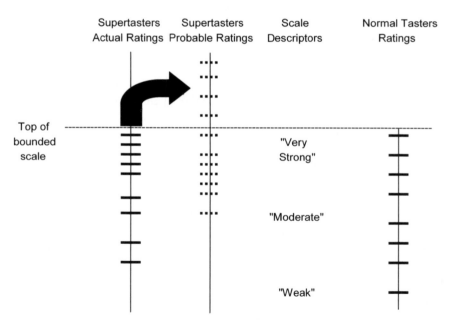

FIGURE 5.1. Supertasters' ratings on a bounded scale. With bounded scales, supertasters and regular tasters may both rate a bitter taste near the top of the bounded category scale even though the supertasters' experience had to be more intense because of their tongues' physical characteristics. The dotted lines on the supertasters' scale indicates where their ratings might fall on an unbounded scale where respondents have the opportunity to consider infinity as a possible response.

particular stimulus more intensely because of their greater numbers of papillae. Bartoshuk (2000, p. 105) concluded that on conventional scales, medium tasters and supertasters will rate PROP near the scale top. While demonstrating individual differences in perceived sensations, this research also shows that ceiling effects with bounded scales can skew supertasters' ratings.

Conclusions and Implications from Psychophysical Research

Although Bartoshuk et al. (2005) and Gracely and Naliboff (1996) described improvements in psychophysical methods, all came to similar conclusions about the methods' ultimate limitations. Bartoshuk (2000) wrote, "It is unlikely that we will ever find a standard that is genuinely perceived identically by all subjects" (p. 450). Gracely and Naliboff (1996) suggested that "other than perhaps the major two dimensions of sensory and affective intensity, the number and organization of pain qualities may be highly situation- and method-specific" (p. 305). Bartoshuk et al. (2005) similarly noted that the meaning of any rating "depends on the sensory context to which it is applied" (p. 122).

On the basis of this brief review of psychophysical methods, three broad conclusions may be drawn that are likely to apply to psychological measurement in general:

1. Improvement in procedures is always possible, once one better understands the methodological aspects of measuring a particular construct or class of constructs. No inherent limitations exist that inhibit the development of better measurement procedures.

2. The act of an individual completing a test always occurs in a *context*, the perceived external and internal aspects of the test-taking situation. In fact, Lockhead (1992, 1995) concluded from his psychophysical research that people cannot directly judge the raw attributes of any object but only the differences and changes over time in those attributes; in essence, people use context to make judgments. Nevertheless, Lockhead (1995) also concluded that people also learn how to perceive constancy in stimuli that appear to change (e.g., a tiger that walks in and out of a shaded jungle). Statisticians may be able to create a statistically adjusted score of a psychological construct that is theoretically context free, but such information will have limited applicability because humans always perceive within a context. Thus, any comprehensive theory of measurement must include context as a central concept inasmuch as context effects appear to operate with all human measurement.

3. Although a new methodology may reduce the effects of a particular error, one or more additional errors (in the context of a testing purpose) will always appear because the new method changes some aspect of the testing context. If different errors interact with one another, a multiplicative effect will be created that further complicates the difficulty of interpreting test scores. Thus, some degree of indeterminacy must always be present when attempting to measure educational and psychological constructs. No measurement procedure can produce an error-free true score, a concept that will remain a useful fiction.

Improving the Principles of Construct Explication

As described in Chapter 3, *construct explication* refers to the process of describing how a particular construct is manifested and how such manifestations can be measured. Construct explication differs from the idea of operationalization in experimental psychology, which refers to choosing a single operation to measure a construct. Measurement psychologists' experience is that no single operation can adequately reflect any construct. Because an inadequate preoperational explication of constructs is a major threat to the construct validity of studies and measures, Cook and Campbell (1979) proposed that "a precise explication of constructs is vital for high construct validity since it permits tailoring the manipulations and measures to whichever definitions emerge from the explication" (p. 65).

In a new science, however, constructs inevitably are explicated imprecisely. Thus, an ongoing goal of most research programs in a relatively new domain such as psychotherapy outcome research should be the evaluation and improvement of current and innovative measurement methods. To deepen knowledge, test developers should explicate constructs, test them empirically, revise the constructs and methods, and recycle the process. Until the test reaches a sufficient degree of precision—as evidenced, for example, by cross-validation of scale items—researchers employing early measurement methods who encounter negative results will not know whether those results should be attributed to incorrect theory or invalid measurement (Torgerson, 1958).

If a researcher intends to improve construct explication in any particular domain, what should she or he be paying attention to? As shown in Figure 5.2, I propose that the construct validity of a test depends on three major factors: Test purpose, test content, and test context. *Test purpose* relates to the inferences for which a test score may be used. That is, what evidence

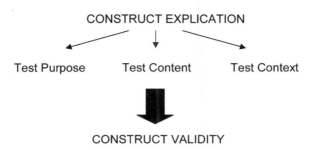

CONSTRUCT EXPLICATION

Test Purpose   Test Content   Test Context

CONSTRUCT VALIDITY

FIGURE 5.2. What influences construct validity? To enhance test validity, test developers should attend to test purpose (i.e., the intended use of its scores), test content (the "what" of items or tasks), and test context (i.e., the perceived internal and external situations related to taking the test). Detection of problems in any of these areas offers an opportunity to investigate methods to improve a test's construct validity.

exists to support that scores on a particular test are useful for a particular purpose? *Test content* refers to the "what" of the test: A test developer has one or more constructs in mind, and existing knowledge about the construct influences the content of items, questions, observations, and so forth. This substantive focus reflects the traditional definition of validity, that is, what a test measures. The *test context* reflects the testing method, the characteristics of the persons taking the test, and all aspects of the perceived testing situation. During test development, the construct explication process should involve the investigation of these three elements in terms of how they influence the measurement of the construct of interest.

Test Purpose

Users of psychological tests are ultimately concerned with interpreting test scores for some purpose. You might be interested in knowing, for example, whether (1) your GRE scores are high enough for you to gain admission to a particular graduate school, (2) your client's scores on an outcome measure indicate that he or she has improved in counseling, or (3) scores on measures you employ during research correlate at a statistically significant level. What scores on any psychological test mean, however, ultimately depends on a series of decisions and procedures that occurred prior to the interpretation stage. As shown below, the interpretation of the meaning of scores on any test depends on what occurs during test (1) *construction*, the procedures employed to create the test, (2) *administration*, how participants completed the test, and (3) *scoring*, how participants' responses were transformed into data.

Construction → administration → scoring → interpretation

Test development should be guided by its intended purposes, and consequently test validity should be evaluated in the context of purpose(s) (Cronbach & Gleser, 1965). The basic premise of this book is that trait-based selection tests have influenced how test developers think about all psychological tests. In terms of test construction, this means that many test developers default to a series of procedures that will produce test scores that primarily reflect stable traits. Although theorists have offered many different approaches to test construction (e.g., Burisch, 1984; Dawis, 1987; Gregory, 1992; Jackson, 1970), in practice tests are often completed via steps such as these:

1. Generate a large pool of self-report items. The items might be created on the basis of a theory, adapted from existing tests, or generated by experts in the test domain.
2. Administer those items to as many people as possible.
3. Subject the resulting scores to some type of item analysis. Factor analysis, a statistical method for understanding the number and type of constructs influencing a test's score, is often the default method. When employing factor analysis, test developers assume that scores on any large number of items reflect a smaller number of more basic factors or traits. These factors consist of a group of highly intercorrelated variables (Vogt, 1993). Factor analysis refers to a set of statistical procedures used to examine the relations among items or tests and produce an estimate of the smaller number of factors that account for those relations.
4. Retain the items selected in step 3 to create one or more scales. Label the scales on the basis of the test developer's judgment of the measured construct.

The major advantages of this approach are ease and low cost. The major disadvantage of this approach is that scores on the resulting test are likely to include sources of invalidity, particularly when the test is employed for nonselection purposes. Selection tests are constructed with items designed to measure stable individual traits. Some researchers and practitioners, however, then employ such tests in an attempt to gauge the effects of interventions and developmental processes. Scores on standardized achievement tests employed in schools, for example, are less likely to show the effects of what is learned in the classroom than mastery or criterion-referenced tests created specifically for evaluating the effects of classroom learning. An analogy is the case of a meteorologist who studies the effect of temperature on plant growth but uses a barometer to measure temperature. Measurements using a barometer for some periods might actually correlate roughly with temperature; during the summer, for example, high barometric pressure is more likely to be associated with warmer temperatures. Consequently, the meteorologist might even find a small relation between barometric pressure and plant growth. That relation, however, will be weaker than the one found with an instrument whose primary purpose is to measure temperature, the thermometer.

Test developers of selection tests choose items in the test construction process that maximize variability among individuals and demonstrate stability over time (Collins, 1991; Dawis, 1992; Guyatt, Walter, & Norman, 1987; Lipsey, 1983; Meier, 1994; Tryon, 1991; Vermeesch et al., 2004). For a test intended to measure psychotherapy outcome, however, a measure's ability to detect change would seem crucial (Vermeersch et al., 2004). Several groups of researchers have proposed guidelines for developing and evaluating treatment-sensitive or change-sensitive outcome measures, and these are introduced below and then described in more detail in the next chapter. Researchers and clinicians whose purposes go beyond selection should reconsider the use of traditional tests or at least explicitly acknowledge the limitations of those methods for nonselection purposes.

Test Content

Knowledge about and understanding of a construct can be shared or differ among test takers. Differences can also exist between test developers and test takers. If test takers randomly differ in their understanding of the meaning of test content, the nomothetic perspective views those individual differences as random error: Such differences will balance out in their effects on test scores, mainly adding what can be considered noise to test scores. For some testing purposes, however, individuals' different interpretations of test instructions, item meaning, or response formats can be seen as idiographic behavior of potential use. To the extent that such idiographic responding is reliable, it may provide, for example, useful clinical information about a particular individual. More on this in Chapter 7.

When test takers construe the meaning of test content in a manner substantially different from that intended by the test developer, the construct validity of the test will be negatively influenced. Two subsequent explanations are that (1) developer's theory, explicated in particular test content, is in error or (2) the test must be changed in a manner so as to more clearly communicate the desired content. Meier (1984; also see Kahn, Meier, Steinberg, & Sackett, 2000, described later in this chapter) provided an example relevant to (1).

Recall from Chapter 3 that Meier (1984) employed Campbell and Fiske's (1959) multitrait–multimethod matrices (MTMM) approach in a study of the construct validity of occupational stress. Convergent validity should be evident when scores between two tests measuring the same construct (1) reflect test takers' shared understanding of the *similarity* of test content and (2), relative to the effect of (1), are substantially neither inflated nor deflated by method variance. Discriminant validity should be present when scores between two tests measuring different constructs (1) reflect test takers' understanding of the *differences* in the test content and (2), relative to the effect of (1), are substantially neither inflated nor deflated by method variance. Thus, demonstrations of a test's convergent and discriminant validity depend on minimizing the effects of method variance relative to test takers' understanding of items' meanings relevant to a particular construct.

Meier (1984) examined correlations among scores from measures of occupational stress to assess convergent validity, and scores on measures of depression and personal orderliness were employed to assess discriminant validity. Typical of many construct validity studies, depression was chosen as a construct for comparison because of questions in the literature about whether constructs such as occupational stress, depression, and anxiety were actually distinct. Because these constructs are primarily measured through self-reports (e.g., no behavioral measures exist), methods selected for this study represented differences in self-report response mode. That is, measures of stress, depression, and orderliness were chosen by the formats of Likert scale, true–false response, and one-item simple self-ratings. Subjects were 320 university faculty members at a large Midwestern university who spent at least 50% of their work time in teaching.

The resulting correlations among measures of occupational stress, depression, and personal orderliness can be found in Table 5.1 (the same as Table 3.1 in Chapter 3). Ideally, correlations between measures of the same construct, using different methods, would be very high. Given that correlations found, for example, among measures of intelligence average above .90, correlations among the three measures of occupational stress might be similarly high. Figure 5.3 displays three correlations of the *same construct/different method* (designated by open circles in Figure 5.3), with the stress measures correlating from .61 to .65, depression .62 to .67, and orderliness .70 to .74. These correlations fall considerably below the ideal .90 level, indicating that (1) one or more of the measures produce scores with a substantial degree

TABLE 5.1. Total Multitrait–Multimethod Matrix

Method	Likert			True–false			Self-ratings		
	1	2	3	1	2	3	1	2	3
Likert									
1. Stress	**88**								
2. Depression	57	**88**							
3. Order	−18	−13	**87**						
True–false									
1. Stress	<u>61</u>	65	−09	**76**					
2. Depression	57	67	−13	69	**80**				
3. Order	−17	−17	74	−14	−23	**86**			
Self-ratings									
1. Stress	<u>65</u>	53	−14	<u>63</u>	59	−12	**73**		
2. Depression	55	62	−12	54	63	−13	60	**57**	
3. Order	−14	−23	70	−12	−20	73	−10	−13	**60**

Note. Decimal points are omitted. Reliability values are in **bold** and <u>underlined</u> numbers are convergent validity estimates.

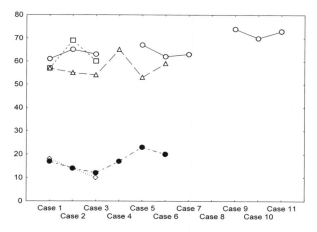

FIGURE 5.3. Plots of MTMM correlations. Open circles designate correlations of the same constructs using different methods. Squares show related constructs measured with the same methods, and diamonds depict different constructs measured using the same method. Triangles show correlations of related constructs measured with different methods, and filled circles depict correlations of different constructs measured with different methods. Negative signs were removed from correlations with personal orderliness.

of construct invalidity, and/or (2) the contribution of method is substantial and decreases the correlation between measures of the same construct.

The contribution of method can also be examined through a comparison of the three correlations of related constructs measured by the same methods (designated by squares in Figure 5.3) and correlations of different constructs measured by the same methods (designated by diamonds). The *related constructs/same method* correlations range from .57 to .60, and the *different constructs/same method* correlations range from −.10 to −.18. Thus, the relatedness of the constructs, as explicated in the measures' item content, appears much more important than the influence of method. The related construct/same mode correlations appear to be roughly equivalent to the same construct/different mode correlations, raising doubts about the discriminant validity (i.e., conceptual separateness) of occupational stress and depression (expected to be related, but theoretically at a lower correlation). Suggesting a similar conclusion, the correlations between related constructs measured using different methods (designated by filled circles) are only slightly below the other sets of correlations reflecting same or related constructs measured using the same or different methods.

What do these findings mean? The relatedness of the test content appears to have a large impact on the correlations. Although occupational stress theorists have suggested that depression and stress are distinct areas (e.g., Pines, 1981), the individuals who completed these measures do not respond to these scales as distinct. In essence, the test developers and test takers do not share the interpretation of the content on the depression and stress tests' items. Although the test developers intended for the depression and stress items to tap into at least moderately different content, participants answered both sets of items similarly. Table 5.2 contains 12 questions from four of the depression and occupational stress scales employed in this study. Can you identify items that belong to either a depression or an occupational stress scale?

Test Context

The idea that *context* affects test takers' behaviors has been recognized in the testing literature—Schwarz and Oyserman (2001), for example, suggested that responses to "self-reports are highly context dependent" (p. 128)—but has not yet received the focus it deserves. Dawis (1987) is among those who have suggested that the method of measurement should be an integral part of construct definition and explication. If the meaning of a construct is affected by the form of its evidence (Kagan, 1988), then in practice, there is

TABLE 5.2. Sample Items from Two Burnout and Two Depression Scales

Item #	Item content
1	I feel fatigued when I get up in the morning and have to face another day on the job.
2	When I wake up in the morning I expect to have a miserable day.
3	I feel emotionally drained from my work.
4	The future looks so gloomy that I wonder if I should go on.
5	I feel like I'm at the end of my rope.
6	I feel blue and depressed.
7	I can't wait for the end of the semester to arrive.
8	I have a lot of self-doubt at work.
9	The best color to describe work for me right now is grey.
10	I often feel anxious about work.
11	I usually feel that life is worthwhile.
12	I work under a great deal of tension.

Note. Items 1, 3, and 5 belong to the Maslach Burnout Inventory (Maslach & Jackson, 1981); items 2, 4, and 6 are from the Costello–Comrey Depression Scale (Costello & Comrey, 1967); items 7, 8, 9, and 10 are from the Meier Burnout Assessment (Meier, 1984); and items 11 and 12 belong to the MMPI Depression scale (Dempsey, 1964).

no such thing as a construct or a method, but only construct–methods. The *test context* reflects the testing method, the characteristics of the persons taking the test, and all aspects of the perceived testing situation. During test development, the construct explication process should investigate these three elements in terms of how they influence the measurement of the specified construct.

If contextual cues are perceived similarly by a group of individuals taking a particular test, the common perception of those cues in that group is a *shared context*. For example, students applying for admission to college or graduate school may recognize the intent of transparent questions and reply with distorted information that favors their selection. Use of a bounded category scale with supertasters may lead them to place many of their ratings at the top of the scale and then spread the remaining responses throughout the scale values so as to appear unbiased. Students of color may decrease their motivation to perform well on a scale perceived as an intelligence test. Supervisors at a company may know that employee performance ratings are largely ignored by top management and rate most of their employees as exemplary despite variations in actual work performances.

The concept of shared contexts differs from the traditional measurement idea of standardized test administration, or *standardization*. In an effort to make test scores comparable across persons, standardization represents an attempt by the test developer and test administrator to provide a uniform test and testing environment for all test takers. The concept of shared contexts, however, suggests that providing a uniform test, although a desirable goal, is a practical impossibility. In any testing situation, an infinite number of influential characteristics in the testing context are potentially present. If the perceived characteristics vary by each test taker, their influence on the test scores of the group as a whole functions as random error. When one or more of those characteristics influence a group of test takers, however, the shared context will systematically influence test takers' scores, often in a way that conflicts with the purpose of the test.

Test developers implicitly depend on shared contexts when they create and administer tests that they intend to be valid measures of a construct. That is, test developers assume, but typically do not evaluate, that characteristics of the testing method, the testing situation, and the test takers all influence test scores in a manner that enhances or at least does not detract from test validity. For example, test developers assume that test takers understand items similarly and in the manner intended by the test developer (Walsh & Betz, 1985). Shared contexts become a source of invalidity, however, when such contexts function in a manner contrary to the test's intended purpose.

In the following sections I discuss how concepts related to shared and differing perceptions of test contexts can provide insight into issues related to measurement issues. I begin with method variance and systematic errors.

Shared Contexts and Method Variance

Fiske (1987) summarized the research on method variance: "The common finding is that when one construct is measured by several distinct methods, the data do not converge as they should. The more distinct and independent the methods, the less the convergence" (p. 301). *Method*, as Fiske employed the term, refers to different types of measurement methods, such as self-reports, interviews, or behavioral observation. *Method*, however, can also refer to aspects of tests that are smaller in scale, such as instructions, item characteristics, or response format. Method variance causes problems when two measures of the same construct, employing different methods, fail to correlate as highly as expected (i.e., fail to evidence convergent validity). Conversely, two measures of different, but related constructs might be more highly correlated than expected (i.e., fail to evidence discriminant validity), at least partially as a result of their similar methods.

The concept of shared contexts provides a new perspective on method variance: Method variance can be redefined as a product of *shared contexts specific to a particular testing method*. That is, some aspects of a method such as self-report or behavioral observation may engender test responses that overlap regardless of the relatedness of the measured constructs. In the next sections I provide examples of context effects engendered by the positive or negative wording of test items, the juxtaposition of multiple instructions and items, response format, test instructions, and item content.

The Context of Positive and Negative Item Wording

As noted in Chapter 3, an example can be found in a test called the Counseling Self-Estimate Inventory (COSE; Larson et al., 1992). On the basis of Bandura's (1977) self-efficacy theory, the test's creators developed the COSE using traditional procedures. As part of test development, 213 counseling students completed the items, whose scores were then factor analyzed and grouped into scales on the basis of the factor analytic results. The first two factors found were a 12-item scale, labeled *Microskills*, and a 10-item scale, labeled *Process*. Table 5.3 displays a few items from both scales. The problem is that the Microskills items are all positively worded, and the Process items are all negatively worded. That is, the content of each scale is confounded with positive or negative item wording that may promote acquiescence or criticalness response biases.

Consequently, it is unclear as to what extent scale scores reflect their intended construct or the bias that is built into the wording of the scales.

TABLE 5.3. Sample Microskills and Process Subscale Items from the COSE

Microskills items	Process items
I am confident that I can assess my client's readiness and commitment to change.	My assessments of client problems may not be as accurate as I would like them to be.
I am confident that the wording of my interpretation and confrontation responses will be clear and easy to understand.	I am worried that my interpretation and confrontation responses may not over time assist the client to be more specific in defining and clarifying the problem.
I am certain that my interpretation and confrontation responses will be concise and to the point.	I am uncertain as to whether I will be able to appropriately confront and challenge my client in therapy.

Certainly there appears to be considerable overlap between the content of the two scales, and it seems plausible that the factor analytic results indicate that test takers primarily responded to the positive or negative wording of the items, rather than the content of the items themselves.

The Context of Item-Instruction Presentation

The complexity of the presentation of test items and instructions can also create a context that may be experienced by test takers as a difficult cognitive task. I recently reviewed a survey on supervision relationships that instructed respondents to reply to each survey item in three ways. Presented with an item such as "The dual relationship of being a supervisor and friend causes problems in the work environment," respondents were asked to do the following:

> First, select the response that most clearly indicates your experience with your supervisees. (This was rated on a 5-point scale from "Not at all" to "A great deal.")
> Second, indicate your opinion of how harmful in general the situation described in the item could be. (This was rated on a 3-point scale from "Low" to "High.")
> Third, indicate how ethical you believe the situation described in the item is if it actually occurred. (This was rated on a 4-point scale from "Very unethical" to "Very ethical.")

Individually, completing any one of the three rating tasks would appear to be a relatively straightforward task for the intended respondents (graduate students and counseling professionals). Completing the three tasks in combination per item, however, is likely to influence respondents' answers on each rating task.

The Context of Response Format

A more subtle example of shared contexts leading to problems with method variance can be found in the work of Meier, McDougal, and Bardos (in press). They reported the development of an outcome measure completed by parents of elementary school children and intended to be sensitive to changes produced by counseling. The data set contained intake and follow-up forms completed by parents over a 5-year period; about two-thirds of the children were male, 60% were Caucasian, and 20% were

African American. The test development process employed three versions of the scale, using a total of 19 items; 14 of those items overlapped all three versions.

As shown below, one version (completed by 139 parents) presented respondents with a response format that included only verbal descriptors of the four available response categories:

Please rate *how often* each of the actions or situations below occurred with your child during the past week. Check the appropriate box.

	Never	Rarely	Sometimes	Often
Pays attention to speakers at meetings such as in church or youth groups.	○	○	○	○
Gets failing grades at school.	○	○	○	○
Behaves differently than other children.	○	○	○	○

A later version (completed by 648 parents) added numbers to the verbal categories:

	Never (0 times)	Rarely (1 time)	Sometimes (2–3x's)	Often (3–7x's)
Pays attention to speakers at meetings such as in church or youth groups.	○	○	○	○
Gets failing grades at school.	○	○	○	○
Behaves differently than other children.	○	○	○	○

Other than the addition of few items and minor changes in format, the major difference between the two versions was the addition of the numeric descriptions (e.g., "0 times") to the category labels (e.g., "Never"). As shown in Figure 5.4, however, a comparison of the 14 overlapping items completed at intake on the two forms found that the form with numeric and verbal categories (Version 5) had higher mean scores for 12 items. Although these differences are small at the item level, they are consistent and become statistically different when aggregated into a scale. The sum of the two versions at intake differed by mean ($t = -2.36$, $p = .02$); the numeric/categorical form had a higher mean (21.09, compared to 19.64) and standard deviation (6.60, compared to 6.37). More important, these differences may have contributed to the ability of the outcome measure to detect changes produced by psychotherapy. Only one item on the category-only version found a statistically significant change over the course of counseling, whereas 11 of

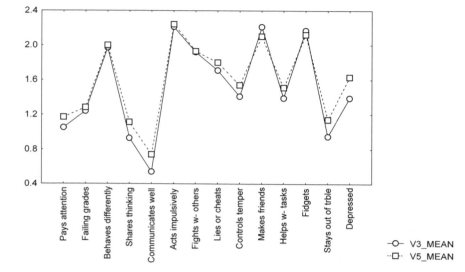

FIGURE 5.4. Comparison of 14 items with different response formats. Version 5 item means (designated by squares), containing both verbal categories and numbers in the response format, are consistently but slightly larger than Version 3 means (circles). When aggregated, the differences become statistically significant.

14 items on the numeric/category version did so. Thus, the context of the response format appears to have influenced respondents' behavior.

Context and Test Instructions

Although many effects of testing context appear to be inadvertent, at least one test varied an important aspect of test context to produce two sets of valid scores. The State–Trait Anxiety Inventory (STAI; Spielberger, Gorsuch, & Lushene, 1970), a widely used measure of anxiety, provides an example of how differences in test instructions can lead to different psychometric properties. The initial goal in creating the STAI was to develop a single set of items that varied by instructions. The STAI consists of two 20-item scales intended to measure trait anxiety (expected to be stable over time and situations) and state anxiety (expected to vary over time and situations). Psychometric evaluations of the two scales shows expected differences; for example, the state anxiety scale evidences lower test–retest reliability, as would be expected. As shown in Table 5.4, many items on the two scales are very similar in content.

The major difference between the scales lies in the instructions provided to respondents. Here are instructions for the 20-item state anxiety scale (emphasis in original):

> A number of statements which people have used to describe themselves are given below. Read each statement and then blacken in the appropriate circle to the right of the statement to indicate how you feel *right* now, that is, *at this moment.* There are no right or wrong answers. Do not spend too much time on any one statement but give the answer which seems to describe your present feelings best.

And here are instructions for the trait anxiety components:

> A number of statements which people have used to describe themselves are given below. Read each statement and then blacken in the appropriate circle to the right of the statement to indicate how you *generally* feel. There are no right or wrong answers. Do not spend too much time on any one statement but give the answer which seems to describe how you *generally* feel.

Thus, the respective scale instructions appear to provide respondents with the necessary context in which to answer very similar items in reference to their perceptions of trait dispositions versus changeable states. In addition, the response formats differ slightly, but in ways that likely encourage state and trait responding. For the trait scale, the options are "almost never," "sometimes," "often," and "almost always"; for the state scale, the response options are "not at all," "somewhat," "moderately so," and "very much so."

Scores on some state anxiety and trait anxiety items, however, do not always respond to the effects of differing instructions and response formats.

TABLE 5.4. Sample Items from the STAI

State anxiety items	Trait anxiety items
I feel pleasant	I feel pleasant
I feel rested	I feel rested
I feel secure	I feel secure
I feel calm	I am "calm, cool, and collected"
I feel content	I am content
I feel nervous	I feel nervous and restless

Spielberger, Sydeman, Owen, and Marsh (1997) noted that scores on the state scale item "I feel upset" increased under stressful conditions. When administered on the trait anxiety scale, however, "I feel upset" failed to correlate with scores on other trait anxiety items and was dropped from that scale. Similarly, scores on the item "I worry too much" remained stable over time and correlated highly with scores on other trait anxiety items, but did not show change under stressful conditions. Spielberger et al. (1997) concluded that "altering the instructions could not overcome the strong psycholinguistic state or trait connotations of key words in some items" (p. 997). Thus, test content may produce an effect stronger than one produced by an aspect of test context.

Context and Item Content

Context effects may even occur on the basis of the implications of item content. Kahn et al. (2000) examined the issue of respondents' interpretation of test language with a well-known outcome measure, the Outcome Questionnaire scale (OQ-45). The OQ contains 45 items that are grouped into three subscales: The Symptom Distress scale contains items related to anxiety and depression, Interpersonal Relations items assess satisfaction with and problems in interpersonal functioning, and Social Role Performance refers to satisfaction and competence in employment, family, and leisure roles. Studies indicate that scores on the OQ-45 demonstrate the usual moderate to high test–retest reliability (Burlingame, Lambert, Reisinger, Neff, & Mosier, 1995) and internal consistency estimates (Lambert & Finch, 1999). Research has found correlations in expected directions and magnitudes between the OQ and related scales such as the Symptom Checklist-90-R (SCL-90-R), Beck Depression Inventory, State–Trait Anxiety Inventory, and Inventory of Interpersonal Problems; other evidence indicates the OQ can distinguish between clinical and nonclinical groups.

Kahn et al. (2000) conducted several small ($n = 5$) focus groups with college students who completed the OQ. Although the developers of the OQ intended its items to be answered in relation to the time period of the past week, focus group participants indicated that they employed a more global, trait-based approach when answering questions. Examination of the OQ indicates a noticeable contrast between the *language* employed in scale items and the time-related *instructions* given to participants. OQ items were developed with questions reflecting broad content areas believed to assess client functioning (Umphress, Lambert, Smart, Barlow, & Clouse, 1997), resulting in items such as "I blame myself for things" and "I get along well with others." Nevertheless, scale directions ask respondents to focus on the present (emphasis added).

> Looking back *over the last week*, including today, help us understand *how you have been feeling*. Read each item and mark the answer that best describes your current situation.

Although the goal of the OQ is to derive recent feelings, global questions phrased in the present tense may elicit generalities rather than specifics. Kahn et al. (2000) created an alternate form of the OQ-45, changing items' tense from a global present tense to a recent past tense. The researchers added the phrase "over the last week" to the end of each item to specify the time frame in which the respondents were to consider their experiences. For example, the item that reads, "I blame myself for things" was changed to "I blamed myself for things last week." One hundred and three students completed the two versions of the OQ about a month apart. With alpha set at .10, 21 of 45 items evidenced a significant mean difference, 47% of the total scale. For most items, the effect of adding the specific time language was to move the mean away from an extreme of the scale. Subscales on the modified OQ evidenced higher coefficient alphas and larger standard deviations.

A plausible interpretation of these results is that the modified OQ elicited more state-like responses from respondents than did the original scale items. That is, respondents may have interpreted the original OQ items as requests for global, trait information. If so, this finding may also explain one of the major problems with the original OQ, which is that the three subscales are more highly correlated than expected. The global connotation of OQ items means that respondents' scores reflect their general distress or neuroticism instead of the specific constructs intended to be associated with items and subscales.

Shared Contexts and Systematic Errors

Systematic errors occur when a subgroup of test takers bring to the testing process a set of personal characteristics that interact in unintended ways with aspects of the testing context. These are errors in the sense that the fit between personal characteristics and the test differ from those intended by the test developer and test administrator for a particular test and its purpose. For example, whereas the developer of a test may intend its scores to reflect individuals' true scores on a trait, a group of test takers may attempt to give a favorable impression on test responses so that they may obtain a desired goal or consequence dependent on the testing outcome (e.g., obtaining a job or admission to school). This is a social desirability (SD) response bias.

Historically, test developers have attempted to eliminate SD effects during scale construction and during test taking (Paulhus, 1991). Although no consensus about best methods has been reached, strategies have included:

1. Instructing test takers to respond honestly (e.g., Benjamin, 1988). Little research is available to document this instruction's effectiveness (Martin, 1988).
2. Developing instruments such as the Social Desirability Scale (Crowne & Marlowe, 1964) to identify and eliminate test items (during scale development) or test takers (during concurrent administration of other tests) that correlate too highly with social desirability scores. Similarly, judges may rate new test items on a scale ranging from extremely desirable to extremely undesirable in an effort to detect relatively neutral items. Research results suggest considerable agreement among groups of judges, including preschool children, different psychiatric populations, and even judges from different cultures, on the desirability of specific items (Edwards, 1970; Jackson & Messick, 1969).
3. Providing items with two alternatives of equal social desirability value (Edwards, 1970). Some evidence suggests this strategy is ineffective (Waters, 1965).
4. Presenting subtle items that may be less transparent and therefore less easily faked (Martin, 1988). As noted later in this chapter, research results are mixed.
5. Warning respondents that methods to detect distortion exist. Hough et al. (1990) cited four studies that found support for the efficacy of these approaches (Haymaker & Erwin, 1980; Lautenschlager & Atwater, 1986; Schrader & Osburn, 1977; Trent, Atwater, & Abrahams, 1986).

In contrast, contemporary efforts to understand SD investigate a variety of contextual effects. For example, Gerbert et al. (1999) examined whether medical patients would change their self-reports about socially desirable behaviors depending on whom they expected to see their responses: the researcher alone, or the researcher and the patients' physicians. Gerbert et al. also assessed whether disclosure would differ across five assessment methods (written, face-to-face interview, audio interview, computer interview, and video interview). Topics included four areas Gerbert et al.

(1999) designated as sensitive (HIV-risk behaviors, alcohol use, drug use, and domestic violence) and three designated as less sensitive (tobacco use, dental health, and seat belt use). Results indicated that patients' disclosures did not differ depending upon whom they expected to see their results. As shown in Figure 5.5, patients did report slightly higher incidences of HIV behaviors, alcohol use, drug use, and domestic violence with more technologically sophisticated methods. Interestingly, one-third of patients in this study thought that their health might improve by discussing survey results with their doctors.

In contrast, Jennings, Lucenko, Malow, and Devieux (2002) found that adolescents mandated to an inpatient substance abuse treatment program or a juvenile detention center reported *fewer* risky behaviors on items with explicit sexual or drug content in a computer-based interview than they did a in a face-to-face interview. Jennings et al. (2002) interpreted these findings by suggesting that in contexts where fear of reprisal may threaten

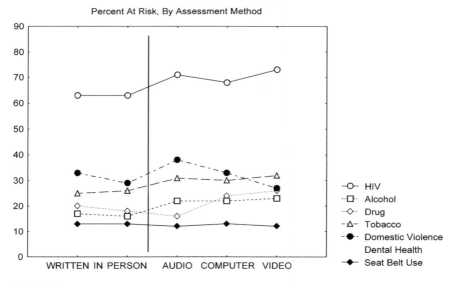

FIGURE 5.5. Test subject and assessment method influences responses. Data collected employing more technologically advanced assessment methods are to the right of the solid vertical line. With technologically sophisticated methods, patients reported higher incidences of the constructs with socially undesirable content (i.e., HIV behaviors, alcohol use, drug use, and domestic violence).

valid reporting, an interviewer may establish rapport and trust that is missing from computer-based methods. On the other hand, Johnson et al. (2001), using a total of 901 interviews with British residents answering sensitive questions about sexual experiences, found no difference between a paper-and-pencil interview and a computer-assisted self-completion interview (CASI). Kurth et al. (2004) also found mixed results regarding differences between audio computer-assisted self-interviews (ACASI) and clinician-administered sexual histories, both completed by 609 clients ages 14–65 of a U.S. public STD (sexually transmitted disease) clinic. Women, for example, reported higher frequencies in ACASI of same-sex behavior (19.6 vs. 11.5%) and amphetamine use (4.9 vs. 0.7%) but lower frequencies of STD symptoms (55.4 vs. 63.7%). Men responded similarly to both types of interviews, reporting only higher frequencies of homosexual sex in ACASI (36.9 vs. 28.7%).

Taken as a whole, these results suggest that social desirability results from an interaction of person characteristics and testing context. Thus, items with sexual content may provoke socially desirable responding in some cultures, but not others, and the age of respondents may similarly influence SD responses. One cannot predict, without a deeper understanding of the individuals who complete the test and the testing context, that a sensitive question will result in any particular pattern of response (e.g., reports of lower or higher frequency of behaviors).

Shared Contexts and Social Roles

The concept of shared contexts also has heuristic value in the connections it provides to such related disciplines and domains as social psychology, narrative therapy, family psychology and systems theory, multicultural counseling, linguistics, memory and cognition, and philosophy. Shared contexts is a concept that invites both qualitative and quantitative researchers to investigate measurement issues and advancements. Below I describe measurement implications derived from two of these areas, *Grice's Conversational Maxims* and *narrative therapy*.

Conversational Rules

Schwarz and Oyserman (2001) indicated that in a testing situation that involves another person (e.g., a test administrator or interviewer), Grice's (1991) Conversational Maxims apply. These maxims, which suggest that most people share a set of implicit principles about appropriate conversational behavior, have potential applicability to testing methods such as interviews and self-reports. In essence, they indicate that people adopt roles regarding the provision of information in social situations. Grice's guidelines include:

1. A *maxim of relation*. Speakers in a conversation will offer information relative to the purpose and context of the conversation. Applied to a testing situation, test takers will be motivated to notice explicit and implicit cues that provide information relative to the purpose and context of a test.

Grice also indicated that a person's understanding of a conversational context will deepen over the course of the conversation. Thus, a test taker's understanding of the testing context may also change as the testing process proceeds. For example, in psychotherapy outcome assessment, questions focus on client problems; for many clients, however, it seems likely that the meaning of the problem changes over the course of therapy. Similar to *testing and instrumentation effects*, Golembiewski, Billingsley, and Yeager (1976) proposed that the pre–post changes demonstrated on psychotherapy outcome measurements can result from (1) *alpha change*, in which altered scores validly correspond to changes produced by an intervention; (2) *beta change*, in which respondents alter the intervals of the scale, on the basis of a new understanding of what is being assessed; and (3) *gamma change*, a shift in the entire meaning or conceptualization of the instrument, perhaps as a result of seeing scale content in a new light. Consequently, a psychotherapy client who changes his or her understanding of the scale intervals or content between assessments is essentially responding to different measurement devices. If this contextual shift occurs in a group of clients, they will be providing data containing a systematic error that will make it more difficult to determine the amount or type of change resulting from psychotherapy.

2. A *maxim of quantity*. Speakers will provide the amount of information they believe is expected. In a written test with a fixed response format, the amount of information desired is clearly evident. In other contexts, such as an interview, the amount of information desired is less clear and may be specified by the interviewer formally or informally. This maxim also predicts that a subset of test takers are likely to respond systematically to some tests by providing too little information (i.e., sparse responding) or too much information. A bounded scale, as shown below, containing a clear range of minimum and maximum responses may lead some respondents to spread out their responses throughout the scale (Gracely & Naliboff, 1996).

	Not at all		*Somewhat*		*Very much*	
Rate the degree to	1	2	3	4	5	6
which your tooth hurts.						

3. A *maxim of manner*. Speakers will provide information as clearly as possible. Thus, individuals assume that the most obvious meaning is correct; if no meaning is obvious, individuals will search the context for clues. Determining the meaning of test-related information will become more difficult if test takers differ in terms of culture, language, and relevant experience. For example, respondents process and provide more complex information when completing questions in their native language (Church et al., 1988; Marin et al., 1983). Some research suggests that individuals' understanding of constructs measured by psychological tests affects their scores on those tests (e.g., Kahn & Meier, 2001). Similarly, if persons completing the MMPI rate 25% of the items as ambiguous and 50% as difficult to understand (Angleitner et al., 1986), it is not surprising that respondents might make systematic errors such as acquiescence or criticalness by focusing on such simple cues as positive or negative wording. In ambiguous test contexts, respondents will search the test context for clues about how to respond.

This maxim also bears on attempts by some test developers to avoid reactivity and transparency problems by making test items more subtle. More subtle items are likely to engender more searching for cues by test takers, with responses likely to contain more noise because they will reflect the diverse randomness of found cues. In support of this interpretation is Hough et al.'s (1990) review of the literature that found few benefits for use of subtle items (e.g., Duff, 1965; Holden, 1989; Holden & Jackson, 1979; Jackson, 1971; McCall, 1958; Nelson & Cicchetti, 1991; Wiener, 1948). Similarly, Graham (1990) reviewed studies of obvious and subtle items designed to indicate emotional disturbance that Wiener (1948) proposed for the MMPI. He concluded that obvious items are more highly correlated with nontest behaviors than subtle items and that MMPI Subtle–Obvious subscales do not accurately detect faked responses. More recent research conducted by Nelson, Pham, and Uchiyama (1996) also supports Graham's conclusions.

Narrative Therapy

A basic premise of narrative therapy (NT) is that all people are "active, impassioned meaning makers in search of plausible stories" (White, 2004,

p. 38). Personal narratives allow individuals to perform three important tasks: (1) store large amounts of information, particularly information relevant to personal goals, (2) make quick decisions (Dimaggio & Semerari, 2004), and (3), perhaps most important for therapeutic purposes, organize information about social interactions and experiences that explains and guides action in social situations (Boothe & Von Wyl, 2004).

Shared narratives about one's family, gender, race, culture, religious group, work and school organizations, and other groups to which one belongs may provide the basis for common perceptions of context. Shared narratives may also be created around one's roles within social groups. For example, fathers and mothers may organize their experiences into narratives relevant to those roles and pay particular attention to narratives they hear from other people relevant to those parenting roles. Similarly, someone who has a particular professional role in a work organization is likely to possess narrative elements that overlap with information stored in the narratives of persons with similar professional roles. Similar to the concept of a *meme* (Pleh, 2003), a piece of information passed from one mind to another, shared narratives may function to spread understanding of contexts through language.

Narratives produced through shared contexts should influence the behavior of therapists and clients alike. A puzzling finding in counseling and psychotherapy is the inconsistency of change estimates across different sources. For example, therapists and expert judges typically rate clients who have completed psychotherapy as evidencing more change than do the clients themselves (Lambert, 1994). As Lambert and Lambert (2004) put it, "The lack of consensus across sources of outcome evaluation, especially when each source presumably is assessing the same phenomena, has been viewed as a threat to the validity of data" (p. 124). From a NT perspective, each source (i.e., therapist, expert judge, client, parent, teacher, significant other) will store information and create a narrative at least partially on the basis of her or his roles. For example, therapists may notice more evidence of improvement because they expect their efforts to be successful: Researchers have found that many therapists believe that treatment success is inevitable if they follow generally accepted procedures (Kendall et al., 1992).

Shared Role Contexts

A group of test takers who share one or more roles relevant to a testing context may behave similarly. Shared roles among test takers might help to explain the inconsistencies found among some raters. Recall that Christensen et al. (1992) found considerable differences in mothers' and fathers' reporting on the Child Behavior Checklist about their children ages 3–13. Mothers reported more negative behaviors than did fathers; parents disagreed about the occurrence of a behavior twice as often as they agreed. Christensen et al. (1992) found more consistency with behaviors described as more disturbed, overt, and specific. In traditional families, mothers may share a similar context of greater contact with their children and thus notice more subtle negative behaviors than would fathers (who would still notice the more obvious negative behaviors). Similarly, Kazdin (1988) noted low correlations between parent and child reports, a problematic finding only if a single testing context exists that should be equally accessible to and reported by all observers. Achenbach (2006) provided a more recent summary of research demonstrating low intercorrelations among different types of observers.

The mother–father differences may be an example of groups of test takers differing systematically in their perceptions of test-related contexts. For example, some research indicates that others rate an individual at least as accurately as he or she rates him- or herself (e.g., Dunning et al., 2004). Yet other researchers have shown the extent to which one person can hold a distorted view of another (Brody & Forehand, 1986; Martin, 1988; Vernon, 1964). Research indicates that a moderate degree of agreement exists between self- and other reports of daily behaviors from two members of the same household (Schwarz & Oyserman, 2001). The highest agreement (a correlation as high as .80) occurs for behaviors in which both individuals participated. In other words, when individuals share a context, their reports are more highly correlated (see also Achenbach, 2006). The correlation drops to .4 when one individual performed the behavior in the absence of other and did not discuss the behavior (Schwarz & Oyserman, 2001).

Similar patterns can be found in research examining correlations among different sources who assess identical or similar behaviors. Gresham and Elliott (1990), for example, reported correlations of a Social Skills total score for elementary and secondary school students (sample sizes ranged from 163 to 676) as rated by students themselves, their parents, and their teachers. From the perspective of shared roles, we would expect correlations between parents and teachers to exceed those between students and parents or students and teachers. As shown in Table 5.5, that is the pattern found by Gresham and Elliott for elementary school students. Interestingly, the correlations among all three groups become roughly equal when examined for secondary school students, suggesting that students begin to notice and

TABLE 5.5. Correlations among Students, Parents, and Teachers on Social Skills Total Scale

Students' level	Teacher–parent	Teacher–student	Parent–student
Elementary	.36	.22	.12
Secondary	.33	.41	.36

interpret their behaviors more similarly to their parents and teachers as they get older.

Similarly, social psychology researchers have documented differing perceptions about causality between persons who perform behaviors (called actors) and persons who observe those actors (Jones & Nisbett, 1971; Ross, 1977; Weiner, 1985). The basic finding, which Ross termed the *fundamental attribution error*, is that actors attribute their actions to environmental factors such as task difficulty, whereas observers tend to view behavior as resulting from stable internal traits. Jones and Nisbett (1971) attributed different perceptions to the different salience of information available to actors and observers. Actors who perform what Jones and Nisbett (1971) termed "preprogrammed and prepackaged" (p. 85) response sequences tend to monitor the environmental stimuli that initiated the sequence. They concluded that

> In short, the actor need not and in some ways cannot observe his behavior very closely. Instead, his attention is directed outward, toward the environment with its constantly shifting demands and opportunities. (p. 85)

For the observer, however, the focus is the actor's behavior. Ross (1977) reviewed research that found that whatever or whoever was the focus of attention tended to be labeled as the causal agent. And given the human tendency toward cognitive balance and consistency, Jones and Nisbett (1971) argued that observers tend to impose trait conceptions on others' behavior; trait schemas are more likely to be employed for ratings when the observer must report on longer time periods (Schwarz & Oyserman, 2001). In other words, actors and observers may not be sharing the same contexts in which they produce test-relevant data. Consequently, test validity when test takers differ systematically would appear to depend on which group of test takers provides data more closely matching test purpose. With mothers and fathers providing information about children's behavioral problems, for example, mothers might be expected to have greater access to samples of behavior relevant to identifying children with chronic or severe problems.

Test takers may also draw inferences about the meaning of a test from such cues as the characteristics of the test administrator as well as the type of language used in test instructions, items, and format. To the extent that contexts are not shared between test taker and administrator/author (e.g., an African American urban male teenager taking a test administered by a Caucasian, suburban middle-aged female), the likelihood of systematic errors such as social desirability will increase. Such mismatches (which may be influenced by such demographic characteristics as ethnicity, age, and gender) can frequently occur and may be a major reason that training in areas such as survey administration and psychological assessment emphasizes the development of rapport between test administrator and test taker, particularly in one-to-one testing situations (O'Muircheartaigh, 1997).

The research on stereotype threat, discussed in Chapter 3, provides an example of problems that can result when groups of test takers have different perceptions about the testing context (Katz, 1964). Steele (1998) reported that "stereotype threat occurs when one recognizes that a negative stereotype about a group to which one belongs is applicable to oneself in a particular situation" (p. 680). In a situation such as taking a standardized intellectual test, stereotype threat occurs when members of a group produce less than optimal performance on a test because of a negative stereotype about that group's expected performance (Beilock & McConnell, 2004; Steele & Aronson, 1995). Steele and Aronson (1995) found that in a testing situation where African American students were led to believe that the test was diagnostic of intellectual ability, they underperformed on difficult items in relation to white students. In a testing situation where the task was presented as unrelated to ability, no difference was found between African American and white students' performances. In another study, Steele and Aronson (1995) found that simply recording their race appeared to produce the stereotype threat effect in African American students. Thus, differing perceptions about the implications of the test context appears to have influenced test performance.

Applications

If test purpose, test content, and test context are the major concerns during the construct explication process, it follows that tests may be improved by attending to aspects of these three domains. What follows are suggestions for improving tests related to this chapter's illustrations of principles related to test purpose, content, and context.

Recommendations Related to Test Purpose

As described earlier, the intended uses of the test should drive the test construction process as well as considerations about how the test is administered and scored. Although these issues are discussed in depth in the next chapter, a brief introduction is appropriate here, focused on measuring change resulting from psychosocial interventions.

TESTS FOR MEASURING CHANGE

Researchers have gradually recognized the potential importance of employing treatment-sensitive measures (e.g., Guyatt et al., 1987; Lipsey, 1983, 1990; Vermeersch, Lambert, & Burlingame, 2000; Vermeersch et al., 2004). More recent approaches to test development with outcome measures have focused on methods of selecting change-sensitive items with adequate psychometric properties (Meier, 1997, 2000, 2004; Vermeersch et al., 2000; Vermeersch et al., 2004). It is important to note that items and measures that show change do not correspond to the same items groupings identified by techniques such as factor analysis (Kopta, Howard, Lowry, & Beutler, 1994; Weinstock & Meier, 2003). Kopta et al. (1994), for example, examined psychotherapy outpatients' scores on the SCL-90-R, a widely used symptom checklist. They found that scores on items could be categorized according to the three rates of change the items displayed in response to treatment: Acute items, quick response to treatment; chronic distress items, moderate response rate; and characterological items, slow response rate. Acute items that evidence rapid response to psychotherapy included content tapping anxiety, depression, and obsessive–compulsive symptoms. The items grouped in these three categories do not correspond to the single category found in factor analyses of the SCL-90-R conducted at a single time point (e.g., Cyr, McKenna-Foley, & Peacock, 1985) or to the nine symptom dimensions reported by Derogatis (1983).

Meier (1997) noted that although relatively little theoretical work has focused on the construction of test items for assessing change, a growing body of literature does exist that examines tests designed for evaluating educational and psychological interventions (cf. Tymofievich & Leroux, 2000). Criterion-referenced tests, for example, are composed of items based on specific criteria toward which an intervention is targeted (Popham, 1993). In a mastery learning class, students might take a reading comprehension test that involves reviewing assigned readings and then attempting to answer correctly at least 90% of the items. Item selection in criterion-referenced tests (Swezey, 1981) includes (1) task analysis of the criteria, (2) determination of costs associated with measuring different aspects of criteria, (3) creation of an item pool, and (4) a pilot study in which items are administered to mastery and nonmastery subjects to determine which items can discriminate between the two groups. The item selection process focuses not on finding stable items, but on those that demonstrate the effects of an intervention to produce change to criterion.

Similarly, researchers employed longitudinal methods in areas such as developmental psychology to attempt to measure intraindividual differences over time. Although such researchers are interested in distinguishing between static (trait) variables and dynamic (state) variables, Collins (1991) observed:

> Little in traditional measurement theory is of any help to those who desire an instrument that is sensitive to intraindividual differences. In fact, applying traditional methods to the development of a measure of a dynamic latent variable amounts to applying a set of largely irrelevant criteria. (pp. 138–139)

In research on longitudinal measurements of physical activity and behavior, Tryon (1991) reviewed studies that found that physical exercise alleviated reactive depression in a variety of samples. Measurement issues in these studies center on finding reliable instruments that can demonstrate significant within-subject change in physical activity over time. Tryon (1991) proposed three criteria for the selection of items and tasks suitable for a test of an intervention:

1. Items should evidence change resulting from the presence of an intervention; for example, items should demonstrate expected changes from pretest to posttest.
2. Items should not change when respondents are exposed to control conditions; that is, item change should not occur over time independent of an intervention.
3. Changes in scores from pre-intervention to post-intervention demand that such alterations not be attributable to measurement error. Thus, measures should not be affected by such nonintervention factors as social desirability, practice effects, or expectancies for improvement.

In the next chapter I provide a detailed example of an application of these ideas with a new test intended to measure change resulting from counseling and psychotherapy.

SOCIALLY DESIRABLE RESPONDING
AND THE TRANSPARENCY OF TEST PURPOSE

Test developers and researchers have also investigated whether making the test purpose transparent to users, or concealing the test purpose, has an effect on socially desirable responding. Cronbach (1984) suggested that making the testing purpose transparent is most common in situations where respondents are anonymous (as in some types of opinion polling) or when respondents may potentially benefit from valid self-disclosure (as in symptom reports in preparation for a clinical intervention). At the other extreme is a strategy of concealment whereby test developers attempt to hide the test purpose. For example, developers frequently create innocuous titles for tests (e.g., "Human Services Inventory" instead of the Maslach Burnout Inventory; Maslach & Jackson, 1981) or provide test takers with a plausible but false rationale for the testing purpose (Cronbach, 1984).

Research examining the effects of making test purpose transparent has yielded mixed results. Early work by Terman and Miles (1936, cited in Loevinger, 1957) found that traits could be measured more accurately when the intent of the measurement was hidden from the test taker. Some research indicates that more subtle items (versus items that make the test purpose obvious) may prevent socially desirable responding and make it more difficult for psychiatric patients to generate normal responses. Hough et al.'s (1990) review of the literature, however, provided little support for use of subtle items (e.g., Duff, 1965; Holden, 1989; Holden & Jackson, 1979; Jackson, 1971; McCall, 1958; Nelson & Cicchetti, 1991; Wiener, 1948). Graham (1990) reviewed studies of obvious and subtle items designed to indicate emotional disturbance that Wiener (1948) proposed for the MMPI. He concluded that obvious items are more highly correlated with nontest behaviors than subtle items and that MMPI Subtle–Obvious subscales do not accurately detect faked responses. More recent research conducted by Nelson et al. (1996) also supports Wiener's conclusions.

In testing contexts where awareness of test purpose inhibits valid responding, another possibility is to make measurement unobtrusive, that is, to collect data from individuals without their knowledge. Unobtrusive measures have been proposed as a viable alternative and supplement to traditional assessment strategies (cf. Webb et al., 1981). Examples of unobtrusive measurement include simple observation in naturalistic settings, observation in contrived situations, examination of archival records, or obtaining physical traces (Kazdin, 1980; Webb et al., 1981). Abler and Sedlacek's review (1986) provided several applied examples of unobtrusive measurement. In one study, researchers attempting to determine the effectiveness of an assertiveness training program posed as magazine salespersons and telephoned former participants to determine the program's effects (McFall & Marston, 1970). Another group of researchers found that prospective college students who made more errors filling out orientation applications were more likely to drop out (Sedlacek, Bailey, & Stovall, 1984). Epstein (1979) reported a study in which students' self-reports of tension were significantly correlated with the number of erasures on exam answer sheets, number of absences, and number of class papers that were not turned in.

UNOBTRUSIVE MEASUREMENT

Computers make increasingly realistic simulations possible and the Internet makes their widespread use possible. Such simulations may be programmed to collect user performance unobtrusively (Johnson et al., 1987; Schatz & Browndyke, 2002). Multimedia programs that utilize audio and visual material in addition to text may be used to create assessment simulations for use in business, industrial, educational, and clinical settings. Computer-assisted instruction (CAI) programs can employ simulations to perform the dual functions of teaching and assessment (Fulton, Larson, & Worthy, 1983; Meier & Wick, 1991). Meier and Wick (1991) described a simulation designed to demonstrate blood alcohol levels for subject-selected drinking experiences. Unobtrusively recorded reports of subjects' alcohol consumption in the simulation were (1) significantly correlated with self-reports of recent drinking behavior, drinking intentions, and attitudes toward alcohol, and (2) uncorrelated with a measure of social desirability. Similarly, Worthen, Borg, and White (1993) discussed the use of computers in continuous measurement in educational settings. If a particular curriculum was computer-based, testing could be embedded in the instructional material and thus be relatively unobtrusive. Worthen et al. noted that such an approach fits very well with mastery learning where progression to the next level of instruction depends on demonstration of successful performance on the current material.

Several problems are inherent, however, with unobtrusive measurements (Webb et al., 1981; Kazdin, 1980; Meier & Wick, 1991). First, considerable effort may be necessary to obtain an unobtrusive measure. It is much easier, for example, to administer a self-report scale to participants in alcohol treatment than to create a simulated bar or observe subjects drink on weekend nights. Second, collecting unobtrusive measurements without arousing subjects' suspicions may be difficult. Third, construct validity is seldom addressed with unobtrusive measures. The behaviors of individuals in naturalistic or contrived situations, for example, may not be direct reflections of a unidimensional construct. Finally, and most important, unobtrusive measures may pose ethical problems. In a research context, it is appropriate to reveal the nature of unobtrusive measurement at debriefing. When working with actual clients, however, the clinician is faced with the dilemma of maintaining the client's trust versus using surreptitious means for data collection via unobtrusive measurement.

Recommendations Related to Test Content

From a nomothetic perspective, the basic concern centers on how to help test takers understand the content of the test as the test developer intended it. From an idiographic perspective, the concern is helping test developers understand how test takers make sense of test content. I begin with discussing approaches to improving test takers' understanding of content on nomothetic tests.

As noted earlier in this chapter, test takers often find test items, instructions, and formats ambiguous. Consequently, test developers need to learn about respondents' perceptions of test content. For interviews, research indicates that respondents increase their comprehension when interviewers are allowed to provide explanations and elaborations of interview questions. In addition, Schwarz (1997) noted that pretesting questionnaires have proven useful particularly "for question comprehension problems, which are only discovered in field pretesting when respondents ask for clarification or give obviously meaningless answers." Schwarz and Oyserman (2001) recommended use of various *cognitive pilot tests*, including procedures whereby:

1. The test developer reads test instructions and questions and attempts to make sense of the test. Test developers rarely read and complete the tests they create—otherwise, the tests would make more sense.

2. Respondents provide information about their thought processes about test content through their paraphrasing of test questions, through researcher probes about question meaning, and by respondents thinking aloud as they complete the test. Schwarz and Oyserman (2001) noted that these procedures can be done concurrently or retrospectively, but each

approach has advantages and disadvantages. Asking respondents to think aloud about how they answered questions in the past requires less effort but may contain more error, whereas the opposite is likely to be true for asking respondents to think aloud as they answer questions at the moment.

3. Test developers create vignettes that illustrate different examples of item meaning. The vignettes indicate what should and should not be included or considered in a response. Design of the vignettes should focus on providing contexts for respondents to help them answer items by focusing on what happened, where it happened, and who was involved.

4. Test developers ask potential respondents how they would answer different examples of the each test question. The version chosen for the test is the one that provides the interpretation that is intended by the test developer.

One way to think about the content issue is from the perspective of discriminant validity. That is, how can the test developer provide content that differentiates the target construct from similar and different constructs? Researchers have described a number of methods that may be useful. A *concept map*, for example, is a graphical representation of one or more concepts linked with associated pieces of knowledge (Trochim, 1999). A test developer might ask one or a group of individuals to develop concept maps that distinguish between two related constructs, and the information in those maps might provide information about item content or tasks that could be employed to enhance discriminant validity. Another method, *back translation*, is employed in checking the accuracy of translating a test from one language to another (Dawis, 1987). The procedure involves taking a test in one language, translating the content to a second language, and then asking one or more additional individuals to translate the content back to the original language. If the process has been accurate, the back translation version should be similar or identical to the original test. For purposes of discriminant validity, a test developer might create two sets of items based on two similar, but possibly different constructs. A set of judges would then attempt to identify which construct each item is supposed to measure. If differences exist between the two constructs, and the item sets are valid representations of each construct, then the judges' back translation should fall into similar or identical groupings as originally created by the test developer. These and similar procedures such as focus groups provide avenues for a better understanding of how test takers understand test content and a subsequent opportunity to revise tests based on that understanding.

Recommendations Related to Test Contexts

A good rule of thumb is that the more interpretation and inference that must be made during a testing process, the more likely that error will occur. As Rosenthal (1976) observed, "Some observations require a greater component of interpretation than others" (p. 16). In most sciences, Rosenthal (1976) indicated, the introduction of more advanced instruments reduces the effects of human observers. These procedures do not replace the human observer, but place the observation in a context that reduces the likelihood of error. A tape recording of a conversation, for example, allows an experimenter to replay segments or record the entirety of the discussion—tasks impossible for most experimenters to perform during the interview itself.

The following approaches focus on procedures beyond the test construction phase and issues surrounding simple item content. The focus is on enhancing validity by improving such contextual components as response format and test instructions.

Provide Testing Contexts That Help
Test Takers Remember Better

Decomposition strategies are designed to provide respondents with recall cues and better estimation strategies. The basic strategy can be described as providing test takes with more contextual information, but through a variety of methods. Schwarz and Oyserman (2001) noted that a question such as "Do you drink alcohol?" can be improved by separating it into more specific questions such as "Do you drink beer?" "Do you drink wine?" and so on. Schwarz and Oyserman (2001) reported that research on decomposition strategies finds that test takers increase their frequency of reports but not always their accuracy. Consequently, they recommend the use of decomposition with behaviors expected to be infrequent, but memorable.

The Descriptor Differential Scale (DDS; Gracely & Kwilosz, 1988) described earlier in this chapter offers another approach to decomposing test items and formats. In essence, each question format is decomposed to create multiple items by format option. The idea is to present multiple question formats to the individual so that he or she can compare each with information stored in memory. For example, a typical self-report item and response format might look like this:

	Never	Rarely	Sometimes	Often
I feel embarrassed:	1	2	3	4

Instead, the DDS approach might translate this single item into multiple items with a presence/absence response format:

I felt embarrassed every day this week:	Yes	No
I felt embarrassed every other day this week:	Yes	No
I felt embarrassed once this week:	Yes	No
I never felt embarrassed this week:	Yes	No

Similarly, Schwarz and Oyserman (2001) noted that instead of asking, "Which of the following services have you used during the last month?" and following the question with a list of services, respondents can be asked to indicate, for each service, whether or not they have used the service.

Translating a traditional scale into the DDS format increases the number of items (thereby enhancing the benefits of aggregation by reducing random error), makes answering items into a detection task (i.e., a judgment of present/absent, which is easier to perform than a rating task), and allows those items to be randomly presented in a written questionnaire or computer-administered format (thus minimizing the cues present in the item order) (Gracely & Naliboff, 1996). Checking the pattern of item responses enables the test scorer to check internal consistency of individual responses. For example, a person who indicated that he or she felt embarrassed every day this week should also answer "yes" to the other positively worded questions about embarrassment. But some problems will remain with this bounded scale, and increasing the number of items in a DDS version may lead to greater test taker fatigue and lower motivation.

Test takers may also evidence improved memory performance when asked to provide frequency estimates of events or behaviors instead of completing more ambiguous rating tasks (cf. Steege, Davin, & Hathaway, 2001). Schwarz's (1999) recommendation was to suggest that respondents be asked to provide frequency information with a unit provided. For example, one could ask:

How many hours a day do you work?   _____ hours per day

Here the memory task involves recalling the number of hours an individual works in a day. Such an approach might be particularly useful in situations of repeated measurements in which respondents know they will be asked to provide such information. Using a response format with descriptors such as "many" or "a few," in contrast, may be problematic because of differences between respondents' understandings of such terms.

Given the discussion of problems with bounded scales earlier in this chapter, a related recommendation is to experiment with unbounded scales. Unbounded scales essentially allow respondents the opportunity to consider infinity as a possible response. For example, you could present a person with an audio tone and ask the person to provide any number of his or her choosing to represent its magnitude. Subsequent tones could then be rated in relation to the number assigned to the first tone, with the possibility existing that a very large number could potentially be assigned to a louder tone. Similarly, instead of asking smokers to rate the number of cigarettes smoked during the past week on a bounded scale of "Never" to "Frequently," smokers could simply estimate or record the number of cigarettes smoked during the past week (i.e., a potentially large number).

Additional alternatives to improve memory performance include restricting reference periods to short and recent reference periods, providing sufficient time to search memory, and using the life history calendar (Schwarz & Oyserman, 2001). For example, instructions to respondents may be written to specify ratings or reports of information for relatively brief, recent reference periods (e.g., today or the past week). Disadvantages here include an increase in zero responses and a failure to improve recall rates when the referenced events or behaviors are (1) rare and important or (2) occur with high regularity. Providing sufficient time means that respondents may engage in repeated attempts to recall additional information. With the life history calendar, respondents are provided with a calendar grid that contains, for example, a column for each day of the week along with rows providing relevant contexts (e.g., activities, persons the respondent saw, and so forth). The idea is to provide respondents with contextual cues that prompt memories relevant to the measurement task.

PROVIDE CONTEXTS THAT MINIMIZE SOCIAL DESIRABILITY

To minimize social desirability errors, Schwarz and Oyserman (2001) provided several recommendations that apply primarily to personal interviews. These include embedding threatening questions among less threatening ones and setting up an interview environment that enhances privacy and confidentiality. Regarding the former, Schwarz and Oyserman (2001) suggested that (1) socially desirable questions be asked only when other people are not present, (2) socially desirable questions be presented in writing, with responses returned in a sealed envelope, and (3) in situations where bystanders cannot be avoided, question responses be phrased (e.g., "yes" or "no," a number) so that other people will not know the question content.

The selection paradigm can encourage large-scale testing in which little rapport is developed between test administrator and test taker. In small groups or individual testing situations, however, the *administrator–respondent relationship* can enhance the test taker's willingness to provide honest answers. For example, when the administrator is a clinical interviewer who has or is developing a therapeutic relationship with the client, the clinician may emphasize that it is in the client's best ultimate interests to report accurately about such sensitive topics as alcohol and drug use, sexual activity, and suicidal ideation. It may simply be impossible to avoid socially desirable responding in some situations, such as employment testing or educational achievement testing, where the stakes are high and rapport is low.

Meier and Schwartz (2007) stumbled on the social desirability problem in an analysis of item-level outcome data provided by middle and secondary school students receiving counseling and psychotherapy in community mental health agencies. Two hundred and fifteen clients completed a brief outcome measure (either 12 or 14 items) at intake and follow-up periods. Scores on 7 outcome items showed statistically significant ($p < .10$) change over time, but 5 of these items *worsened* over time. Interestingly, the content of these 5 items appears susceptible to socially desirable responding, particularly in middle and high school students: "People think I behave strangely," "I smoke cigarettes," "I tell an adult at home before I go out," "I cheat," and "I follow directions." The other two items, "I act without thinking" and "I get failing grades," are more likely to reflect impulsive behaviors that would be a target of therapeutic interventions for many of these clients. (Other examples of events producing divergent effects on scale items exist. Ekkekakis, Hall, and Petruzzello, 1999, for example, found that exercise caused scores on State–Trait Anxiety Inventory items assessing cognitive antecedents of anxiety to decrease, whereas items assessing perceived activation increased.)

As shown in Figure 5.6, all 5 of the SD items worsened from intake to the follow-up period. Overall, 10 of the possible 16 items evidenced increased symptomatology or dysfunction from intake to follow-up. On the other hand, the impulsivity item evidenced statistically significant improvement and positive change on the academic performance item approached statistical significance.

So why would these middle and high school students in the Meier and Schwartz (2007) study report more problems after they began counseling? One explanation is that their trust in the mental health agency, and subsequent willingness to provide more honest answers to survey questions in-

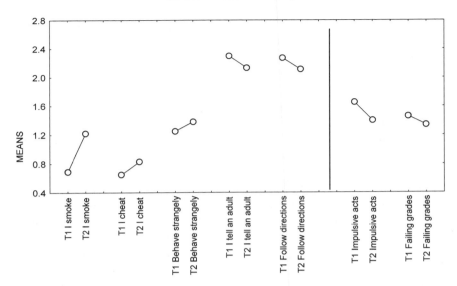

FIGURE 5.6. Plot of intake and follow-up means for items with statistically significant change. Seven items demonstrated a statistical change over time ($p < .10$) from intake (T1) to follow-up (T2). Means to the left of the vertical line indicate a worsening from intake to follow-up, while the means to the right indicate an improvement over time. On socially desirable items that asked about smoking, cheating, strange behavior, telling an adult when going out, and following directions, students reported a worsening of such behaviors from intake to follow-up.

creased after they developed a rapport and working relationship with their counselor. This was most apparent on items that tap into behaviors these clients initially perceived as undesirable to adults, such as smoking, cheating, and (not) following directions. In addition, the fact that several items describing likely therapy targets evidenced improvement suggests that a factor other than a criticalness error was influencing this client sample. Thus, a plausible, if preliminary, conclusion is that if a clinician can establish a safe interpersonal context, clients are more likely to increase the frequency of their reports of socially threatening information. This result needs to be replicated in future research as well as investigated in nonclinical testing contexts.

The Meier and Schwartz (2007) results may also explain an important puzzle in the outcome literature with children and adolescent clients. Kazdin (2000) noted that more than 1,000 controlled studies of psychosocial interventions for children and adolescents exist. Effect sizes (ESs) in these studies for all interventions average around .70 for children and adolescents, with interventions tending to be more effective for adolescents than for younger children. These findings, however, are complicated by research that indicates that the strength of treatment effects appears to depend on whether services were delivered in a field setting, such as a community mental health clinic, or in controlled studies, using more cooperative volunteers, conducted in a laboratory clinic (i.e., the type cited by Kazdin, 2000). Meta-analyses examining the effects of psychotherapy provided in laboratory settings versus field settings indicate that the latter produces ESs around 0 (Weisz, Weiss, & Donenberg, 1992). In other words, studies conducted in field settings indicate that the counseling and psychotherapy provided there has, on average, no effect. In addition, Weisz et al. (1998) found only nine published studies (over a period of 50 years) that examined the effects of child treatment in field settings. This small number likely results from a file drawer problem whereby researchers find that their studies of treatment effects in field settings produce no evidence of beneficial effects and thus do not submit them for publication.

The Meier and Schwartz (2007) results indicate that difficulties will exist in interpreting the results of outcome research conducted in field settings using methodological strategies originally developed for use in laboratory settings. That is, researchers and evaluators in both field and laboratory research employ some version of a pretest, followed by the implementation of an intervention, and conclude with a posttest and, if resources allow, additional follow-up measurements. The Meier and Schwartz (2007) results suggest that pretest data with many adolescent clients will be tainted by underreporting on socially desirable items. Thus, adolescents at pretest will appear healthier and higher functioning than they actually are, making it more difficult to find differences in posttest scores that would potentially evidence statistically significant improvement after counseling and psychotherapy. The Meier and Schwartz (2007) data also imply that some adolescents will provide more valid information on such items at an undetermined future point in their treatment, presumably when they develop sufficient trust in their therapist. These data may represent a more valid starting point to compare to posttest scores.

STRUCTURE INTERVIEWS

The traditional clinical interview has usually been unstructured; that is, the interviewer has few or no preestablished guidelines or procedures for gathering information. Although the interviewer conducting an unstructured interview may have a list of questions, these questions may be asked in a different order with different interviewees, item wording may be changed over time, follow-up questions may or may not be asked, and how to interpret interviewee responses may be left to the judgment of the interviewer.

Contemporary assessors have targeted this lack of structure as a major source of interview problems (Judge, Higgins, & Cable, 2000; Mayfield, Brown, & Hamstra, 1980; Schwab & Heneman, 1969; Weiss, 2004). One of the major purposes of the clinical interview is to arrive at a diagnosis. Matarrazo (1983) reviewed studies indicating that interviewers, even two experienced clinicians with the same patient, could produce little agreement when using unstructured diagnostic procedures. Morrison (1988) suggested that such problems were primarily a result of two factors: (1) *criterion variance*, in which clinicians held different criteria for including and excluding patients into diagnostic groups, and (2) *information variance*, in which clinicians employed different questions with patients and thereby produced different information. Similarly, Swezey (1981) employed the term *error of standards* to describe inconsistencies among raters who employ different standards when assessing individuals' behaviors.

Helzer (1983) defined a *structured interview* as one that includes a predetermined description of

1. The clinical information to be obtained.
2. The order of questions.
3. The coding and definitions of symptom questions.
4. The guidelines for probing responses so as to obtain codable answers.

Clinicians have employed such procedures to develop explicit diagnostic criteria and a structured format for assessing them. Resulting interviews such as the Schedule for Affective Disorders and Schizophrenia (SADS; Endicott & Spitzer, 1978) and the Diagnostic Interview Schedule (DIS; Robins, Helzer, Croughan, & Ratcliff, 1981) have demonstrated significant increases in reliability over previous interviews (Endicott & Spitzer, 1978).

Wiesner and Cronshaw (1988) and Wright, Lichtenfels, and Pursell (1989) conducted meta-analyses that demonstrated that the addition of structure to employment interviews significantly increased validity estimates. Wright et al. (1989) found a validity estimate of .39 for structured interviews and suggested that this number "approaches that found for many cognitive ability tests" (p. 197) as reported by Hunter and Hunter (1984). Structured interviews work, Wright et al. (1989) maintained, because they (1) are closely based on a job analysis of the employment position, thus reducing error from information irrelevant to the specific job, (2) assess individuals' work intentions, which are often linked to work behavior, and (3) use the same set of questions and standards for scoring answers, thereby increasing reliability.

Thus, when a clinician wants to employ an interview to ascertain a client's status with a particular psychological construct, research results support the use of a structured interview. If the interview is employed to assess outcome resulting from a psychosocial intervention, however, the clinician should also determine whether evidence exists indicating that the interview can detect change.

TRAIN RATERS

Just as increased variability in interview procedures introduces error, untrained raters also tend to produce data with less validity. In such disparate areas as behavioral assessment (Hartman, 1984; Paul, 1986), performance appraisal (Gronlund, 1988) and process research (Hill, 1982), test developers have increasingly focused on rater training as a method of decreasing rater error. As Paul, Mariotto, and Redfield (1986a) observed, "The schema[s] employed by untrained or minimally trained observers are generally loose, with fuzzy category boundaries based on prototypes" (p. 1–50). Rater training is designed to reduce schema-produced biases, increase rater motivation, and improve observational skills (McIntyre, Smith, & Hassett, 1984). Behavioral assessors record overt behavior, for example, in staff and clients (Paul, 1986). Observers are trained to record specific behaviors and then assigned to make those observations in specified settings. Describing the elements of one type of behavioral observational training, Hartman (1984) indicated that observers should

1. Complete a general orientation. In research studies, observers should be provided a rationale explaining that they should remain blind to study hypotheses, avoid generating hypotheses, and avoid private discussions of rating problems.
2. Memorize verbatim information such as coding procedures and examples as contained in the observation training manual.
3. Be trained to predetermined standards of accuracy, first through written tests, and then with increasingly complex practice observations, each followed by feedback and discussion of rating problems.
4. Practice observations in the actual setting, with an emphasis on maintaining high observer motivation.
5. Receive periodic evaluation and retraining.

Elements 4 and 5 seem particularly important for maintaining the reliability of behavioral observers. Research has indicated that reliability estimates (i.e., interobserver agreement) drop from a .70–.80 range under evaluated conditions to .30–.40 under nonevaluated conditions (Nay, 1979). In other words, when observers know their work will be evaluated, they provide reliable observations; in other conditions, they may not.

What types of rater training work best? Dickinson and Baker's (1989) meta-analysis of 15 training studies found some support for rater discussion of material during training, practice performing ratings, feedback, and discussion of feedback. Bowers (1973) found that some studies show greater consistency between self and other ratings as raters' familiarity with the target person increases (Norman, 1969), and other research has demonstrated an increase in the judges' rating accuracy when they receive correct feedback about the target (Fancher, 1966, 1967). However, Fancher (1967) also found that judges with greater conceptual sophistication were less accurate in predicting behavior. Bowers (1973) interpreted this finding as indicating that when experienced judges encounter data discrepant from their schemas, they modify the information rather than their schemas. This may be an instance of the hypothesis confirmation bias.

One of the major problems with research in this area is knowing when ratings are in error. In a work setting, for example, what is there to compare a supervisor's ratings with? Laboratory studies in which actual performance is videotaped, however, allow comparison between ratings and actual performance (Murphy & Davidshofer, 1988). These studies indicate that valid ratings are related to a variety of factors, including supervisors' motivation to rate validly, variability of performance, memory aids, and the social context in which rating occurs (Murphy & Davidshofer, 1988). Researchers such as Boice (1983), Allport (1937), Taft (1955), Hartman (1984), and Hill (1982) have identified other factors associated with valid ratings, including higher intelligence, gender (i.e., women are better raters), and attention to detail. Other authors (e.g., Groth-Marnat, 1990; Vernon, 1964), however, have suggested that differences in variables such as age and gender are subtle or nonexistent.

Summary and Implications

Most testing errors appear to be related to three factors: (1) test purpose, (2) test content, and (3) test context. The third element, test context, has been largely overlooked from a theoretical perspective. Although the influence of situations has been recognized in behavioral assessment, context is a more encompassing concept because it can be employed to describe the internal and the external, the objective and the subjective, and what is shared among individuals and what is unique to an individual. Research suggests that scores on all psychological tests, even those as basic as tests of perception, are influenced by context. Test takers, for example, attempt to discern the intent and meaning of tests by searching for clues in test contexts, including instructions, item language, and response formats (Schwarz, 1999). Although the effects of such contexts may sometimes be small, they may still be significant relative to other effects on test scores, such as the moderate effects of many psychosocial interventions.

Individuals may share contexts and these shared contexts can influence test-related behaviors. An example provided in this chapter was of a self-efficacy scale whose item responses appeared to be more strongly influenced by the positivity/negativity of their wording than by item content itself. In addition, test instructions provide an orientation to test takers that influences similar responding, the implications of the language of test items have been shown to alter individuals' item responses, and groups of individuals may also share personal characteristics, such as a desire to present themselves favorably, that can lead to similar responses to test items.

The social norms of the testing situation can influence the characteristics of responses, as when interviewees provide the amount and type of information they believe is expected on the basis of interviewer clues. Information about an individual's social roles may be stored in personal narratives that influence test response. An individual's gender, age, or ethnicity may influence social narratives that guide how that individual behaves in a testing situation, independent of the person's amount or type of a psychological attribute of interest. Some research suggests, for example, that African American students may underperform, when they believe that a test measures intellectual ability, on the basis of the stereotype threat implicit in such a testing situation.

A variety of methods might be employed to evaluate the potential effects of test context. Cognitive pilot tests may be useful for identifying test takers' misunderstandings of test items, instructions, and formats. Deconstruction procedures, such as those employed with the Descriptor Differential Scale (DDS), may be useful for simplifying test materials and enhancing test takers' memory of important events and characteristics. Enhancing or measuring the rapport between client and counselor may be important for understanding when clients feel comfortable enough to respond more honestly as compared with giving socially desirable responses.

The paradox of context in measurement is that it represents a universal principle that can only be applied and observed in an idiographic manner. That is, everyone appears to employ some aspect of context as a means for making sense of and completing psychological tests. The actual effects, however, will not be nomothetic in nature, but will depend on a time- and place-specific interaction between a particular individual and that person's perceived context. Perhaps this seeming contradiction particularly explains why the concept of context, while noticed historically by measurement theorists (e.g., Sternberg, 1984), has yet to take a significant hold in measurement paradigms.

Providing more structure for interviews and more training for raters may also improve test reliability and subsequently enhance validity. A basic method for improving validity in outcome measures employed in counseling and psychotherapy may be to include a step in the test development procedures where the change-sensitivity of test items and tasks are evaluated. These and related ideas are discussed in detail in the next chapter.

General Measurement-Related Writing Assignment

For the three measures you chose (see Chapter 4), conduct a brief literature review (searching sources such as *PsycINFO, Tests in Print, Mental Measurements Yearbooks*, and *Test Critiques*, or test manuals for published tests) and find at least three sources who report reliability estimates for one or more of those measures. In a table, report the author/year of each source as well as the specific reliability estimate (e.g., a test–retest correlation of .80).

Change-Related Writing Assignment

For the three measures you chose, conduct a brief literature review (searching sources such as *PsycINFO, Tests in Print, Mental Measurements Yearbooks*, and *Test Critiques*, or test manuals for published tests) and find at least three sources who report reliability estimates for one or more of those measures. These can be traditional reliability estimates (such as coefficient alpha or test–retest) as well as evidence that test scores remain stable in any type of control group. In a table, report the author/year of each source as well as the specific reliability estimate (e.g., a test–retest correlation of .80).

QUESTIONS AND EXERCISES

1. This in-class exercise is designed to be used in conjunction with the reading and presentation of Chapter 5; consequently, it should be done at the begin-

ning of class or before the reading is completed. Below are 16 items adolescent clients were asked to complete before they began counseling at a community mental health agency. Some of the adolescents' responses suggested they responded to these items in an SD manner. Put a check by the five items that you believe are most likely to elicit socially desirable responding in this adolescent client population.

> I listen to my friends when they talk about their problems.
> I become angry when others tease me.
> I fight with others verbally.
> I fight with others physically.
> I get failing grades.
> People think I behave strangely.
> I act without thinking.
> Other people like me.
> I smoke cigarettes.
> I tell an adult at home before I go out.
> I cheat.
> I use alcohol or drugs.
> I follow directions.
> I feel sad.
> Family members discuss emotional issues.
> Family members fight with one another.

Tally the class's responses and see if they match the five items Meier and Schwartz's (2007) analyses suggested were reflecting SD bias. Can you suggest possible explanations for matches or mismatches between the two lists? In my class, for example, students thought that the item "I use alcohol or drugs" would be affected by social desirability, but it was not one of the top five found by Meier and Schwartz (2007). One explanation for why it wasn't in the top five is that students would rarely admit to alcohol/drug problems, even after they began counseling and started to trust their counselor, because it would mean that they would be referred for separate alcohol/drug counseling.

2. For 3 minutes, write down what you consider the major ideas of this section, chapter, or class. At the beginning of next week's class, share with the group.

3. In small groups or individually, describe the major conclusions and implications from the review of measurement issues in psychophysical research.

4. In small groups or individually, summarize and draw implications for testing for Grice's three conversational maxims.

5. In small groups or individually, compare and contrast the ideas of test purpose, test content, and test context.

CHAPTER 6

Nomothetic Approaches to Measuring Change and Influencing Outcomes

History and Background
Examples of Nomothetic Measures
Reliability of Nomothetic Measures
Validity of Nomothetic Measures
Applications
Summary and Integration

History and Background

Recall from Chapter 2 that *nomothetic* measurements observe characteristics of populations, whereas *idiographic* measures focus on individuals. *Outcome assessment* refers to the use of a test to measure the effects of counseling and psychotherapy. A key component of psychotherapy research and practice (Strupp, Horowitz, & Lambert, 1997), researchers use outcome measures to conduct efficacy (i.e., laboratory-based) and effectiveness (community-based) studies that examine the effects of psychosocial interventions (Hill & Lambert, 2004). Because the primary purpose of an outcome measure is to assess client changes, an instrument's sensitivity to change is directly related to its construct validity (Vermeersch et al., 2004). Most measures employed for outcome measurement in clinical and research efforts are nomothetic in nature.

Researchers have demonstrated that outcome measures differ considerably in their ability to detect the types and amount of change resulting from psychotherapy. Lambert et al. (1986), for example, compared the Zung, Beck, and Hamilton depression scales as outcome measures and found "that rating devices can by themselves produce differences larger than those ordinarily attributed to treatments" (p. 58). Lambert (1994) summarized other research that found that (1) measures based on specific targets of therapy produce greater effects than more distal assessments, (2) therapist and expert judge ratings produce larger effects than client self-reports, and (3) global ratings produce larger effects than assessments of specific symptoms. He concluded that "there are reliable differences in the sensitivity of instruments to change" (Lambert, 1994, p. 85). Yet researchers who rely on clinical trials, with random assignment to treatment and control groups, frequently appear unaware that their choice of outcome measures has serious implications for their findings. Until researchers have a better understanding of the influence of outcome measures on treatment efficacy and effectiveness, their conclusions should be tentative.

In practice settings, one of the most important current uses of outcome measures is to employ data from such measures to justify funding from managed care companies and other sources (Botcheva, White, & Huffman, 2002; Brown & Reed, 2002; Gibbs, Napp, Jolly, Westover, & Uhl, 2002; Thayer & Fine, 2001). Pressure to produce positive outcome data is persistent across the range of field settings, from university counseling centers to hospitals and community agencies. Little guidance and few appropriate outcome measures, however, are available to help clinicians make good choices about assessing change. Froyd et al. (1996) found that counselors, faced with a decision about outcome measures, often employ traditional tests such as the Minnesota Multiphasic Personality Inventory (MMPI) that were not constructed for assessing change. Similarly, many of the best-known scales employed for outcome measurement with children and adolescents, such as the Child Behavior Checklist and Conners Rating Scales (Achenbach, 1994; Conners, 1994), are lengthy diagnostic and screening instruments. As Hill and Lambert (2004) noted, "most outcome measures have not been developed with an eye toward choosing items that are sensitive to change, and little is known about this aspect of test validity" (p. 117). Vermeersch et al. (2004) identified the MMPI as an example of an inappropriate outcome measure because "it is excessively long, very expensive, and contains many items that are not sensitive to change" (p. 38; but see Butcher, 1990, for a different perspective). Although research participants may be willing to spend an hour completing a battery of measures, in many community mental health settings, for example, clients will not complete tests or tasks that they perceive as too long (i.e., more than one page in length or requiring more than 5 minutes to complete) or unrelated to the provision of counseling services.

Examples of Nomothetic Measures

Well-known scales such as the Child Behavior Checklist, Conners Rating Scales, and the MMPI are lengthy measures initially designed for diagnostic and screening purposes. Four examples of measures frequently employed to assess outcome in clinical research and practice are described below. Two measures are domain specific to depression and anxiety, and the remaining two provide examples of a global outcome measure and a comprehensive outcome measure.

Beck Depression Inventory

A self-report scale, the Beck Depression Inventory (BDI) contains 21 multiple-choice items assessing 21 different aspects of depression (Beck & Steer, 1987). Developed on the basis of observations of depressed and nondepressed individuals, each item refers to different aspects of depression and contains four statements of increasing severity. Depression symptoms and attitudes include mood, guilt feelings, suicidal wishes, irritability, sleep disturbance, and appetite changes. Scores on the BDI in previous research have shown high internal consistency, high correlations with other measures of depression, and sensitivity to change resulting from a variety of medication and counseling interventions (Kendall et al., 1987). However, some research indicates that more than 50% of individuals classified as depressed by the BDI changed categories when retested, even when the retesting period consisted of only a few hours or days (Kendall et al., 1987). In addition, the BDI has been shown to exhibit sudden, substantial increases and decreases between psychotherapy sessions (Kelly et al., 2005). The instability of some BDI items raises questions, when assessing counseling outcome, about the ability to attribute change in scores on this instrument to counseling or to other influences.

State–Trait Anxiety Inventory

Based on a conceptual understanding of anxiety as a signal to an individual of the presence of danger, the State–Trait Anxiety Inventory (STAI) consists of two 20-item self-report scales to measure state and trait anxiety (Spielberger et al., 1970, 1997). The State Anxiety scale assesses state anxiety, an emotional state that can vary by situation; the Trait Anxiety scale focuses on more stable aspects of anxiety. The State and Trait scales show expected differences, such as lower test–retest reliability for the State scale; both scales evidence high internal consistency across most samples. The State Anxiety scale has been shown to be treatment sensitive, particularly in detecting the effects of counseling interventions aimed at decreasing test anxiety. Most measures of anxiety and depression correlate moderately to highly, raising questions about their construct validity.

Global Assessment of Functioning

Over the past several decades the most widely used brief outcome measure has been the Global Assessment of Functioning (GAF) scale, a single-item 100-point rating scale that clinicians complete to estimate a client's overall functioning and symptomatology (Endicott, Spitzer, Fleiss, & Cohen, 1976). The global rating is intended to summarize symptoms and functioning across diverse domains, ranging from work functioning to suicidality, over daily, weekly, or monthly periods. GAF ratings employed for outcome assessment are typically completed at intake and termination, although managed care companies often require counselors to report such ratings for individual clients over more frequent time intervals while counseling is ongoing. Despite its widespread use, little psychometric data are available for its current form, although researchers have reported modest test–retest reliability values in the .60–.80 range. As Davis and Meier (2001) noted, the basic problem with the GAF is its transparency: The counselor can easily manipulate the rating, making the client appear as distressed as necessary to justify treatment, but at a potential cost of validity. Many counselors also do not view GAF information as particularly relevant: A recent survey found that counselors considered global GAF-type data among the least useful information for outcome assessment (Bickman et al., 2000).

Outcome Questionnaire

The Outcome Questionnaire (OQ-45) is one of the newest comprehensive outcome scales (Lambert & Finch, 1999). Lambert and colleagues developed the OQ and describe the scale as easy to score, of low cost, sensitive to change over short periods, and able to measure characteristics associated with mental health functioning. Intended for persons 18 and older, the 45-item test can be completed in about 5 minutes. Sample items include "I feel blue" and "I am satisfied with my relationships with others." The OQ produces a total scores and three subscales: The Symptom Distress subscale contains items related to anxiety and depression; Interpersonal Relations items assess satisfaction with and problems in interpersonal functioning; and Social Role Performance items relate to satisfaction and competence in employment, family, and leisure roles.

Studies indicate that the OQ-45 has adequate test–retest reliability and internal consistency. The OQ also correlates in expected directions and magnitudes with related scales such as the Symptom Checklist 90-R, Beck Depression Inventory, State–Trait Anxiety Inventory, and Inventory of Interpersonal Problems and can distinguish between clinical and nonclinical groups. Research indicates that some OQ-45 items evidence change in response to treatment (e.g., Vermeersch et al., 2004), and a study with college students also indicated that students show improvement on OQ items even when they are not in counseling, although not at the same rate as treated individuals. An additional concern is that all three subscales of the OQ-45 are highly intercorrelated, suggesting that the total score on the scale should be considered an indication of general distress. As described below, some of the most interesting outcome research now being conducted has demonstrated that by using OQ scores to provide feedback to counselors, the rate of clients' failing treatment can be reduced.

These tests are potentially useful outcome measures with significant sources of invalidity. The BDI's strong relationship to measures of anxiety remains to be explained; the STAI's usefulness for assessing outcomes with the types of anxiety (particularly social anxiety) and depression found in psychotherapy clients needs to be further explored. The transparency of the GAF's global score means that clinicians can easily manipulate this score, and the overlap among the subscales of the OQ-45 raises questions about its construct validity. More fundamental, researchers should examine these measures' construct validity for outcome purposes, including their sensitivity to change with different client populations and different types of interventions. Hill and Lambert (2004) observed that "most outcome measures have not been developed with an eye toward choosing items that are sensitive to change, and little is known about this aspect of test validity" (p. 117). How could the field think about such problems in a way that would offer methods for improved assessment?

Reliability of Nomothetic Measures

The usual definition of *reliability* refers to a measurement method's ability to produce consistent scores. Thus, one might check the reliability of a measure of a trait by administering it twice to the same group of individuals one week apart and then correlating those scores. If the correlation is high (generally above .80), this means that scores on the measure have good test–retest reliability (Nunnally, 1967; Meier & Davis, 1990). A low estimate (e.g., below .70) presents a problem for subsequent interpretation of the meaning of these scores.

A variety of methods exist for estimating the reliability of test scores (Cronbach, 1984; Crocker & Algina, 1986). For example, you could calculate *internal consistency* (the average correlation between any item and the sum of the items), *test–retest reliability* (the correlation between two administrations of the same test given to the same persons, described in the preceding paragraph), or *interrater reliability* (the correlation between two raters who observe the same phenomenon). *Coefficient alpha*, a measure of internal consistency, currently is the most frequently used method for quantitative data because it requires only a single administration of the measurement method and is easily computed using programs such as SPSSx and SAS.

Assessing the stability of nomothetic outcome measures would seem a contradiction since, as discussed in the next section, the most important characteristic of an outcome measure is its sensitivity to change. What causes the items on an outcome measure to change, however, is the crucial issue; valid outcome items in this context are those that change only in response to an intervention (Meier, 1997). Ideally, outcome items would not change as a result of repeated administration or natural developmental processes such as maturation, although rigorous application of such a standard may be unrealistic. Pragmatically, test–retest reliability of outcome measures should be evaluated with control samples or nonclinical samples; the test–retest range should approximate the periods between use of outcome measures with clinical samples. Coefficient alpha should also be a useful measure of reliability with nomothetic outcome measures when aggregated test scores are intended to reflect a single construct.

Validity of Nomothetic Measures

Recall the two major definitions of validity: what a test measures, or what inferences can be drawn from test scores. If a test is labeled as a measure of social anxiety, what evidence exists that it does measure the construct of social anxiety? Similarly, does evidence exist that test scores can be employed for certain purposes, such as diagnosing individuals with social anxiety? These concerns apply also to measures of change in counseling and psychotherapy. With an outcome measure designed to assess anxiety, for example, the test developer should provide evidence that anxiety (and not depression, for example) is the construct being assessed by items and aggregated scores on the test. Similarly, evidence should also be provided that the measure demonstrates a response to an effective intervention. As Vermeersch et al. (2004) stated, "the sensitivity to change of a measure is directly related to the construct validity of the instrument, because the primary purpose of outcome measures is to document clients' changes following a course of therapy" (p. 38). Various criteria related to this central idea have been proposed. Vermeersch et al. (2004), for example, suggested that (1) change should occur in theoretically expected directions (i.e., clients should improve while completing counseling) and (2) clients receiving counseling should evidence more improvement than persons who do not receive an intervention (i.e., untreated controls).

The test development literature offers little general guidance about which validity analyses are most useful. Murphy and Davidshofer (1988) concluded that "it would be fair to say that any type of data or statistic might be useful in determining" validity (p. 103). Anastasi (1986) reached a similar conclusion: "Almost any information gathered in the process of developing or using a test is relevant to its validity" (p. 3). Focusing on the intended use and purpose of test scores, however, does assist the test developer or test evaluator to decide on the types of evidence that will be useful for evaluating a test. As described in the next section, data related to a test's sensitivity to change resulting from psychosocial interventions is central to evaluating the validity of outcome measures.

Change-Sensitive Tests

One explanation for differences in the sensitivity of measures to change is that individual items on those measures may be more or less able to detect the multiple effects of any psychosocial intervention. To identify such items, Meier (1997, 2000, 2004) proposed a set of intervention item selection rules (IISRs) designed to identify intervention-sensitive items. This approach is based on the assumptions that (1) items differ along a trait–state continuum and (2) different test construction and item analysis procedures are necessary to select items and create scales that reflect intervention effects. Intervention-sensitive items should remain relatively stable over time when no intervention is present (i.e., be reliable), but should change in response to an intervention (i.e., evidence state effects). This perspective also implies that scores on traditionally developed outcome assessments will reflect more trait variance than the desired state effects resulting from psychotherapy. If correct, traditional tests will produce scores that reflect only small amounts of variance resulting from psychotherapy effects, amounts be too small for purposes other than examining, in large samples, such general questions as whether differences exist between treatment and control groups.

The major statistic employed to evaluate the amount of change resulting from psychotherapy is effect size (ES). Since the seminal work of Smith and Glass (1977), the use of ES has become the major statistical technique for describing the amount of change in both research and clinical settings (Smith & Glass, 1977). Researchers compute ES employing some variation of the following formula, where posttest scores are subtracted from pretest scores and then divided by the standard deviation of all pretest and posttest scores:

$$ES = \frac{Mean\ (posttest\ scores) - Mean\ (pretest\ scores)}{Pooled\ standard\ deviation\ for\ posttest\ and\ pretest\ scores}$$

The resulting standard score can be employed as an indicator of the degree of change resulting from the intervention. Smith and Glass (1977) employed ESs in their meta-analysis of psychotherapy effects to determine that (1) different psychotherapy approaches produced ESs of about the same size and (2) among the methodological indicators examined, ES correlated most highly with a rating of the transparency or reactivity of the outcome measures used.

Initial research with outcome measures developed using change-sensitive criteria provides evidence that such measures possess different psychometric characteristics than tests developed with traditional approaches. Figure 6.1 shows data from studies in which change-sensitive scales produced larger effect sizes than comparison scales in intervention studies. Key studies, primarily using actual clients receiving services in university counseling centers and community mental health centers, include:

1. Weinstock and Meier (2003) subjected intake and follow-up items on a 56-item self-report checklist completed by 615 university counseling center clients to principal component analysis (PCA, a type of factor analysis) and an IISR evaluation. As predicted, the items identified through the IISRs were different from those found in the PCAs and, when combined into scales, had larger effect sizes. Scales formed with intervention-sensitive items demonstrated lower test–retest reliability and internal consistency estimates but, as shown in Figure 6.1, larger pre–post change than items formed by PCA analyses.

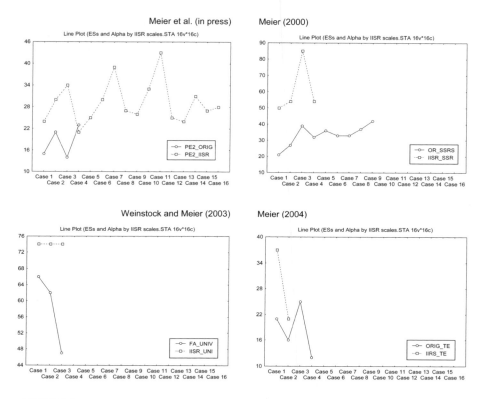

FIGURE 6.1. Change-sensitive scales produce larger effect sizes. Outcome measures with change-sensitive items consistently evidenced larger effect sizes than scales developed through traditional methodologies.

2. One hundred and sixteen parents completed a social skills rating scale at intake and follow-up periods as part of treatment for their children in a community health center (Meier, 2000). Results indicated that scales composed of items that met IISR criteria had higher effect sizes than the original scales developed through traditional item selection methods.

3. Meier (2004) applied the IISRs during the initial development of an outcome measure, completed by teachers, for 88 elementary age children receiving psychosocial services from several community mental health agencies. As shown in Figure 6.1, the major scale formed with these change-sensitive items displayed the largest effect size when compared with a scale composed of the original item pool.

4. Application of the IISRs to a diverse sample of 896 elementary

school children, two-thirds of whom were boys, receiving counseling from community mental health agencies resulted in scales composed of change-sensitive items with larger effect sizes than scales composed of the original item pool (Meier et al., in press).

These studies establish a fundamental conclusion: Test items differ and can be evaluated on the basis of their ability to discriminate the amount of change that takes place during a psychosocial intervention. The Weinstock and Meier (2003) study also provides evidence that the selection of a subset of change-sensitive items can be replicated across samples. This sets the stage for subsequent research and practice applications.

For research purposes, the results of change-sensitive item-level research should allow a more precise comparison and integration of results using data from outcome measures employed across multiple studies. Meier and Vermeersch (2007) provided an example of employing IISR analyses for research on therapy outcomes by examining change at the item level in three outcome studies employing a total of 7,344 clients (Vermeersch et al., 2000, 2004; Weinstock & Meier, 2003). Although the psychotherapy literature indicates that nothing beyond a general positive improvement across domains should be present in such a heterogeneous data set, Meier and Vermeersch (2007) found that depression and anxiety-related items evidenced larger effect sizes than items assessing other domains. They suggested that depression and anxiety may represent a *common outcome factor* related to negative affect and that alleviation of negative mood states may be a ubiquitous effect of all therapeutic interventions.

Meier and Vermeersch (2007) also noted that the large depression/anxiety effect could explain the puzzling, but consistent finding in the psychotherapy outcome literature of equivalent gains across therapy types. Given the theoretical range of psychotherapy orientations as well as the large number of different psychotherapy techniques employed in such research (Meier & Davis, 2005), psychotherapy researchers have been puzzled by the finding that different types of counseling and psychotherapy show no differences, or in other words, they produce equivalent gains (Smith & Glass, 1977; Wampold, 2001). If large-scale psychotherapy studies and meta-analyses of such studies contain heterogeneous sets of clients, counselors, interventions, and outcome measures, improvement in depression and anxiety may represent the largest common contribution to total ES across treatments. If so, the large depression/anxiety contribution will account for the equivalent gains result. Specific effects may still occur, but the Meier and Vermeersch (2007) findings suggest that they will be smaller than the depression/anxiety effect when examined in large data sets of psychotherapy clients receiving diverse interventions.

In both efficacy and effectiveness research, employing treatment-sensitive measures would appear to be an important ingredient in enhancing power to detect the small to moderate effects and interactions produced by psychosocial interventions. The IISR studies have found (1) gender differences, indicating differential response to counseling for boys and girls (Meier, 2000; Meier et al., in press); (2) ceiling effects, indicating that problems such as interpersonal communication skills deficits were perceived in some clinical groups as strengths in the beginning of counseling (Meier et al., in press); and (3) specific items that showed improvement or worsening, such as fidgeting and academic performance (Meier, 2004), that can provide useful progress feedback to individual counselors as well as to entire counseling agencies (Weinstock & Meier, 2003).

Taken as a whole, the results of these studies lend support to the idea that use of trait-based, individual difference methods of item evaluation and selection are less valid for measuring constructs that change. In essence, employing traditional tests to measure counseling outcome may be akin to eating soup with a fork. Intervention–sensitive tests appear to detect intervention–related states and offer advantages, as compared with traditional psychological tests, in both the clinical and research realms. Nevertheless, some limitations exist. IISR studies require resources that may be unavailable to many researchers. For example, control groups may help to rule out alternative explanations for change such as practice and demand characteristics. Most of the IISR studies conducted in field settings to date have not included control groups, meaning that the resulting scales might be better described as change sensitive but not necessarily treatment sensitive (because explanations for change beyond the provided interventions cannot be ruled out).

Using Outcome Data for Clinical Feedback

In fields such as education and medicine, researchers and practitioners have employed outcome-related data to improve the results of ongoing interventions (Cross & Angelo, 1988; Sapyta, 2004). The basic premise is that if *feedback* is provided to persons involved in or providing an intervention, further improvement is likely. In contrast, lack of feedback with many types of tasks has been shown to result in deteriorating performance (Bilodeau & Bilodeau, 1961, cited in Gentile, 1990; but also see Kluger & DeNisi, 1999, for a more complex description of feedback effects). Research supports the basic concept: Kluger and DeNisi's (1996) meta-analysis of feedback studies found that persons receiving feedback on various tasks outperform persons who do not. Similarly, Sapyta's (2004) meta-analysis of 30 randomized clinical trials in which health professionals received feedback about client health status in community settings showed a mean ES of .21, indicating better outcomes for clinicians who received feedback about progress.

How does feedback work? Saptya, Riemer, and Bickman (2005) suggested that for feedback to be useful, an individual (1) needs to be committed to a goal (e.g., wants to achieve a good clinical outcome), (2) must be aware of a discrepancy in regard to that goal (e.g., a client fails to make progress), and (3) must believe the goal to be achievable (i.e., outcome and efficacy expectations). In other words, the main function of feedback is to indicate whether or not a goal has been accomplished. Yet Claiborn and Goodyear (2005) noted that "feedback is often not specified as a theory-based component of psychological treatment, perhaps because it is so fundamental to and pervasive in the change process" (p. 215).

Despite research showing that most clients improve (e.g., Smith & Glass, 1977), other evidence indicates that counselors experience difficulty making good judgments about client progress and choice of interventions. As Saptya et al. (2005) noted, "Therapists are trained, are supervised, and practice in the absence of information about client treatment response from objective sources" (p. 147). Despite 30 years of research, no consensus among researchers exists to support the idea that training, clinical experience, or supervision influences mental health outcomes (Sapyta et al., 2005); yet most clinicians receive feedback about their work solely through supervision and clinical experience. Gray and Lambert's (2001) review of research on clinicians' judgment of client progress concluded:

> Clinicians are not effective in gauging patient response to treatment, especially in early treatment sessions. However, when they are provided with feedback on poor treatment response, they develop a perspective on their patient's clinical progress that enables them to recalibrate treatment and make a substantial impact on improvement rates. (p. 26)

Similarly, Persons and Mikami (2002) noted several large-scale studies of psychotherapy in which 50% or more of the counseled participants failed to improve. They also noted, "We have found in our caseloads, and we believe that readers who examine their own caseloads will also find, a surprising number of patients who have been in treatment for a disconcertingly long time without making significant progress" (Persons & Mikami, 2002, p. 143).

Other research suggests that even when they notice a lack of progress, many counselors fail to adjust their approach. For example, Kendall et al. (1992) surveyed 315 psychotherapists to investigate the amount of treatment failure in their practice and their explanations for such failure. Their survey found that about 11% of each counselor's clients were not making progress and yet the majority of counselors had no alternative plans for these failing clients. In contrast to previous research in which therapists rated themselves as the most important influence on treatment failure, therapists in this survey rated clients' inability to benefit from therapy as the most important reason for lack of progress. Despite this belief, most clinicians failed to cite the severity of client problems as a reason for treatment failure. Although research indicates that the severity of clients' problems strongly influences therapeutic improvement (Lueger, 1998; Meier & Letsch, 2000), therapists' written comments indicated that they generally believed that no problem was too severe to be treated by psychotherapy. Kendall et al. (1992) concluded that "therapists failed to take into account the severity of their clients' symptoms when explaining both probable causes of their clients' lack of progress, and when evaluating their clients' functioning" (p. 278). With failing clients, then, these counselors neglected to adjust their approach and misperceived at least one major reason for a lack of improvement.

Given the difficulties that most people exhibit in making judgments about causality (Alloy & Abramson, 1979; Jenkins & Ward, 1965; White, 2000), it is not surprising that counselors would experience similar problems in their work (Garb, 1998; Hannan et al., 2005; Haynes, Spain, & Oliveira, 1993). Garb (1998) summarized research that found little overlap among clinicians' case formulations of the same clients; these conceptualizations describe causal links between process and outcome elements in individual clients. DeWitt, Kaltreider, Weiss, and Horowitz (1983), for example, studied teams of clinicians who interviewed the same sets of clients who presented with abnormal grief reactions after the death of a parent; the researchers concluded that the formulations among treatment teams differed. Garb's (1998) review also found that agreement among clinicians' conceptualizations has been moderate to poor when clinicians (1) differ in theoretical orientations, (2) rate the source of schizophrenic symptoms, and (3) identify client problem areas or nominate a primary target behavior to be changed. Clinicians have been found to mistake the simple presence of such symptoms as low self-esteem, depression, and suicidal thoughts as evidence of past sexual abuse (Garb, 1998). Client and clinician gender, race, sex roles, age, and religion have also been found to influence case conceptualizations (Garb, 1998). Garb (1998) concluded that "because case formulations are frequently made on the basis of clinical experience and clinical intuition, and because reliability and validity have often been poor for case formulations, clinicians may frequently want to defer from making judgments about the causes of a client's problems or they may want to try to use empirical methods to derive causal inferences" (p. 101). Ziskin (1995) reached similar conclusions:

> Even if there were not a massive body of research strongly suggesting that clinicians actually have limited capacity to manage complex information and often stumble over a few variables, it should be clear that the obstacles facing the clinician who hopes to integrate all of the data are not merely difficult hurdles, but impossible ones.... Perhaps it would not be entirely unfair to say that a large percentage of clinicians do in fact evidence a shared myth about their own judgment capacities. As far as we can tell, there seems to be no plausible way one can legitimately support these beliefs on the basis of scientific evidence. (p. 261)

A reasonable conclusion from this research is that particularly with clients who fail to improve, counselors would do well to employ more systematic methods in place of or in addition to their professional judgment (Haynes et al., 1993; Mumma, 2004). A few contemporary practitioners and researchers have demonstrated the benefits of employing structured feedback and clinical support tools as part of the therapeutic process (Clement, 1994, 1999). Lambert and others have applied the feedback concept explicitly in what has been termed *patient-focused research*, whereby clinicians receive direct feedback about a client's progress (Howard, Moras, Brill, Martinovich, & Lutz, 1996). Lambert et al. (2001) examined the effect of providing feedback to therapists working with two types of college counseling clients, those who were evidencing improvement and those who were not. Clients completed the OQ weekly, and therapists received progress reports to indicate which clients had an adequate rate of change, an inadequate rate of change, or were failing to make any progress. Lambert et al. found that OQ scores at termination were higher for clients who were initially not making progress, but whose therapists were receiving feedback, as compared with clients who were not making progress and whose therapists received no feedback. In contrast, clients who were not progressing, and whose therapists received no feedback, worsened over time.

Interestingly, clients already making progress did not evidence additional gains in the feedback condition. This makes sense in that feedback theories focus on the role of negative feedback in a regulatory system (e.g., Carver & Scheier, 1981; Lord & Hanges, 1987). In such a system a person notices a discrepancy between a goal and present performance and becomes motivated to reduce this discrepancy (Bandura, 1997). Thus, therapists who participate in clinical feedback systems are more likely to attend to information that indicates that clients are not making progress. In contrast, information that confirms expected progress may not elicit further attention; as described below, research indicates that most therapists do expect most clients to progress.

Lambert, Harmon, Slade, Whipple, and Hawkins (2005) summarized the results of four studies that evaluated the effects of clinical feedback with more than 2,500 cases. The studies uniformly found that a feedback system enhances outcomes for patients with a negative response. That is, among clients not making improvement at the beginning of therapy, those whose therapists received feedback showed less deterioration and more improvement over time than clients whose therapists did not receive feedback. More specifically, in these studies, 21% of clients who were not making progress continued to deteriorate when their therapists were not given feedback; in contrast, only 13% of clients deteriorated among those who were not making progress but whose therapists received feedback about that lack of progress. Twenty-one percent of clients improved who were not making progress and whose therapists were not given feedback, as compared with 35% who were not making progress and whose therapists were given feedback. Lambert et al. (2005) reported that therapists given feedback about their clients' lack of improvement tended to keep those clients in treatment for more sessions, and concluded, "we recommend widespread application of feedback systems in routine care" (p. 171).

Brown and Jones (2005) reported related research with a feedback system involving more than 7,000 clinicians employed in a large managed care company. They found that, contrary to previous research results (cf. Meier & Letsch, 2000), persons with severe problems entering therapy that utilized feedback can show improvement. Clients in their system evidence considerable attrition, with the modal number of sessions attended equal to one. Because many clients stopped treatment after fewer than five sessions, Brown and Jones (2005) inferred that the decision to stop apparently rests with clients and not clinicians. Reviewing patterns of treatment use, they concluded that clients and therapists did not overutilize services and "that the most effective method to manage cost is to ensure that patients receive effective treatment because patients receiving effective care naturally tend to utilize fewer sessions" (Brown & Jones, 2005, p. 191). Miller, Duncan, Sorrell, and Brown (2005) reported on the use of a similar outcome management system that employed a four-item outcome measure and a four-item therapeutic alliance scale, both completed by the client. Feedback to the clinician that included both outcome and alliance information boosted success rates (Miller et al., 2005). Miller et al. (2005) also found that persons who completed the therapeutic alliance scale at intake were more likely to evidence improvement than persons who did not. Previous research by Meier and Letsch (2000) found that parents who completed an intake and a follow-up outcome measure for their children in counseling rated their children as more socially skilled and as having less severe problems than parents who completed only an intake rating. These results suggest that a client's willingness to complete an outcome measure may serve as a proxy for problem severity and likelihood of improvement through psychosocial services.

Use Measures with a Strong Theoretical Basis

As with traditional tests, items created for change-sensitive tests should be theoretically based as much as possible (Meier, 1997). Many contemporary measurement theorists believe that test validation is closely related or identical to traditional hypothesis testing (cf. Ellis & Blustein, 1991; Landy, 1986). Landy (1986) maintained that "the validity analyst is carrying out traditional hypothesis testing" (p. 1186); Loevinger (1957) similarly indicated that when test developers examine individual items during the test construction process, they are testing hypotheses. Theoretical grounding also provides an important context for understanding the meaning of changing values of items in a change-sensitive assessment.

Intervention-sensitive items should be grounded in a theory of the psychotherapeutic intervention (Meier, 1997). For example, if depression and anxiety measures such as the BDI and STAI were based on theories that explained the relationship, similarities, and differences between anxiety and depression, the high correlation between measures of anxiety and depression would likely be reduced or at least made more understandable. Similarly, a deeper theoretical basis for the items that make up the subscales of the OQ-45 should reduce their intercorrelations or provide a stronger explanation than methodological error.

During test construction, test developers should search existing theoretical and empirical literatures to develop items responsive to the intervention(s) and clinical populations in question. The first step would be to conduct a literature review in preparation for creating items and tasks about problems thought to be affected by different interventions with the clinical population of interest. With children and adolescents, for example, questions about problems such as smoking or sexual activity might be usefully guided by developmental research (e.g., Karcher & Finn, 2005). Thorough explication of the constructs expected to be influenced and unaffected by the intervention should result in a large initial item pool, providing the capacity to investigate general and specific intervention effects. Test developers might consider explicitly including (1) items from theories that conceptualize the process and outcomes of an intervention in different ways as well as (2) items not expected to be intervention sensitive. As in dependent measures designs (Cook & Campbell, 1979), demonstration of change in intervention-sensitive items and stability in items not expected to change would be another strong method of demonstrating construct validity for change-sensitive tests. Current theories in counseling and psychotherapy, however, are not deep enough to make predictions about what specific outcomes will and will not change in response to particular interventions.

Bandura's (1977) self-efficacy theory provides an example of a nomothetic theoretical approach that offers a degree of specificity about what outcomes should change as a result of psychosocial interventions. Bandura proposed self-efficacy theory as an universal explanation for behavior change. As shown in Figure 6.2, *outcome expectations* refers to knowledge or beliefs about what specific behaviors will lead to desired outcomes. *Self-efficacy expectations*, however, refers to beliefs clients hold about whether they can perform those specific behaviors. Students may know, for example, that if they study every night for 2 weeks before a major test, they are likely receive a grade of A on that test. However, many students may not believe that they can study that consistently and consequently do not attempt the task. Considerable research evidence (Bandura, 1977, 1986, 1997) supports the hypotheses that efficacy expectations strongly determine (1) what actions individuals will initiate and persist in and (2) the types of affect individuals

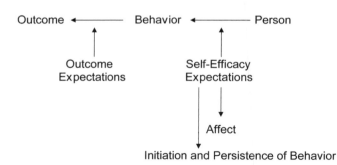

FIGURE 6.2. Outcome and efficacy expectations. Bandura (1997) proposed that individuals' expectancies about their ability to perform behaviors linked to desired outcomes strongly influenced their initiation and persistence of those behaviors. Those expectancies also influence what affect individuals experience. From Bandura (1997). Copyright 1997 by the American Psychological Association. Reprinted by permission.

will feel around certain tasks. For example, students with low self-efficacy for studying behaviors are likely to feel anxious about studying. Bandura (1977) intended this theory to be applicable to all clients and problems and proposed a set of interventions (e.g., modeling, direct performance of behaviors) specifically selected to improve efficacy expectations. The theory has proven to be robust, generating empirical support from such diverse domains as physical and mental health, athletic performance, and career choice (Bandura, 1997). In essence, self-efficacy expectations present an efficient means of measuring outcome-related constructs because of their strong relation to both behavior and affect.

A strong theoretical basis for change, however, is insufficient to guarantee that derived outcome measures will be reliable and valid. Persistent measurement issues with self-efficacy, for example, can be found in the research literature. Basic issues such as acquiescence and criticalness bias can make interpretation of positively and negatively worded self-efficacy scales problematic (see examples in Guskey & Passaro, 1994; Larson et al., 1992). More complex problems include (1) a lack of discriminant validity between self-efficacy and related constructs, including outcome expectations (Eastman & Marzillier, 1984; Lee, 1984; Marsh, Dowson, Pietsch, & Walker, 2004; Meier, 1988; Tschannen-Moran & Hoy, 2001); (2) questions about mediators of self-efficacy's relations to behavior (Meier, McCarthy, & Schmeck, 1984); and (3) evidence that different assessment methods, including the degree of specificity of the measured self-efficacy domain, influence individuals' production of efficacy and outcome expectations (Arisohn, Bruch, & Heimberg, 1988; Pajares, 1996; Tschannen-Moran & Hoy, 2001). Meier et al. (1984), for example, studied self-efficacy as a predictor of writing performance in a sample of 121 freshmen in 16-week remedial, required, or honors writing courses at a large Midwestern university. Using a self-efficacy for writing measure based on course objectives, they found a statistically significant relationship between students' self-efficacy for writing and judges' ratings of their essays. The researchers also found that students' locus of control (i.e., a measure of general outcome expectations) mediated the relationship: The self-efficacy for writing of students classified as internals (who believed that their behaviors led to desired outcomes) correlated .61 with writing performance, whereas the self-efficacy students classified as externals (who believed outcomes were not in their control) correlated only .10 with writing performance. Thus, the establishment of positive outcome expectations may precede the development of efficacy expectations. It is also possible that once positive efficacy expectations develop, outcome expectations may be reduced in their effect on behavior (cf. Lee, 1984).

Use Brief Measures

Until recently, perhaps the single most important rule for the selection and use of an outcome measure in practice settings was brevity. Several reasons account for brevity's importance. Brief measures are more likely to be easy to score and cost less. Most community mental health agencies have relatively small amounts of money to spend on outcome assessment; most clinicians and clients want to spend as little time as possible completing such measures. Yet the use of traditional scales as repeated measures for outcome assessment is likely to be problematic in situations where clients and informants have discretion about whether or not to complete such measures (Meier & Letsch, 2000). Because perceived survey length influences completion rates (Dillman, 1978), brevity is important for engaging the cooperation of clients and other sources of information such as parents, custodians, counselors, and teachers. Research indicates that clinicians and clients have a 5-minute time limit for completing outcome measures (Miller et al., 2005). Use of longer measures likely means less cooperation and poor data quality. In addition, managed care companies and traditional insurers tend to employ outcome measures such as the GAF as a simple accounting device that provides information about whether or not the client is improving. There is often little or no interest, for example, in more complex issues such as the amount of change, the type of change, or whether information on the test could be employed to provide feedback. Consequently, the type of information produced by brief measures is often of limited use to clinicians.

Tests that contain only change-sensitive items should be briefer tests with greater practical utility for clinicians and clients. IISR scales containing a concentration of change-sensitive items will be shorter in length than traditional tests that possess both a large number of trait items and only a smaller subset of change-sensitive items. The challenge for test developers, however, will be to balance the need for brevity versus the stronger reliability and validity estimates associated with longer measures.

Applications

Creating Change-Sensitive Measures

As noted earlier in the chapter, Meier (1997, 2000, 2004) described a set of intervention item selection rules (IISRs) designed to identify intervention-sensitive items either during test construction or in subsequent item evaluations. The development of an IISR scale can be considered a test of the hypothesis that selected items and tasks reflect a change-sensitive aspect of a construct. Test developers who employ IISRs contrast the major hypothesis, that item change results from the intervention, against a potentially large number of plausible competing hypotheses related to test and experimental validity (Meier, 2004). Intervention effects compete with such other factors as (1) state effects, including situations and development/ maturation), (2) trait effects, including personality characteristics and psychopathology, (3) measurement error, such as reactivity in self-reports and practice effects, and (4) sampling error, including systematic missing data. Consequently, effect size at the item level due to any particular state effect is likely to be small.

To provide an example of creating an outcome measure via IISRs, this section describes the development of an intervention-sensitive scale, the Parent Elementary form of the Behavioral Intervention Monitoring and Assessment System (PE-BIMAS; Meier et al., in press). The PE-BIMAS's purpose is to assess change in children completing counseling in field settings, a combination rarely studied in psychotherapy research (Kazdin, 2000). In the following discussion, PE-BIMAS items are evaluated by IISR guidelines in preparation for creating aggregate scales, and the psychometric properties of those scales, particularly their change sensitivity, are then assessed.

PE-BIMAS items were created on the basis of a review of the literature on children's behavior problems (Stiffman, Orme, Evans, Feldman, & Keeney, 1984), other measures of children's distress and functioning (Meier, 1998), and suggestions from mental health professionals. The Stiffman et al. (1984) review identified categories including hiding thoughts from others, deviancy, internalizing behaviors (e.g., anxiety, depression), externalizing behaviors (e.g., fighting), and problems in cognitive, social, and academic functioning. To avoid acquiescence and criticalness biases, items were worded in both a positive (labeled Strengths) and negative (Distress/Problems) direction; this process resulted in the creation of a 32-item scale labeled the Original Scale.

Parents often are the primary source of information about their children because of their accessibility, knowledge of behavior across situations and time, and key role in referral to treatment (Kazdin, 1994). With the PE-BIMAS, a parent or another adult familiar with the child first provided brief demographic information about the child and then assessed a variety of behaviors and emotional states. Raters were instructed to report how often each of the behaviors, events, or situations described in PE-BIMAS items occurred during the past week. Parents answered each PE-BIMAS item by checking a box on the following scale: Never (0 instances in the past week, coded as 0), Rarely (1 instance, coded as 1), Sometimes (2–3 instances, coded as 2), and Often (3–7 instances, coded as 3).

All parents or guardians of children and adolescents who sought counseling at several multibranch community mental health agencies completed an intake version of the PE-BIMAS at their first visit. These agencies provide individual, family, and group interventions to children and families in urban, suburban, and rural communities and are staffed primarily by master's-level counselors. Peer difficulties, family conflict, illegal activities that bring children into court, emotional and physical problems, lack of self-confidence, child abuse, and hyperactivity are among clients' presenting problems. Parents completed an informed consent form describing the need for program evaluation of the agency and indicating they could decline participation and continue to obtain services. These agencies had experienced difficulty in obtaining outcome assessments at termination, and consequently they adopted a procedure whereby follow-up forms were administered to all clients currently receiving services at quarterly intervals (i.e., approximately four times a year; cf. Lewis & Magoon, 1987). A unique intake form was collected per client, but multiple follow-up forms were possible. In instances where multiple follow-ups were collected, the PE-BIMAS form completed at the longest time point since intake was chosen; the mean amount of time between intake and follow-up in the PE-BIMAS database was 7.2 months (SD = 5.1, range 1–38 months).

Over a period of 5 years this procedure resulted in the compilation of a database of 2,002 intake and 2,588 follow-up forms. Of that total, 896 distinct clients (45% of intakes) had completed at least one intake and one follow-up form. Of those 896, 742 (83%) reported data about client gender (66% identified as male, 34% as female), and 706 (79%) reported client race (60% white, 20% African American, 8% Hispanic, 4% biracial, 2% Native American, 3% Asian, and 3% other). Six hundred and one parents (67%) reported client school grade (12% in kindergarten, 14% in grade 1, 13% in grade 2, 14% in grade 3, 19% in grade 4, 15% in grade 5, 11% in grade 6, and remaining 2% in grades 7–10).

Each IISR is explained in detail below and displayed in Table 6.1. Note that IISR 4 is the pivotal guideline, specifying that baseline assessments at intake should be compared with one or more assessment periods following an intervention to detect change (Cronbach et al., 1980; Speer & Newman, 1996). To address IISR 9, clients were randomly assigned to one of two groups, resulting in Subsample A and Subsample B, both with a sample size of 448. Use of the total sample or both subsamples in each IISR analysis depended on the rationale for that guideline as well as the size of the avail-

TABLE 6.1. Brief Description of Intervention Item Selection Rules

Rule	Description
1	Ground scale items in theoretical and empirical literature relevant to applicable interventions, clinical populations, and target problems.
2	Aggregate items at appropriate levels.
3	Assess range of item scores at pretest.
4	Items evidence change in intervention conditions.
5	Items evidence change in theoretically expected direction.
6	Examine whether differences in change exist between intervention and comparison groups.
7	Examine whether intake differences exist between comparison groups.
8	Examine relations between item scores and systematic error sources.
9	Cross-validate results to minimize chance effects.

able sample. Because of parents' reluctance to complete what they perceived as lengthy questionnaires, the scale was reduced to a one-page form. The 32-item Original Scale was thus reduced to a 16-item scale on the basis of item analyses that evaluated item–total correlations, change sensitivity, and content validity. After several periods of data collection, staff requested that other items (principally related to family functioning) be added to the scale and others dropped. Thus, three versions of the PE–BIMAS were eventually employed, with 16, 17, and 17 total items; 14 items overlapped these versions. For the PE–BIMAS database, these changes resulted in data collection for 19 total items. Five items (*Sleepy or tired, Starts conversations, Well-behaved at home, Family members fight, and Limits set with children*) possess a smaller sample size than the overlapping 14 items.

IISR 1. Ground items in theoretical and empirical literature. Relevant research and theory provide a context for understanding the meaning of changing scores on an intervention-sensitive measure. In areas where research and theory are thin, qualitative studies may need to be conducted first to suggest and evaluate potential item content. A review of the literature pertinent to program effects, clinical populations, and target problems should provide the test developer with ideas for creating items and tasks. Pertinent to this study, in the area of child and adolescent psychotherapy Kazdin (2000) noted that more than 1,000 controlled studies of psychosocial interventions for children and adolescents exist and that because effect sizes (ESs) for all interventions average about .70 for children and adolescents, maturation alone cannot account for such gains. Meta-analytic studies indicate that adolescents show greater gains from psychotherapy than children; most of the difference can be attributed to the benefits received by adolescent girls (Weisz et al., 1998). Applied to this study, these findings suggest that (1) some PE-BIMAS items should evidence positive change, but that these effects will be small, and (2) girls may be more likely to show positive change than boys.

IISR 2. Aggregate items at an appropriate level. Because an item response contributed by an individual on one occasion may be influenced by random error (Messick, 1989a), item responses should first be aggregated across individuals. Aggregation of individual item responses into scales increases the reliability and validity of measurement of the studied construct. Epstein (1979, 1980) demonstrated that aggregation of test scores across occasions decreases random error and provides further increments in test reliability and validity. Intervention-sensitive items are not aggregated across occasions, but summed across individuals and items, and then compared across time periods in which interventions take place to determine if change effects are present at the level of aggregated item responses.

IISR 3. Assess range of item scores at pretest. Ceiling and floor effects inhibit detection of desired changes in intervention-sensitive tests because they can restrict the potential range of scores. Thus, interventions may cause changes that are undetected because mean item scores fall too close to the top or bottom point on a rating scale. A ceiling effect occurred in this study when an item's standard deviation was added to the item mean and the resulting sum exceeded the highest value of the scale (3). A floor effect occurred when the item's standard deviation was subtracted from the item mean and the result was less than the bottom range of the scale (0). Table 6.2 displays intake means of raw responses for the two subsamples. Items are arranged by positive wording (i.e., Strengths) and negative wording (Distress/problems); for both sets of items, higher scores indicate greater frequency. No floor effects were found, but three Strengths items in both subsamples had a ceiling effect: *Communicates clearly* (in Subsample A, 2.28 + .77 > 3), *Starts conversations* (2.34 + .75 > 3), and *Limits set with children* (2.64 + .60 > 3).

IISR 4. Items should evidence change in intervention conditions. Intervention-sensitive items should demonstrate change over time with clients who receive psychosocial interventions (cf. Cronbach et al., 1980). Paired *t*-tests were computed to examine change in item scores from intake to follow-up. Because these analyses are exploratory in nature, and the expected effects at the level of an individual item are likely to be small, an alpha level of .10 was set to detect statistically significant change (cf. Meier, 2000). As shown in Table 6.3, 12 of 19 items evidenced statistically significant change in one

TABLE 6.2. Intake Means and Standard Deviations

Item content	Subsample A		Subsample B	
	M	SD	M	SD
Strengths				
Controls temper	1.48	0.93	1.51	0.92
Helps with household tasks	1.49	0.96	1.52	0.95
Stays out of trouble	1.86	0.90	1.96	0.82
Pays attention to speakers	1.88	0.85	1.85	0.77
Shares thinking	1.93	0.86	1.95	0.84
Well-behaved at home	2.00	0.85	1.98	0.80
Makes friends easily	2.17	0.82	2.07	0.87
Communicates clearly	2.28	0.77	2.36	0.75
Starts conversations	2.34	0.75	2.30	0.81
Limits set with children	2.64	0.60	2.75	0.50
Distress/problems				
Gets failing grades	1.30	1.08	1.28	1.00
Sleepy or tired	1.40	0.85	1.45	0.87
Feels depressed	1.64	0.92	1.55	0.92
Family members fight	1.67	0.99	1.68	0.98
Lies or cheats	1.80	1.02	1.75	0.97
Fights with others	1.93	0.92	1.75	0.85
Behaves differently	1.97	0.86	2.02	0.83
Fidgets	2.11	0.96	2.16	0.91
Acts impulsively	2.23	0.83	2.27	0.79

Note. For all items, higher scores indicate greater frequency. Items are presented by ascending means of Subsample A. *Italicized* items evidence a ceiling or floor effect. Sample size per item in each subsample ranges from 446 to 448 except for items *Sleepy or tired, Starts conversations, Well-behaved at home, Family members fight,* and *Limits set with children,* whose sample sizes range from 170 to 278 at intake.

or both subsamples: *Controls temper, Pays attention to speakers, Stays out of trouble, Communicates clearly, Shares thinking, Feels depressed, Behaves differently, Acts impulsively, Fights with others, Family members fight, Lies or cheats,* and *Gets failing grades.*

IISR 5. *Items should evidence change in the theoretically expected direction.* The 12 items that evidenced significant change on at least one subsample in Table 6.3 improved from intake to follow-up. Although clients worsened in at least one subsample on *Makes friends easily, Limits set with children,* and *Helps with household tasks,* these changes did not reach statistical significance.

IISR 6. *Evaluate item change in intervention and comparison groups.* Item change in intervention groups can be compared with item change evident in comparison groups (cf. Rounds & Tinsley, 1984). For example, a subset of items may evidence more or different change in persons completing an intervention in relation to persons enrolled in a comparison condition such as a waiting-list control group. Two or more interventions may produce patterns of differential item change, results that can be of considerable practical importance (e.g., for matching client problems and interventions). Client characteristics, when indicated by previous research or theory, may also provide an opportunity to compare intervention effects at the item level. In the PE–BIMAS database, information was available that allowed creation of a best available control group and a gender comparison group.

A best available control group was created by searching the PE–BIMAS database for instances when a follow-up form had been completed 30 or

TABLE 6.3. Results of Change Analyses for PE-BIMAS Items

Item content	Subsample A			Subsample B		
	M Diff	Std Err	t	M Diff	Std Err	t
		Strengths				
Communicates clearly	.13	.04	3.47**	.05	.03	1.33
Stays out of trouble	.13	.04	3.08**	.05	.04	1.13
Controls temper	.13	.05	2.80**	.14	.05	2.93**
Pays attention to speakers	.12	.04	2.78**	.16	.04	4.07**
Well-behaved at home	.07	.05	1.51	.05	.05	1.02
Shares thinking	.06	.04	1.36	.09	.04	2.10*
Limits set with children	.05	.04	1.12	−.03	.04	−0.63
Starts conversations	.06	.08	0.78	.06	.07	0.75
Makes friends easily	.00	.04	0.03	−.06	.04	−1.51
Helps with household tasks	−.00	.05	−0.02	.02	.04	0.45
		Distress/problems				
Feels depressed	.22	.05	4.69**	.14	.05	3.17**
Behaves differently	.13	.04	2.91**	.18	.04	4.01**
Family members fight	.16	.06	2.79**	.11	.06	1.96*
Acts impulsively	.10	.04	2.59*	.14	.04	3.38**
Fights with others	.10	.04	2.46*	.14	.04	3.37**
Lies or cheats	.12	.05	2.43*	.11	.04	2.55*
Gets failing grades	.10	.05	1.98*	.10	.05	1.98*
Fidgets	.08	.05	1.60	.07	.04	1.60
Sleepy or tired	.01	.09	0.10	.07	.08	0.83

Note. Items are arranged by descending absolute *t*-value of Sample A. Underlined items evidence statistically significant change in both Subsamples A and B; *italicized* items evidence statistically significant change in either Sample A or B. A negative mean change score indicates that scores for this item worsened from initial to follow-up period. Table reprinted with permission from Meier, McDougal, and Bardos (in press), Sage Publications.

*p < .10; **p < .05.

fewer days since completion of the intake form. Thirty-one such matches were found, although 13 of the participants had additional follow-up forms that also allowed them to be assigned to the intervention group. For control group participants, 3 of 19 items evidenced statistically significant change: *Communicates clearly* improved during this brief time period ($t = 3.00$, $p < .01$), whereas *Fidgets* ($t = -2.56$, $p < .05$) and *Family members fight* ($t = -1.74$, $p < .10$) significantly worsened. Nine of the 19 items evidenced a worsening trend for the control group during this brief period. Although these results suggest that no positive change occurred for the majority of items during a brief retesting period, one item, *Communicates clearly*, improved as a result of a brief intervention or a practice effect.

As noted above, Kazdin's (2000; see also Webster-Stratton, 1996; Weisz, Weiss, Han, Granger, & Morton, 1995) review found that girls evidence more improvement than boys do as a result of psychosocial interventions. Meta-analytic results, however, indicate that this finding may primarily be due to gains by adolescent girls (Weisz et al., 1998). Because of missing reports of demographic information, gender analyses were not conducted by random subsample but for the entire sample of clients' parents who had provided information about gender ($n = 493$ for boys and 249 for girls). As shown in Table 6.4, both boys and girls evidenced statistically significant improvement on six items: *Pays attention to speakers, Controls temper, Communicates clearly, Feels depressed, Acts impulsively,* and *Fights with others.* Boys evidenced more improvement than girls on four Distress/ Problems items, changing on *Behaves differently, Gets failing grades, Lies or cheats,* and *Family members fight.* Girls demonstrated more improvement on three Strengths items, improving at a statistically significant level on *Stays out of trouble, Shares thinking,* and *Limits set with children.* Boys also evidenced a statistically significant decrease on the Strengths item, *Makes friends easily.* These results indicate that boys and girls experienced some differential effects as a result of the psychotherapeutic interventions they received.

IISR 7. Examine the equivalence of items' scores at intake between groups. Equivalence at intake was examined in this study's data set with the two randomly created subsamples. Paired *t*-tests were employed to assess differences between item means, and two items differed at intake: *Makes friends easily* ($t = -1.78$, $p < .10$) and *Family members fight* ($t = -2.37$, $p < .05$). Random assignment resulted in statistically equivalent groups, providing confidence that cross-validation analyses (IISR 9) can be interpreted appropriately.

IISR 8. Examine the relationship between scale items and systematic error sources. This IISR indicates that item scores on change-sensitive tests should

TABLE 6.4. Results of Change Analyses for PE-BIMAS Items by Gender

Item content	Subsample A			Subsample B		
	M Diff	Std Err	t	M Diff	Std Err	t
		Strengths				
Pays attention to speakers	.12	.06	2.09★	.18	.04	4.73★★
Controls temper	.16	.07	2.41★	.12	.04	2.69★★
Communicates clearly	.14	.05	2.72★★	.07	.04	1.99★
Makes friends easily	.06	.06	1.01	−.07	.04	−1.84★
Stays out of trouble	.14	.06	2.36★	.07	.04	1.76
Shares thinking	.13	.06	2.20★	.05	.04	1.29
Well-behaved at home	.05	.06	0.84	.06	.05	1.16
Starts conversations	.04	.09	0.47	.06	.07	0.82
Limits set with children	.11	.05	1.92★	.02	.04	0.43
Helps with household tasks	.02	.06	0.39	.00	.04	0.00
		Distress/problems				
Feels depressed	.12	.06	1.98★	.27	.05	5.92★★
Behaves differently	.09	.06	1.59	.21	.04	4.98★★
Acts impulsively	.15	.06	2.60★★	.16	.04	4.04★★
Fights with others	.12	.06	2.12★	.15	.04	3.88★★
Gets failing grades	.08	.08	1.08	.15	.05	3.21★★
Lies or cheats	.07	.07	0.99	.12	.04	2.96★★
Family members fight	.14	.08	1.70	.10	.06	1.85★
Fidgets	.13	.06	2.04	.07	.04	1.60
Sleepy or tired	.05	.09	0.55	.07	.08	0.82

Note. Items are arranged by descending absolute *t*-value of the boys' sample. Underlined items evidence statistically significant change for girls and boys; *italicized* items evidence statistically significant change for one gender. A negative mean change score indicates that scores for this item worsened from initial to follow-up period.

not be associated with systematic error sources. If scores on an item are highly correlated with social desirability at pretest, for example, its mean may be elevated, thereby decreasing its probability of demonstrating intervention effects. The data provided by Meier and Schwartz (2007) in Chapter 5 is a likely example of social desirability influencing scores on intervention-sensitive measures. However, if clients have learned that data from outcome measures are being used to evaluate the counselor, and these clients desire to make the counselor appear effective, clients' scores may be inflated. In such an instance items particularly susceptible to socially desirable responding might overestimate the intervention's impact. A variety of response styles, such as acquiescence and criticalness, and response sets, such as social desirability, malingering, and dissimulation, represent sources of systematic error that can influence item response. Such items should be dropped or balanced during test construction. In this study, however, no data were available for evaluating this IISR.

IISR 9. Cross-validate IISR analyses. Given the possibility of chance findings in this set of IISR analyses, cross-validation of item selection results is important. As shown in Table 6.3, nine items have *t*-values with statistical significance below .10 for both randomly constructed subsamples: *Controls temper, Pays attention to speakers, Feels depressed, Behaves differently, Acts impulsively, Fights with others, Family members fight, Lies or cheats,* and *Gets failing grades.* Consequently, these items can be considered cross-validated in terms of their sensitivity to change across subsamples.

Psychometric Properties of Aggregate Scales

The preceding IISR analyses provide a basis for understanding the relevant properties of scale items and lay the foundation for subsequent decisions about which items to include in multi-item scales. As shown in Table 6.5, additional psychometric analyses at the scale level provide relevant reliability and validity information.

1. Because the PE–BIMAS scale was intended to reflect a broad range of potential problems and strengths, it could also be employed as a screening instrument. This scale will be labeled the *Total Scale,* consisting of the 14 overlapping items across the three versions employed during test construction. The performance of all 19 items will be examined through two subscales, the 10-item *Strengths* and the 9-item *Distress/Problems* subscales. Because not all of these items were present in all three versions of the PE–BIMAS, the sample size was reduced when calculating scale properties (see Table 6.5).

2. The items that evidenced no ceiling or floor effects (IISR 3), changed from intake to follow-up in the total sample (IISR 4), changed in the expected direction (IISR 5), did not show positive change in the control condition (IISR 6), showed equivalence between subsamples at intake (IISR 7), and were cross-validated (IISR 9) will be combined into an 8-item *Positive Change* scale. This brief scale is the most methodologically sound of the IISR scales.

3. Emphasizing the centrality of IISR 4, all 12 items that changed from intake to follow-up in either subsample will be grouped into a 12-item *Positive Change* scale. Containing a larger number of items, this broad-based scale has increased reliability as compared with the 8-item change scale (see Table 6.5).

TABLE 6.5. Descriptive Statistics, Coefficient Alphas, and Effect Sizes for PE-BIMAS Scales

Scale (No. of items)	Initial				Follow-up				Pooled	
	n	M	SD	alpha	n	M	SD	alpha	SD	ES
				Original scale						
Total (32)	111	53.02	13.10	.88	122	54.90	12.02	.88	12.60	.15
				Screening scales						
Total (14)	891	20.79	6.53	.80	894	19.36	6.91	.84	6.76	.21
Strengths (10)	579	9.40	4.23	.72	644	8.78	4.34	.76	4.30	.14
Distress/problems (9)	581	14.65	4.37	.72	647	13.62	4.59	.76	4.51	.23
			Intervention-sensitive scales							
Positive change (8)										
Total sample	892	13.46	4.26	.73	895	12.39	4.47	.78	4.40	.24
Boys' sample	477	13.88	4.32	.75	478	12.51	4.58	.79	4.50	.30
White	275	13.41	4.31	.76	276	11.89	4.60	.80	4.52	.34
Girls' sample	238	12.89	4.21	.71	240	11.98	4.53	.77	4.39	.21
Positive change (12)										
Total sample	579	18.20	5.67	.77	646	16.70	6.18	.82	5.99	.25
Boys' sample	283	18.85	5.61	.78	324	17.01	6.36	.82	6.09	.30
White	155	18.09	5.47	.78	177	15.71	6.37	.83	6.08	.39
Girls' sample	139	17.69	5.90	.76	159	15.98	6.48	.83	6.27	.27
Boys' change (10)										
Total sample	580	15.98	4.92	.74	647	14.65	5.27	.78	5.14	.26
Boys' sample	284	16.57	4.82	.74	324	14.84	5.42	.79	5.22	.33
White	155	16.09	4.69	.74	177	13.82	5.49	.80	5.25	.43
Girls' sample	139	15.47	5.11	.74	159	14.16	5.45	.80	5.32	.25
Girls' change (9)										
Total sample	579	11.74	4.02	.68	644	10.75	4.25	.73	4.17	.24
Girls' sample	139	11.53	4.33	.68	159	10.14	4.49	.75	4.46	.31
White	72	10.81	4.15	.68	84	9.63	4.65	.78	4.45	.27
Boys' sample	283	12.20	3.97	.68	322	11.01	4.42	.75	4.25	.28

Note. From Meier, McDougal, and Bardos (in press). Reprinted by permission of Sage Publications.

4. The 10 items that displayed positive change with boys are labeled the *Boys' Change* scale, and the 9 items that evidenced change with girls will be the *Girls' Change* scale (IISR 6).

As shown in Table 6.5, reliability estimates are high to average for the Original 32-item scale and the three Screening Scales; the Screening Scales' alphas had an intake mean of .75 and a follow-up mean of .79. Reliability estimates for the group of intervention-sensitive scales are similar: At intake, IISR scales' alphas averaged .75, and at follow-up, .80. Reliability values indicate that all scales have sufficient internal consistency for subsequent use and interpretation.

Because participant heterogeneity can decrease the power to detect treatment effects (Lipsey, 1990), scale results were computed and reported for the largest homogeneous subgroups in this data set (i.e., for total sample, boys and girls, and white boys). Effect size (ES) was calculated by subtracting the follow-up mean from the initial mean and then dividing that difference by the pooled (intake and follow-up) standard deviation. As shown in Table 6.5 and graphed in Figure 6.3, the Original and Screening scales have lower ESs than intervention-sensitive scales. The mean ES for the three Screening scales equaled .19 (SD = .05), and the mean ES for the IISR scales across all subgroups was .29 (SD = .06). More homogeneous subgroups had higher ESs: Boys' IISR scales ranged from .30 to .33, and Caucasian boys' scales from .34 to .43. The 10-item Strengths scale (which includes 3 items with ceiling effects) and the 32-item Original Scale (whose statistics are based on a smaller sample size previously collected at the same agencies) had the lowest ESs of .14 and .15, respectively.

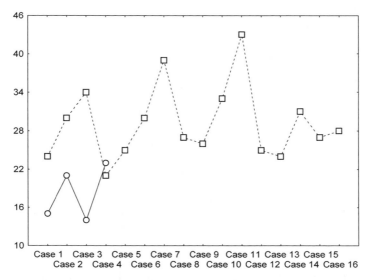

FIGURE 6.3. IISR scales effect sizes exceed Original Scales' ESs. Effect sizes (ESs) for IISR-developed scales are designated by squares, and circles show ESs for the Original Scale and three Screening Scales.

In summary, application of the IISRs to parent ratings of 896 child clients resulted in the creation of brief change-sensitive scales. Scores on these scales demonstrated adequate reliability, significant correlations in expected directions with measures of social skills and problem behaviors, and larger effect sizes than scales containing the original item pool. Twelve PE-BIMAS items evidenced statistically significant change in at least one of two randomly constructed samples; 9 of these 12 change-sensitive items were cross-validated across both samples. On the basis of the research literature, no a priori reason existed to predict which items would show change, and changes on these 12 items were spread across content domains, including depression, impulsivity, and physical aggression. In addition, boys consistently evidenced higher ESs than girls across different change scales; boys' change items were similar to girls' but also included improvement on other domains, including academic performance. The academic improvement finding for boys is particularly worthy of additional study because some funding sources for counseling services, particularly in school settings, may be predicated on the assumption that a link exists between school achievement and mental health variables (cf. Finn, Pannozzo, & Voelkl, 1995).

Using Change-Sensitive Tests in Program Evaluations

Program evaluation refers to a collection of applied research methods employed to gauge the effectiveness of programs intended to help individuals with various needs (Posavac & Carey, 2003). Program evaluation can encompass such related purposes as assessing the need for programs, determining whether the programs were implemented as intended, and the ratio of costs and benefits of implemented programs. In the context of the current discussion, *program evaluation* refers to efforts to evaluate the clinical services provided by one or more clinicians. Funding sources such as the United Way, city, state, and federal government agencies, and grant providers often mandate that some type of program evaluation be provided as a requirement of receiving or continuing funding.

In practice, there are often serious obstacles to conducting program evaluations in mental health agencies. Evaluations usually involve extensive discussions and decisions about program objectives and outcomes, research design, choices and procedures related to measures and data collection, and the establishment and maintenance of a database for evaluation-related data. Mental health agencies may lack the capacity to conduct competent evaluations in terms of staff with evaluation skills as well as money to hire outside evaluators. Clients and staff often lack motivation to complete lengthy questionnaires or brief questionnaires at frequent intervals. The result is that evaluations often boil down to basic pre–post designs using brief, qualitative, and quantitative measures that provide information related to whether clients demonstrate improvements related to program objectives. Given the need for brief measures, it follows that scales such as the GAF are likely to be employed in many program evaluations of mental health services.

The data collection process often must be simplified as much as possible. For example, Meier and Letsch (2000) examined missing data rates in a large urban mental health agency that served more than 1,000 children, adolescents, and their families annually. To measure outcome, the agency employed the 55-item Social Skills Rating System (SSRS), Parent Elementary Form (Gresham & Elliott, 1990). The agency had great success in collecting intake data as clients began treatment, but considerable difficulty in persuading clients to complete the same form at termination. Meier and Letsch found that only about one out of four children had intake and termination outcome assessments (as completed by their parents) and only one of two possible clinician-rated GAFs. Subsequent to this study, the agency agreed to collect follow-up outcome data with all clients every 3–4 months (cf. Lewis & Magoon, 1987) and later hired a part-time psychologist to oversee the data collection efforts. In addition to the GAF, the agency also agreed to employ brief intervention-sensitive scales developed using IISR methods. These efforts led to data collection rates of nearly 50% for complete outcome data sets (i.e., clients with at least two complete outcome assessments). The larger data sets provide more confidence that subsequent evaluation results apply to the agency's entire client population.

For example, an evaluator employed data from IISR derived scales (the previously described Parent Elementary [PE] scale and a similar measure, the Parent Secondary [PS] form) to conduct annual program evaluations for an urban mental health agency. One evaluation included client satisfaction data, qualitative comments from parents about the agency and its services, and outcome results based on data provided by the change-sensitive scales. As shown in Table 6.6, two separate programs at the agency were evaluated.

Table 6.6 contains excerpts from the evaluation report pertaining to the evaluation of the two programs using the change-sensitive scales. The officials of the funding agency to whom this report was directed had specified that they desired the outcome data reported in a particular way: Did at least 50% of the children receiving counseling achieve at least a 10% improvement on the outcome measure? Previous research with this agency's clients had identified two separate sets of eight items on the PE and PS

TABLE 6.6. Using Outcome Data in Program Evaluations: Excerpts from an Evaluation Report

Treatment Program 1

Outcome 2: Parents will report positive behavioral change, improvement in functioning, and decrease in psychiatric symptoms in their child following counseling.

The criterion for this outcome was that at least 50% of children achieve at least a 10% decrease in scores on the Treatment Outcome subscales of the Parent Elementary (PE) form and the Parent Secondary (PS) form. The eight-item Treatment subscale of the PE form and the eight-item Treatment subscale of the PS form were employed because previous research had shown them to be sensitive to psychosocial treatment effects. Use of treatment-sensitive scales is important because meta-analyses of treatment outcomes studies have found that the typical treatment delivered to children in community mental health centers produces, on average, no change.

During 2005, 273 parents completed the PE form at a follow-up interval, who had also completed an intake PE form previously. Forty-nine percent reported at least a 10% decrease in symptoms from intake to follow-up on the Treatment Outcome PE subscale.

Of the 266 parents who completed the PS follow-up form in 2005, 50% reported at least a 10% decrease in symptoms from intake to follow-up on an eight-item Treatment Outcome subscale. Fifty-five percent of parents of male clients and 46% of parents of female clients reported at least a 10% decrease.

Thus, the criterion for this outcome was met for parents of secondary school children and just missed for parents of elementary school children.

forms that demonstrated change over time while clients were in counseling. Parents' ratings on these eight items were then summed at intake and termination, with higher scores indicating more symptoms or problems. The intake score was then divided by the termination score to produce an improvement ratio per individual. For example, if a client's summed ratings at intake equaled 9, and the sum at termination equaled 8, the improvement ratio equaled $(9/8 =)$ 1.125. Thus, this person's termination score improved 12.5% from intake.

A frequency tabulation of all improvement ratios was performed, and the number that exceeded 10% was then tabulated. As described in Table 6.6, 49% of parents of elementary school children who received counseling in the Treatment Program 1 met the 10% improvement standard, and 50% of parents of secondary school children in the clinic program met the standard. Thus, the goal of reaching at least 50% of children evidencing 10% or greater improvement was just missed for elementary school children and just met for secondary school clients.

A second example of an evaluation takes a different approach, examining and reporting change at the level of individual items. As excerpted in Table 6.7, individual items on earlier versions of the PE and PS forms were examined for change from intake to follow-up for different agency programs. Interestingly, results indicated that counseling decreased depression in both elementary and secondary school clients. Parents of secondary school students also reported that their children evidenced statistically significant improvement on items assessing anger, cheating, persistence, paying attention, unusual behaviors, and shame. Similarly, parents of elementary school students reported that their children evidenced improvement at a statistically significant level on items assessing paying attention, unusual behaviors, and fidgeting. In contrast to the first report, which focused on *amount* of improvement, this evaluation report focused principally on *what changed* during counseling.

An Evidence-Based Approach to Supervision

Clinical supervision, the process of a counselor overseeing the work of a student, is a ubiquitous aspect of all counseling and psychotherapy training programs (Holloway, 1995). Supervision can be (1) performed with an individual student or a group of students, (2) scheduled on an as-needed basis or in regular weekly sessions, and (3) accomplished through students' verbal reports of sessions with clients as well as through live, audiotaped, or videotaped observations of those sessions. Supervisory skills include establishing a working relationship with supervisees, conceptualizing supervisee issues, being aware of supervisor–supervisee interpersonal patterns, giving appropriate feedback and support to supervisees, and helping supervisees do all of the above with their clients. Although many supervision approaches simply translate particular psychotherapy theories for use in the supervision setting, other theories focus on developmental aspects of supervisees (Stoltenberg & Delworth, 1987) and social role aspects of the process (Bernard & Goodyear, 1992).

Despite all of the considerable applied, research, and theoretical effort expended on the topic of supervision, no consensus exists in the literature about whether supervision improves client outcomes (Sapyta et al., 2005). One plausible explanation is that feedback about client progress employed in most supervision is based on the supervisees' subjective impressions about such progress. Sapyta et al. (2005) noted that clinicians get little direct feedback about their work, and thus it is not surprising when research documents instances when practicing clinicians fail to gauge the client's response to counseling and psychotherapy (Gray & Lambert, 2001).

Earlier in this chapter I described patient-focused research in which feedback about client progress, based on outcome data, is provided directly

TABLE 6.7. Using Outcome Data in Program Evaluations: Excerpts from an Evaluation Report

Client Improvement

Two multi-item scales were employed to evaluate treatment outcome. The first, the Parent Secondary scale, contains 12 items. Cumulative data were available for 107 parents who completed at least one initial and one follow-up scale.

Dependent measures t-tests were computed for each item and for the total score (posttest score minus pretest). Results were statistically significant for the total score ($t = 3.55, p < .01$), indicating significant improvement in secondary students over time as perceived by their parents. At the individual item level, 11 of 12 items evidenced positive change, with 7 of those showing change at a statistically significant level:

> *Gets embarrassed or feels ashamed.*
> *Behaves differently from others.*
> *Has trouble paying attention.*
> *Acts sad or depressed.*
> *Becomes very angry.*
> *Quits a job without finishing it.*
> *Lies or cheats.*

An intake form and at least one follow-up form were available for 196 parents who completed the Parent Elementary scale. As above, dependent measures t-tests were computed for each item and for the total score (posttest score minus pretest). Results approached statistical significance for the total score ($t = 1.85, p = .07$), indicating significant improvement in elementary students over time as perceived by their parents. At the individual item level, 12 of 16 items evidenced positive change, with 3 of those showing change at a statistically significant level:

> *Pays attention to speakers at meetings such as in church or youth groups.*
> *Behaves differently than other children.*
> *Fidgets.*

However, these results may be confounded by differences in improvement evidenced by boys and girls. Elementary-age boys benefited more than girls: The total score for girls did not show change over time ($t = 0.66, p = .51$), whereas the score for boys did change ($t = 2.06, p < .05$). At the level of individual items, 14 of 16 items for boys showed positive change, with 6 items evidencing statistically significant change:

> *Pays attention to speakers at meetings such as in church or youth groups.*
> *Behaves differently than other children.*
> *Acts impulsively.*
> *Controls temper when arguing.*
> *Stays out of trouble.*
> *Feels depressed.*

to the clinician. How might such evidence be useful in supervision? In general, outcome data employed as an indication of progress might encourage *praxis*, the idea of balancing action and reflection with a client. Whereas most counselors' eclecticism translates into a trial-and-error approach to counseling, a supervisor might help students to integrate and apply their previous learning related to counseling theory and assessment with specific clients (Meier, 1999, 2003). For example, although students' knowledge of meta-analytic studies of psychotherapy outcome might lead them to believe that their clients should evidence progress in counseling, a supervisor might help students select an appropriate outcome measure (e.g., a BDI) that best fits a particular client (e.g., a client who presents with depression).

Another possibility would be for supervisee and supervisor to spend a portion of each supervision period attempting to identify likely candidates for treatment failure. A procedure would first be established for regular collection of outcome data for all clients and a system implemented for providing timely summaries of those data to supervisor and supervisee (cf. Harmon, Hawkins, Lambert, Slade, & Whipple, 2005). Because some research suggests that persons who benefit from therapy often demonstrate a relatively quick response (e.g., Kelly et al., 2005), a plausible schedule is to ask clients to complete a measure such as the OQ-45 at the first, third, fifth, and every subsequent fifth sessions. Special attention might be paid to clients who do not make progress or evidence deterioration over the first 5–10 sessions. In such instances supervisors might help student therapists consider alternative conceptualizations that might lead to implementation of a different therapeutic approach.

A supervisor's perspective on client outcome data might also provide supervisees with a more objective reaction to outcome data. Supervisees may understandably view negative trends in client data as critical of their work; supervisors may more reasonably suggest that such data are feedback indicating that the case conceptualization and counseling approach be re-examined (Mash & Hunsley, 1993; Meier, 2003). For example, Mash and Hunsley (1993) suggested that once failure to improve is evident, therapists should examine such factors as the quality of the working alliance, the degree to which the treatment was faithfully implemented, and the client's motivation, problems with affect, and verbal communication skills; these are essentially alternative conceptualizations to be considered. Evidence of treatment failure appears particularly important to recognize, inasmuch as research suggests that many clinicians assume that if they implement generally accepted approaches, success must follow (Kendall et al., 1992). Even with empirically supported procedures, therapists do not know if they will be successful with any particular client (Streiner, 1998). As shown in Figure 6.4, even with treatments shown to be effective on average, some clients may evidence poor outcomes or no improvement. Finally, supervisors who know the psychotherapy research literature may also help supervisees to place outcome data in context by acknowledging the limits of any one measurement device and the usefulness of obtaining additional information, from other methods or sources, when making important clinical decisions.

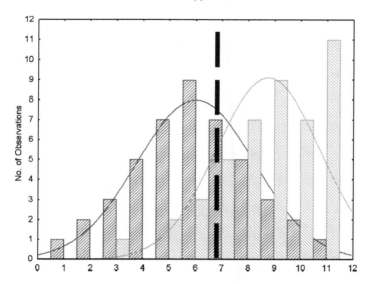

FIGURE 6.4. Typical distribution of outcome scores for control and treatment groups. This hypothetical frequency distribution shows the status after treatment of individuals who received treatment (left distribution) and individuals who were untreated (right distribution). The black dashed vertical line shows a hypothetical cut point for scores on an outcome measure. Scores to the left of the line indicate normal functioning on this measure, and scores to the right indicate a level of clinical problems. As is the case in actual treatment studies, these individuals evidence an array of responses to treatment, including individuals who show no change (and still possess substantial problems).

This evidence-based approach to supervision should also include consideration about how to present and review client data. Graphics can be particularly useful for representing case conceptualization and sets of outcome data. Mattaini (1993) suggested that graphs can help counselors to organize and simplify complex clinical information, recognize trends in data, and recall clinical data. Representing outcome data in a time series graph, for example, can help supervisor and supervisee see trends over time, raise questions about the causes of those trends, and develop new hypotheses related to the causes of clients' behavior (Mattaini, 1993; Meier, 2003).

Finally, some evidence suggests that graduate students can be taught to improve their conceptualization and assessment skills. Meier (1999) reported that students in a semester-length counseling process course who were taught to implement a structured approach to case conceptualization and clinical assessment increased their self-efficacy for doing these tasks. Some students in this course resisted the close supervision of this approach, fearing the negative feedback about the absence of positive client change. Differences in case conceptualization and assessment skills were also present in students. For example, less skilled students tended to choose case conceptualization elements that were too concrete or too ambiguous. More skilled students often selected more abstract constructs for their conceptualization (e.g., selection of "processing client's storytelling" as a key element).

Summary and Integration

The ideal nomothetic outcome measure produces scores that are reliable, valid, and relevant to feedback about clinical progress. In other words, scores should demonstrate stability over time in the absence of an intervention, change in expected directions in response to an intervention, and be sensitive enough to intervention effects to demonstrate short-term and long-term changes for use in client progress feedback. Ideally, the measure would also be brief and theoretically based. Its length would be as short as one page for use in settings such as community mental health centers, where clients and staff often view assessment as secondary to the process of treatment. An outcome measure's theoretical basis should include a theory related to employed intervention(s), whose expected effects are reflected in the content of the outcome measure's items or tasks. In addition, a measurement theory that provides information about testing purpose(s) and relevant contextual and situational influences should be employed to guide the construction and administration of the outcome measure.

The efficiency of nomothetic measures means they may be the best choice for studies whose purpose is to examine the effects of therapy with large groups of clients. This includes basic research as well as program evaluations of organizations providing psychotherapy services, such as community agencies and college counseling centers, and studies intended to provide information relevant to public policy decisions. Persons (1991) criticized psychotherapy outcome studies, however, for including nomothetic, atheoretical measures of outcome that fail to reflect the theoretically based, idiographic approach that many clinicians employ in practice. That is, Persons maintained that psychotherapy outcome studies designed to examine the efficacy of one or more approaches to therapy do not reflect the actual practices, particularly assessment practices, followed by practitioners of those methods with individual clients. In particular, Persons (1991) observed that all psychotherapy approaches propose "an individualized treatment based on the results of an individualized assessment" (p. 99) of the client.

As discussed in the next chapter, idiographic measures may be more appropriate for assessment of individual clients for the purpose of guiding and evaluating treatment progress. Even measures designed to be sensitive to change in studies of groups of clients completing counseling are unlikely to be as sensitive as measures designed for a specific, individual client.

General Measurement-Related Writing Assignment

For the three measures you chose, conduct a brief literature review (searching sources such as *PsycINFO, Tests in Print, Mental Measurements Yearbooks*, and *Test Critiques*, or test manuals for published tests) and find at least three sources who report validity estimates or information for one or more of the three measures. It is likely to be relatively easy to find estimates of convergent validity, but try to find at least one estimate of discriminant validity as well. For selection tests, try to find estimates of predictive validity. In a table, report the author/year of the source as well as the specific validity estimate (e.g., a convergent validity correlation of .50 between two tests of the same construct).

Change-Related Writing Assignment

For the three measures you chose, conduct a brief literature review (searching sources such as *PsycINFO, Tests in Print, Mental Measurements Yearbooks*, and *Test Critiques*) and find at least three sources who report validity estimates or information for one or more of the measures. In particular, is there any evidence that the test(s) is sensitive to change? In a table, report the author/year of the source as well as the specific validity estimate.

QUESTIONS AND EXERCISES

1. For 3 minutes, write down what you consider the major ideas of this section, chapter, or class. At the beginning of next week's class, share with the group.

2. What are the types of reliability estimates?

3. In a small group or individually, list and explain the nine IISRs.

4. In a small group or individually, discuss how the discovery of a common outcome factor could influence current psychotherapy theories and clinical assessment.

5. In a small group or individually, summarize the theory and research on feedback.

CHAPTER 7

Idiographic Approaches to Measuring Change and Influencing Outcomes

History and Background
Reliability of Idiographic Measures
Validity of Idiographic Measures
Applications
Summary and Implications

History and Background

In the history of psychological measurement, the nomothetic paradigm has dominated, accompanied by selection testing's assumptions regarding the presence of the same traits in all individuals. The nomothetic approach has been effective for selection purposes. With large samples, one could usually find bell-shaped distributions of psychological characteristics, thus mirroring the natural distributions of phenomena found in other sciences. Use of multiple-item tests decreased random error, and group testing was efficient and inexpensive, at least compared to testing methods that focused on the use of a single test taker and assessor.

But psychologists such as Allport (1937) took nomothetic proponents to task because of their emphasis on groups of individuals instead of the individuals themselves. Idiographic psychologists were interested in developing laws that generalized across persons instead of groups of persons (Lamiell, 1990). As Danziger (1990) wrote, "If the subject is an individual consciousness, we get a very different kind of psychology than if the subject is a population of organisms" (p. 88). For Allport, there were no psychological laws to be found outside the study of individuals. Idiographic study and assessment usually occurs in the context of a relationship between assessor and individual. Such a relationship allows a greater understanding of the interaction between an individual's perception of traits and other factors, such as psychological states and external situations, that change over time. It follows, then, that improvements in the prediction and understanding of an individual's behaviors might be possible if measurement were idiographically focused (cf. Magnusson & Endler, 1977; Walsh & Betz, 1985). Although overlap occurs, it is a truism in psychology that individuals experience and manifest psychological traits and states in different ways.

Nomothetic approaches may be best understood as a first wave of measurement methods in psychology. That is, economic forces pushed selection tests to the forefront because selection tests employed efficient, low-cost nomothetic assumptions and methods. To the extent that resources become available to employ single assessor and single test taker methods, idiographic methods should ascend because of their potential for improving validity, particularly in clinical settings (Mumma, 2004). This chapter examines a set of such idiographic approaches, focusing first on basic principles and then applications and detailed examples.

Reliability of Idiographic Measures

For nomothetic, trait-based tests, the two most popular means of demonstrating reliability are coefficient alpha and test–retest reliability. As described in the preceding chapter, *internal consistency* refers to the average correlation between scores on any one item and the sum of scores on all items, whereas *test–retest reliability* refers to the correlation between two administrations of the same test given to the same persons. Coefficient alpha is by far the most frequently employed index of reliability because it requires only a single administration of a test and the statistical software required to compute it (SAS, SPSS) is widely available.

Both coefficient alpha and test–retest reliability have potential problems for evaluating reliability with idiographic measures designed to evaluate outcomes. To the extent that idiographic measures are composed of multiple items or tasks thought to reflect a single construct, coefficient alpha is an appropriate statistic. If an idiographic measure employed with an individual client is a single operation, however, as is often the case in clinical practice, then coefficient alpha cannot be computed. Hoffman and Meier (2001), for example, described the use of three idiographic outcome measures specific to a particular client, Doris, a 30-year-old, white, single student who was referred by an instructor to a college counseling center to discuss emotional issues. Her counselor assessed Doris on three measures specific to her problems: (1) the number of physically violent and emotionally explosive incidents Doris reported for the past week; (2) a review of her psychiatrist's notes on the level of depression; and (3) Doris's report of the number of times per week she smoked marijuana. None of these measures produces data thought to be reflective of the same construct, and there is no reason to believe that scores on these measures should be highly correlated or stable over time.

A more appropriate approach to assessing the reliability of idiographic measures is to examine their stability during a *baseline* period prior to the implementation of treatment. In a baseline, behavior is measured repeatedly for the purpose of demonstrating relative stability before an intervention (Bloom & Fischer, 1982; Hartman, 1984; Heppner et al., 1999). Many clinicians traditionally employed the first two or three sessions with individual clients to obtain intake information and build rapport; if therapy is being financed by managed care companies, however, this may be unrealistic as the time-limited treatment may need to begin immediately (Davis & Meier, 2001). Baseline data collected during a preintervention period can provide greater confidence that any subsequent changes that occur result from the intervention.

Suppose that a hypothetical client rates feelings of anxiety daily on a scale of 1–10, with 10 indicating very intense anxiety; the client then reports the average daily rating for the previous week. Figure 7.1 displays this client's average anxiety ratings for the first 3 weeks of therapy. Of note in this figure is the relative stability of the ratings for the three time periods of the baseline. This is the ideal situation in a baseline, suggesting that the measure can evidence stability in the absence of an intervention. However, if the data show an increase or decrease across the baseline, it becomes more difficult to attribute subsequent changes to the intervention alone. In the second graph in Figure 7.1, for example, the average weekly anxiety rating, in the absence of any intervention, is steadily declining during the baseline period. Even if this trend continued during the start of therapeutic intervention during Session 4, it would be difficult to attribute continued improvement to the intervention and not to other factors.

Validity of Idiographic Measures

To measure idiographic clinical outcomes in an individual, a test should be able to detect the multiple effects of the chosen intervention(s). A key ad-

Stable Baseline Period

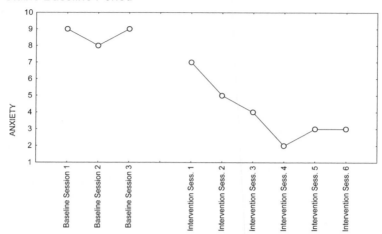

Unstable Baseline Period

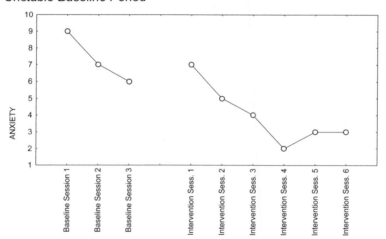

FIGURE 7.1. Sessions 1, 2, and 3 were employed to gather baseline data for anxiety. In the first graph, the data show relative stability over the baseline period, providing evidence for the stability of the anxiety measure and making subsequent improvements more attributable to treatment. In the second graph, anxiety decreases during the baseline. This trend raises questions about (1) the ability of the measure to show stability in the absence of an intervention and (2) the extent to which decreases in anxiety can be attributed to any interventions.

vantage of idiographic measures is that they are intended to provide intervention-sensitive data and that the choice of what to measure can be altered
or modified over the course of treatment (Bickman et al., 2000; Cone, 1988;
Kiresuk, Choate, Cardillo, & Larsen, 1994; Mash & Hunsley, 1993). A client
who presents with depression, for example, may report symptoms shared
by others (e.g., sleep disturbances) as well as symptoms relatively unique to
that individual (e.g., increased irritability around a spouse). Therapists often
target client-reported symptoms, and idiographic measures represent a brief
and efficient means of gathering data about the targeted symptoms.

Particularly with nomothetic measures and experimental methods, the
prototypical assessment procedure is a pretest and a posttest. Here individuals complete one or more measures before and after an intervention for the
purpose of detecting change (in intervention groups) or relative stability
(in control groups). In this context measurement is separate and distinct
from the intervention. In clinical situations with individual or small groups
of clients, however, there are advantages to integrating measurement more
closely into the intervention process. These are discussed below with examples from behavioral assessment and self- and other monitoring.

Behavioral Assessment

An idiographic focus is one of the hallmarks of *behavioral assessment* (Hartman, 1984), testing procedures that involve the direct observation of client
behavior. Behavioral assessors target behaviors specific to a particular client, with the assumption that such an approach will be more sensitive to
detecting changes in behavior (Cone, 1988). Behavioral assessment usually
involves repeated measurement of observable behavior for the purpose of
detecting an intervention's effects. Pelham, Fabiano, and Massetti (2005),
for example, described a system designed to identify idiosyncratic problems
in children with attention-deficit/hyperactivity disorder (ADHD) that is
completed by teachers observing students over time in school settings.

Behavioral measures tend to be *criterion referenced* (i.e., scores are compared to some absolute measure of behavior), and nomothetic approaches
are *norm referenced* (i.e., scores are compared among individuals). A therapist
and client, for example, might agree to set "two" as the maximum number
of alcoholic beverages a client may consume in a week; the data produced
by the client has meaning primarily in relation to the established therapeutic standard of "2" in this example. Norm-referenced tests are constructed
to maximize variability among individuals (Swezey, 1981), and items that

measure behaviors infrequently performed by the population are unlikely to be included in such tests. Jackson (1970), for example, suggested that items endorsed by less than 20% of the test development sample be dropped because they will not contribute to total score variability. Yet those infrequent, idiographically relevant items may be the very ones of interest to counselors and psychotherapists.

In contrast to traditional psychological measurement, whereby anyone can be a self- or other observer if enough measurements are gathered to decrease measurement error, behavioral assessment usually involves trained observers. Training consists of learning the contents of an observation manual (containing definitions of relevant behavior and scoring procedures), conducting analogue observations, on-site practice, retraining and debriefing (Hartman, 1984; Nay, 1979; Paul, 1986). Paul's approach to behavioral assessment provides a representative example of the use of trained observers.

Paul (1986) described a comprehensive assessment system designed to produce clinical and administrative data in residential treatment facilities. Paul's work with data collection and feedback systems demonstrated that clinical information can be useful for adjusting therapy, as well as other purposes such as effectiveness research and documenting the effects of staff training. Paul, Mariotto, and Redfield (1986b) described their chief assessment tools as *Direct Observational Coding* (DOC) procedures. DOCs are based on the principle that the recording of the presence or absence of a behavior (e.g., "the client cried in session") enhances validity estimates, whereas greater interpretation (e.g., "report the client's level of depression") can result in lower validity estimates. This approach is a hybrid between idiographic and nomothetic philosophies: Potentially the same information could be collected for each patient, but in practice, different types of information are likely to be useful for feedback about each patient's progress.

Perhaps the most unique aspect of Paul's approach for assessment in inpatient facilities is the hiring of staff whose major function is to move about the facility and assess targeted behaviors. DOCs require *explicit sampling* of individuals and occasions by trained observers. Paul et al. (1986b) concluded that the accuracy and relevance of behavioral observations can be maximized using multiple, discrete, and scheduled observations made by trained observers as soon as possible following a behavioral event. Similar to the recommendations noted in Chapter 6 on training raters, Mariotto and Licht (1986) suggested that behavioral assessors' training include:

1. An orientation stressing the purposes and confidentiality of measurement,
2. Technical manuals that describe coding content and procedures,
3. Practice coding behavior,
4. Objective feedback to coders,
5. *In vivo* coding practice,
6. Certification, through a work sample, of the observer's readiness, and
7. Procedures to maintain observer skills.

Nay (1979) offered a similar set of guidelines for training observers and recommended that a training manual provide:

1. A rationale for observations,
2. A description of applicable settings,
3. Coding definitions,
4. Rules for sampling behavior,
5. Rules for observer behavior,
6. Methods for assessing observer reliability, and
7. Methods for assessing observation validity.

In essence, the manual defines what is included and excluded as a recordable behavior. In other words, the manual describes the process of construct explication.

Paul et al. (1986b) noted two important sources of error that should be monitored with observers: (1) *decay*, random changes in the observer's reliability or consistency of observation, and (2) *drift*, systematic changes in the definition or interpretation of coding categories. Paul et al. (1986b) maintained that such errors could be checked and minimized by obtaining converging data from different assessment procedures, conditions, and operations. Paul et al. (1986b) also provided instructions about *observational schedules*, classifying them into *programmed* (i.e., scheduled or unscheduled) and *discrete* or *continuous*. Recording can be accomplished immediately after behavior or delayed, on single or multiple occasions, and with stable or transitory phenomena. Actions or interactions can be monitored, as well as individuals or aggregations of individuals. Paul and colleagues emphasized that observations be recorded as soon as possible because accuracy and precision tend to decrease as the time period between event and recording increases. Although measurement error decreases with greater data collection, continuous recording of data in all three domains (clients, staff, and time) is usually impractical.

Paul et al. (1986b) also suggested that the units of observation (e.g., behaviors such as talking, sleeping, or smoking) be established before the observation period so that observers are able to focus on key elements. Such units should be discrete samples of behavior, as opposed to global signs, because greater amounts of interpretation by observers are more likely to reflect characteristics of the observer. Error arising from such factors as carelessness or fatigue of the rater will be minimized when measurement data can be aggregated from multiple occasions. Observation of clients and staff may be reactive, but independent raters should be less reactive than clients or staff, inasmuch as their ratings will have less personal significance and evaluative potential.

As shown in Table 7.1, Paul et al. (1986a) were interested in obtaining detailed information about three target domains: clients, staff, and time. Paul et al. (1986b) noted that information about these domains could be provided by and about (1) clients and staff who can provide information about themselves, (2) significant others, (3) residential clients who can provide information about other clients and staff, (4) clinical staff who can provide information about all three domains, (5) records and archives, and (6) trained staff whose only responsibilities are to function as observers. Information about the three domains is collected and summarized regularly so that client progress can be monitored and interventions adjusted as needed.

Licht, Paul, and Power (1986) reported that DOC systems have been implemented with more than 600 clinical staff in 36 different treatment programs in 17 different institutions. The resulting flood of data has produced results of interest to researchers, as well as to clinicians and administrators in the studied agencies. Data from DOC systems have produced evidence of substantial differences in the behavior of various clinical staff and treatment programs. For example, staff–client interactions in 30 studied agencies ranged from 43 to 459 interactions per hour; over a full week, staff members were responsible for as few as 4 clients or as many as 33. DOC

TABLE 7.1. Domains and Sources for Behavior Assessment

Domain	Examples
Clients	Problem behaviors, stable personal–social characteristics (e.g., age, gender, education), and physical–social life environments (i.e., the context in which problems occur)
Staff	Therapeutic techniques, stable personal–social characteristics, and physical–social life environment (i.e., the context in which treatments occur)
Time	Moment when an assessment is obtained and the period of time to which it applies

data also demonstrated changes in staff behavior resulting from training and development procedures and the maintenance of such behavior. Licht et al. (1986) reported that how staff interacted with clients—that is, specific intervention programs—was highly correlated with client functioning and improvement (correlations ranged from .5 to .9 on different variables). In addition, the data indicate that the quality of staff–client interaction was more important than the quantity of that interaction. Licht et al. (1986) emphasized that DOC information may not only aid in the monitoring of treatment implementation, but may be employed as feedback to adapt treatment for improved effectiveness.

Self- and Other Monitoring

Based in classical psychophysics and introspective methods (Kazdin, 1974), *self-monitoring* is a combination of self-report and behavioral observation whereby individuals observe and record behaviors intended to be targets of an intervention. Considered a type of behavioral assessment, self-monitoring provides treatment-sensitive data in a wide variety of treatment domains, including smoking, eating disorders, and depression.

Self-monitoring usually involves recording the frequency of behaviors, but may also focus on other dimensions such as the duration of behavior (Jackson, 1999). In behavior therapy, clients are frequently assigned to self-monitor problematic behaviors in preparation for an intervention. The procedure teaches clients to keep a notebook with them at all times, to record behaviors immediately after they occur, and to record only a single response at a time (Cone, 1999; Hayes & Nelson, 1986); more recent efforts have involved portable electronic devices (Barton, Blanchard, & Veazy, 1999; Riley et al., 2005). Although nomothetic applications exist (e.g., Agras & Apple, 1997), self-monitoring is idiographic in that client and counselor define what particular behaviors are to be observed by that client.

Interestingly, the simple act of recording a behavior such as smoking has been shown to lead to a decrease in the frequency of the observed behavior (Gottman & Leiblum, 1974; Lichstein, 1970; Nelson, 1977a, 1977b). Potentially any client behavior can be self-monitored both to monitor client progress and to function as an additional intervention (Korotitsch & Nelson-Gray, 1999). In this sense self-monitoring procedures are highly reactive. Although this reactivity improves outcomes, it is a problem in situations (such as baselines) where a nonreactive measure is desired (Jackson, 1999). And although several explanations have been proposed for its positive effects (Korotitsch & Nelson-Gray, 1999), self-monitoring increases the likelihood that clients perceive feedback about the occurrence and contexts surrounding problematic behaviors. As discussed in Chapter 6, such feedback appears to be an essential element of any change process.

Cone (1999) noted a variety of measurement and intervention issues that accompany self-monitoring. For example, clinicians often avoid self-monitoring of weight with clients with some types of eating disorder (Wilson & Vitousek, 1999) or of ritualistic behaviors with obsessive–compulsive disorders (Craske & Tsao, 1999). If the target behavior occurs frequently, to avoid observer overload it may be necessary to employ a sampling strategy by time or behavior, whereby a system is devised to observe only a representative portion of behaviors. Phenomena that vary a great deal by time or situations, such as mood, may require a strategy that provides a representative sample but does not overload the self-observer. Hayes and Cavior (1977, 1980) found that data accuracy and reliability were negatively correlated with the number of different events an observer must record, and other reports indicate that the accuracy of self-monitoring improves when the observer expects the data collection to be checked and evaluated (Korotitsch & Nelson-Gray, 1999). Training improves self-monitoring accuracy and includes providing explicit definitions of target behaviors and explicit instructions for data recording (Mahoney, 1977). Interestingly, some research suggests that self-monitoring data can be roughly equivalent to retrospective reports, although this may result from clients estimating regularly occurring behavior (e.g., number of cigarettes smoked in day) (Korotitsch & Nelson-Gray, 1999).

Effects parallel to those of self-monitoring can be found in literature examining the effects of observation of others' behaviors. Bloom, Hursh, Wienke, and Wolf (1992) found that compared to baseline conditions, teachers' frequent measurement and graphing of targeted student behaviors resulted in improvements in those behaviors. These results were found regardless of whether the teachers employed paper-and-pencil or computer systems for measurement, although teachers indicated that they preferred the computer methods and more frequently altered their interventions when they used the computer. When using computers, teachers continued to record data regularly following the formal study. Bloom et al. suggested that one explanation for these results is that data collection helped teachers to focus on the specific objectives for behavior change with their students. Data collection concerning "complying with requests," for example, focused the teacher's attention on the student's action following a request, as well as the reinforcers the teacher employed with that student. Similarly, students often had an increased awareness of their specific behaviors when monitored. Bloom et al. (1992) also found that teachers employed the resulting data to make decisions about their interventions with students. They concluded that "the type of intervention chosen may be a moot point unless student progress is monitored" (p. 189). Thus, self-monitoring and observation of others' behavior may both change behavior because of the feedback provided.

The Use of Natural Language

In an important sense, language is the data of counseling. Verbal and non-verbal communications are the primary media through which therapist and client transfer information and meaning. One method of understanding individuals well is to listen closely to what they say, that is, to study their use of language. A focus on natural language is the essence of various narrative approaches to studying, assessing, and intervening with individuals. In the following discussion, I describe two contemporary approaches to natural language that offer potential insights into improvements in the measurement of psychological constructs. Narrative therapy emphasizes the importance of understanding the meaning of the stories people tell, while the approach employed by Pennebaker and others examines patterns found in word usage.

Narrative Therapy

As described in Chapter 5, narrative therapy (NT) invites us to notice that clients tell stories in therapy and that these stories can be useful in assessing and helping clients. Narrative therapists believe that all people are "active, impassioned meaning makers in search of plausible stories" (White, 2004). In other words, people make sense of their life experiences through stories. Stories are informal theories, a verbal mapping of our personal experiences. Personal narratives allow for three important goals: (1) storage of large amounts of information, particularly information relevant to personal goals, (2) quick decision making (Dimaggio & Semerari, 2004), and perhaps most important for therapeutic purposes, (3) organization of information about social interactions and experiences (Boothe & Von Wyl, 2004). Although proponents of narrative approaches differ to some degree in the ideas they emphasize, all agree that individuals' stories are idiographic in that they possess some degree of uniqueness (Polkinghorne, 2004). This uniqueness is the problem that nomothetic measures cannot handle and that is the focus of idiographic approaches.

In terms of measuring change resulting from counseling and psychotherapy, it seems reasonable to expect NT to direct us to look at changes in stories. But what types of changes? NT authors have proposed a diversity of concepts thought to be central to stories (see Table 7.2). For example, theorists differentiate among types of stories and histories: Hardtke and Angus (2004) distinguished between *micronarratives*, stories told in the therapy hour, and *macronarratives*, the clients' life stories. Angus and McLeod (2004) described *chronicles* or *reports* (stories with no sense of drama or purpose) and *cultural narratives*, stories of the good life. Singer and Blagov (2004) focused on what they term *self-defining memories*, which include the main elements of personality and identity, including personal goals (cf. Hardtke & Angus, 2004, regarding self-image). Self-defining memories of therapeutic interest are those that possess affective intensity and vividness and relate to an important unresolved concern. Singer and Blagov (2004) suggested that "images from these memories serve as metaphoric touchstones in the therapeutic dialogue" (p. 239), helping the client to draw lessons from different, linked experiences. Thus, metaphors also can serve as the focus of assessments (cf. Meier & Davis, 2005). *Repetitive memories* also indicate content related to important goals and issues (Singer & Blagov, 2004); a decrease in the repetitiveness of a particular memory or story is likely to be evident as a result of effective therapy. That is, as specific issues are resolved, clients

TABLE 7.2. Examples of Assessment Targets Suggested by Narrative Therapy

Author (year)	Concept	Description
	General constructs	
Hardtke & Angus (2004)	Micronarratives	Stories told the in therapy hour
Hardtke & Angus (2004)	Macronarratives	Life stories
Angus & McLeod (2004)	Chronicles/reports	Stories with no sense of drama or purpose
Angus & McLeod (2004)	Cultural narratives	Stories of the good life
Singer & Blagov (2004)	Self-defining memories	The main elements of personality and identity, including personal goals; can possess affective intensity and vividness
Dimaggio & Semerari (2004)	Diagnostic stories	Tone or style of story indicates DSM diagnosis (e.g., lack of positive valence indicates depression)
Anderson (2004)	Positive/negative dimension	Depressed individuals may have difficulty identifying positive aspects of experiences
Williams (1996)	Generality/specificity dimension	Stories that are too general may be indicative of working memory problems
Greenberg & Angus (2004)	Affect	Affect shapes many aspects of stories
Singer & Blagov (2004)	Integrative statements	Reports in stories of lessons learned from life experiences

should decrease the frequency of telling a particular story and its emotional valence should be less intense as well.

Narrative therapists suggest that evidence of distress and dysfunction can be present in personal narratives. Everyone possesses a *dominant life story* that describes the major experiences and themes of his or her life. This story, however, cannot encompass all of one's life experiences, and some of the *excluded experiences* may be important to a healthy sense of self. Some types of dysfunction may be evident by the absence of key story elements (Anderson, 2004). All stories should have a beginning, middle, and end, for example, with the absence of one of these components indicating a potential problem in the storyteller (Boothe & Von Wyl, 2004). In addition, some important life experiences may *contradict* the dominant story. For example, a counselor in training who sees himself as a natural helper may find it difficult to accept feedback from a supervisor who tells him that he is a poor listener. Similarly, one's life story may include components that are incompatible with each other, indicating the presence of *multiple, fragmented identities* (Angus & McLeod, 2004). McAdams (1996) suggested that the degree of organization of one's life story is indicative of mental health.

Polkinghorne (2004) indicated that culture provides a repertoire of life stories that can be adopted by persons living in that culture. The plots of some cultural stories, Polkinghorne (2004) maintained, describe social functions that the individual must perform. Some of these cultural stories, however, can be "constrictive and blaming" (Polkinghorne, 2004, p. 53), and narrative therapists then see their therapeutic task as helping clients to create more expansive interpretations of their situations. In the United States, for example, the majority culture presents thin women as attractive and desirable, which contributes to the development of eating disorders (Zinn, 2006). Given that research indicates that positive relationships are strongly related to happiness and that most problems addressed in therapy are interpersonal (Lambert & Finch, 1999), it makes sense that many key themes in clients' narratives will be social in nature.

Some theorists also suggest that particular types or characteristics of stories are associated with specific diagnoses. Dimaggio and Semerari (2004), for example, described clients with borderline personality disorder as telling stories "loaded with extreme judgments—all good or all bad—toward the self and significant others" (p. 267), and Anderson (2004) indicated that depressed individuals have difficulty identifying positive experiences in stories. Stories that are too general may be indicative of working memory problems associated with anxiety and depression (Williams, 1996). Another possible assessment target is *affect* evoked during storytelling (e.g., Boothe & Von

Wyl, 2004; Greenberg & Angus, 2004; Hardtke & Angus, 2004). Greenberg and Angus (2004) emphasize the importance of emotion in narrative work, suggesting that stories themselves are shaped by the emotional themes present. They maintain that emotions are the "primary associative connection" of story elements, the glue that holds the story together. Singer and Blagov's (2004) research with 106 college students investigated the relationship between *integrative statements* in a written description of a vivid memory with personality adjustment (such as self-restraint) and coping. Integrative statements are those indicative of meaning created, with beginnings such as "I learned that . . ." or "This experience taught me. . . ." Singer and Blagov found that moderate self-restraint, but not low or high self-restraint, was associated with greater numbers of integrative memories.

Mayer and colleagues' work on *seductive details* (e.g., Harp & Mayer, 1998; Mayer, Heiser, & Lonn, 2001) offers another potentially useful target of assessment. Harp and Mayer (1998) defined seductive details as "highly interesting and entertaining information that is only tangentially related to the topic but is irrelevant to the author's intended theme" (p. 414). For example, if students are learning in a science lesson about how lightning occurs, adding graphics such as a picture showing how lightning tore through a high school student's football helmet leads to a decrease in learning performance. Harp and Mayer's (1998) studies found that seductive details become an organizing framework that diverts learners from the key ideas by priming "an inappropriate context" (p. 431). They suggest that instructors focus on topics of cognitive interest in material, enhanced by "summaries, illustrations, and text cohesiveness" (p. 432). In contrast, illustrations such as the lightning's effect on the football helmet will increase the learner's affective arousal and prime other schemas or stories (e.g., "That reminds me of the time I was hurt in an automobile accident"). This research implies that for some clients, the emotion or experiential context of a traumatic incident may be so gripping or overwhelming that it hinders them from creating new lessons (cf. the case of Patricia, cited by Mergenthaler, 1996). The seductive details research suggests that for assessment purposes, then, the focus should be on the context of the story, particularly the affectively tinged context, as much as on story actions and events. Context can include the specificity of the story as well as the temporal context and other details of the narrative (Singer & Blagov, 2004).

In addition to assessment content, several formal procedures have been proposed for narrative assessment (e.g., Hardtke & Angus, 2004). Hardtke and Angus (2004) proposed a Narrative Assessment Interview (NAI), a brief semistructured interview designed to be administered at the start of therapy and at follow-up periods. Three questions are administered in the interview: (1) How would you describe yourself? (2) How would someone who knows you really well describe you? (3) If you could change something about who you are, what would you change? The next stage involves a content analysis of the person's answers to each question in order to produce a summary sheet of key information. In general, grounded theory procedures would appear useful for analysis of natural language data (Levitt & Rennie, 2004).

Pennebaker's Word Use Approach

Studies of language appear to be divided between researchers interested in word use versus the meaning of words (i.e., narratives) (cf. Pennebaker, Mehl, & Niederhoffer, 2003). Perhaps as a result, narrative therapists have generally ignored the empirical work of James Pennebaker and colleagues, who have conducted a series of studies, using word use methods, to investigate the effects of writing about personal traumas. In Pennebaker's procedure, participants are given instructions such as, "Write about your deepest thoughts and feelings about a trauma"; they are to do this over a period of 3–5 days for 15–30 minutes a day (Pennebaker et al., 2003). In essence, participants must create a written narrative of a traumatic incident. Research reports of this process indicate that the writing procedure induces affect and meaning making in ways very similar to traditional counseling. This research is based on the assumption that psychological information is conveyed through word use, independent of semantic context (Pennebaker et al., 2003). Computer-based word count systems analyze the content and style of word use to examine grammatical units (e.g., use of personal pronouns) as well as psychological dimensions (e.g., emotional words).

Smyth (1998) conducted a meta-analysis of 13 studies comparing the effects of the Pennebaker written condition with some type of control (e.g., another writing condition, such as, "Write about your plans for the day"). Smyth (1998) reported an overall effect size of .47, indicating that the written emotional expression groups exceeded controls on a wide range of outcome measures, including measures of affect, grade point average, immune system performance, number of health center visits, and reemployment status. The health center visits results mirrored findings in *medical cost offset* studies, in which use of counseling and psychotherapy has been shown to reduce medical and surgical costs (Cummings, O'Donohue, & Ferguson, 2002). These studies also suggested greater benefits for males (perhaps because men's sex role inhibits emotional disclosure to other people) and for writing periods that are spread out over a longer period of time. Writers reported an increase in short-term distress before later improvements became evident, although the amount of short-term distress was unrelated to subsequent change. Studies of word use patterns of persons completing the writing intervention indicate that persons were more likely to benefit if their writing contained more positive emotion words, a moderate number of negative emotion words, and an increasing number of causal and insight words from the beginning to the conclusion of writing (Pennebaker et al., 2003). Pennebaker et al.'s (2003) interpretation of these findings is that "the construction of a story or narrative concerning an emotional upheaval may be essential to coping" (p. 568) and that successful therapy requires individuals to "move from highly specific referential activity and high emotional tone to high levels of abstraction" (p. 568).

Smyth (1998) noted that some theorists believe that traumatic memories are stored differently and not integrated into personal narratives. More specifically, traumatic memories are repetitive in the sense that they intrude into consciousness (Foa & Riggs, 1993). For outcome assessment, a reduction in the frequency of a particular story or a story's themes should be evident following successful therapy. Reflecting the organization concept proposed by McAdams (1996), traumatic memories appear to be disorganized and treatments such as exposure therapy and the writing procedure appear to reduce that disorganization (Pennebaker, 1993). In the writing procedure, attending to the traumatic event for a sufficient period of time appears to lead to increased use of insight words such as "understand" and "realize" (Smyth, 1998). Smyth (1998) concluded that "written emotional expression leads to the transduction of the traumatic experience into a linguistic structure that promotes assimilation and understanding of the event, and reduces negative affect associated with thoughts of the event" (p. 174). Put more simply, people become deconditioned to the trauma and make sense of the experience.

Pennebaker et al. (2003) also expressed enthusiasm for the future study of *particles* (e.g., pronouns, articles, prepositions), which make up to 50% of all words used but consist of only about 200 words:

> Particles serve as the glue that holds content words together....They are referential words that have tremendous social and psychological meaning. To use a pronoun requires the speaker and listener to share a common knowledge of who the referent is.... Pronoun use requires a relatively sophisticated awareness of the audience's ability to track who is who. (p. 570)

Campbell and Pennebaker's (2003) reanalysis of writing protocols found that change in particles and pronoun use between sequential writing days was associated with fewer physician visits. They noted that particle use helps to identify relationships between the narrator and other individuals and objects. On this basis, Campbell and Pennebaker (2003) concluded that "individuals who altered their individual and social perspectives from day to day were the participants most likely to benefit from the disclosure exercise" (p. 64). In other words, participants may have been creating models of social interaction that led to health improvements, at least in terms of physician visits.

The word count approach has its own set of limitations. Because the word count alternatives are computer based, they require dictionaries and rules to sort and count words. To interpret the results of word count studies and design more sophisticated dictionaries requires basic theories about the purpose of word use. As Pennebaker et al. (2003) stated, "no one has yet devised a compelling psychological theory of word usage" (p. 572). Narrative theorists, however, may be able to fill that void. Pennebaker et al. (2003) also cautioned researchers from solely using emotion words to study affect inasmuch as people naturally express feelings through such nonverbals as intonation or facial expression (cf. Barrett, 2006). Noting reports of improvement resulting from writing if individuals employed more positive emotion words and causal or insightful words, Campbell and Pennebaker (2003) noted that "the effects reported have been modest and often inconsistent" (p. 60). A more idiographically based model of word use may be necessary for outcome assessment.

Idiographically Based Feedback Procedures

In Chapter 6, I described patient-focused research conducted by Lambert and colleagues that demonstrated the benefits of employing a nomothetic outcome measure, the OQ-45, with failing clients. A parallel set of procedures employ idiographic measures designed to provide feedback about progress. In these feedback-based procedures, clinicians make explicit connections between case conceptualization, clinical assessment, analysis of intervention-related data, and interventions with clients (cf. Beutler & Harwood, 2000; Persons, 1989). Most texts emphasize the counseling process as consisting primarily of the interventions and interactions that take place in therapy sessions. In contrast, feedback-based approaches make conceptualization, assessment, and analysis of process and outcome information integral components of treatment.

Meier (2003) described the ideal process as a *flexible feedback loop* (see Figure 7.2) that consists of

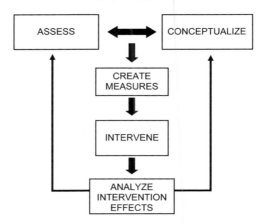

FIGURE 7.2. Sequential relations among assessment, conceptualization, intervention, and analysis of intervention effects. Counselors begin with an initial conceptualization and from there develop ideas about interventions and process/outcome measures (Meier, 1999, 2003). Data analyses of the subsequent assessment information can be fed back into conceptualization, assessment, and intervention procedures to increase the likelihood of client improvement. From Meier (2003). Copyright by Sage Publications. Reprinted by permission.

1. An initial assessment and conceptualization of a specific client,
2. Selection of process and outcome measures that reflect the initial conceptualization,
3. Selection of initial intervention(s) that follow from the conceptualization,
4. Implementation of the measurement and intervention protocol, with regular analysis of qualitative and quantitative data, and
5. Feeding those results back to the clinician (and, perhaps, the client) so that the interventions (and, perhaps, the conceptualization and assessment procedures) can be reconsidered and adapted if necessary.

This and other types of feedback loop can provide clinicians with useful information with which to create treatment plans and adjust conceptualizations and therapeutic interventions as data suggest (Haynes, 1993; Howard et al., 1996; Lambert, 1998; Lambert et al., 2001; Mark et al., 1991; Palmer, 1986). Similarly, Persons (1991) proposed a case formulation hypothesis that states that "all else being equal, outcome ought to be better for a patient treatment with an accurate formulation than for a patient treated with an inaccurate formulation" (p. 103). Persons (1991) also described several studies that provided indirect evidence that interventions based on a valid conceptualization lead to better outcomes.

Whereas Lambert's approach employs the use of a nomothetic measure (the OQ-45), idiographic proponents believe that idiographic measures are more likely to be sensitive to constructs that change during counseling (Bickman et al., 2000; Cone, 1988; Kiresuk, Smith, & Cardillo, 1994; Mash & Hunsley, 1993). In particular, idiographic procedures may be particularly useful for identifying and reducing treatment failure. Perhaps because of the time-consuming nature of feedback-based approaches, in practice they may primarily be useful for clients who are failing to make progress or deteriorating. Noting that "clinicians often lack the skills to handle" treatment failure, Persons and Mikami (2002, p. 140) described a set of principles designed explicitly for dealing with cases of treatment failures. Key among these is to perform continuous monitoring of client progress, using graphical plots of outcome data (cf. Gottman & Leiblum, 1974; Sterling-Turner, Robinson, & Wilczynski, 2001; Yeaton & Sechrest, 1981). Persons and Mikami (2002) suggested that such monitoring focus on (1) intermediate outcomes related to steps that occur before more long-term outcomes are addressed and (2) adherence to the treatment plan, the process by which outcomes will be reached. They also call for periodic review of outcome and process measures to determine whether other constructs might be usefully substituted in the case formulation and subsequently assessed. Key to the entire process, however, is the creation of an idiographic measure for a specific client.

Applications

Five steps are necessary for creating an idiographic measure: (1) Begin with the case conceptualization, (2) explicate constructs, (3) measure behaviors, (4) collect as much data as possible, and (5) analyze the idiographic data using graphs and descriptive statistics. I describe each step in detail using a case example from the literature.

Begin with the Case Conceptualization

Case conceptualizations are verbal and graphic depictions of important process (causes) and outcome (effects) elements for a particular client. The client's description of relevant history and events indicates potential causes of the client's problems, and the client's presenting problem(s) provides information relevant to desired outcomes (Meier, 2003). In general, an ideal case conceptualization includes a brief list of process and outcome elements included in a graphical depiction of the relationship of those elements. The conceptualization can also include a depiction of the treatment plan, describing interventions aimed at particular process–outcome relationships. More detailed guidelines about creating a case conceptualization can be found in a variety of sources (Berman, 1997; Meier, 2003; Needleman, 1999; Nelson & Neufeldt, 1998).

For illustration, consider the case of Mr. F, a 19-year-old Asian American who sought counseling because of intrusive thoughts (Abramowitz, 2002). Mr. F had recurring thoughts about cursing at others during class, looking at people's genitals, and raping a particular female friend. Mr. F maintained that he would never take such actions, but he was very fearful that he might do so. The intrusive thoughts had begun about a year before he enrolled at the university, when Mr. F had thoughts about killing his parents in their sleep. Abramowitz (2002) noted that Mr. F "often would sit in his room thinking about ways he could be careful so as to prevent his thoughts from influencing his actions" (p. 9). Mr. F also reported physical symptoms of anxiety and depression such as frequent indigestion and sleep loss.

Abramowitz's (2002) initial assessment of Mr. F found that he met DSM-IV criteria for obsessive–compulsive disorder (OCD) and major depressive episode. The assessment found that Mr. F avoided knives, the dormitory balcony where he would have thoughts of jumping, classes where he was afraid he would curse, and his computer because he was afraid of sending inappropriate e-mail messages. Mr. F also reported several rituals intended to help cope with his anxiety about the intrusive thoughts, including whispering curse words in public and reasoning about the possibility that he would actually do an inappropriate act. As part of the assessment process, Mr. F also completed nomothetic measures of OCD symptoms, depression (i.e., BDI), unwanted thoughts, and strategies for controlling thoughts. One possible conceptualization of Mr. F's sequence of thoughts and feelings is illustrated in Figure 7.3.

Abramowitz (2002) noted that Foa and Kozak (1986) recommended that phobic clients learn to confront the feared stimulus so that they learn that disastrous consequences do not actually occur. A conceptualization of the treatment plan might thus look like Figure 7.4.

Psychotherapy consisted of twice weekly sessions over 8 weeks, plus a telephone contact between sessions, focusing on *in vivo* and imaginal exposure to the aversive thoughts along with appropriate homework. For example, in one session Mr. F was instructed to not think of pink elephants; he subsequently reported thinking about numerous pink elephants. The thera-

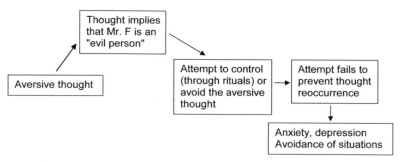

FIGURE 7.3. Case conceptualization for Mr. F.

pist emphasized that attempts to suppress thoughts result in an increase in the unwanted thoughts. Other work included developing a hierarchy of fear thoughts and situations and exposing Mr. F to increasingly stressful steps.

Explicate Constructs

Once process–outcome elements have been specified, the task becomes how to gather data related to those key constructs. Meier (2003) described the process as similar to the procedures behavioral assessors employ: (1) Name the construct, (2) define it, (3) elaborate on its critical components, (4) provide examples, (5) describe questionable instances and whether they should count as data, and (6) describe the units of measurement. Following these steps adds needed structure to the process; simply choosing or creating a measure without following these steps may produce confusion during the measurement procedure or in the interpretation of the resulting data (Meier, 2003).

In the case of Mr. F, Abramowitz (2002) administered the previously described nomothetic tests at the beginning, middle, end, and follow–up to treatment. Although useful for research studies examining the efficacy of treatment, or program evaluation studies documenting the effectiveness

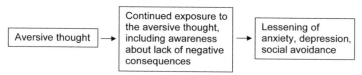

FIGURE 7.4. Mr. F's treatment plan.

of treatment, such a schedule may not provide data timely enough to adjust the conceptualization or treatment as it progresses. Abramowitz (2002) did, however, create idiographic rating scales for three constructs that he labeled *fear of intrusive thoughts, avoidance* (of situations associated with intrusive thoughts), and *neutralizing rituals* (i.e., behaviors believed to lessen anxiety). Abramowitz (2002) described these therapist-completed scales and provided a unit of measurement (0, none, to 8, severe), but did not define the constructs, elaborate on their critical components in the case of Mr. F, or describe questionable instances (e.g., problems in measurement); this relative lack of structure may lead to problems with the resulting data and analyses, as described below. Abramowitz (2002) collected data with these idiographic measures after each of 13 psychotherapy sessions.

Measure Behaviors

Research in behavioral assessment has found that in general, lower reliability and validity estimates are associated with greater interpretation on the part of the observer (Paul, 1986). For example, a therapist could rate a client's overall anxiety in a therapy session (which requires considerable interpretation of what occurs in the session) or record the number of instances the client expressed anxiety verbally in a session ("I'm afraid to take the psychology exam tomorrow because I haven't studied") or nonverbally (e.g., excessive body movements while talking about taking the examination). Greater amounts of interpretation mean that assessment data are more likely to reflect characteristics of the observers and the assessment task than the phenomena being observed (Paul, 1986). For these and other reasons (cf. Paul, 1986), assessment of a construct through well-defined behavioral observation is more likely to produce data with higher reliability and validity estimates.

Interestingly, Abramowitz (2002) implemented a behavioral approach to treating Mr. F, but did not employ more traditional behavioral methods. Instead, he employed (1) nomothetic self-reports of OCD symptoms, depression, unwanted thoughts, and strategies for controlling thoughts, and (2) idiographic therapist ratings of fear of thoughts, avoidance of situations, and neutralizing rituals. The most likely reason for these choices was the availability of resources. Self-reports and therapist measures are of relatively low cost in terms of time and money, as compared with behavioral observation. If additional resources were available, behavioral approaches such as self-monitoring (Cone, 1999) or analogue measures (Haynes, 2001) might have provided additional useful data.

Collect as Much Data as Possible

Once the measurement procedures are chosen, collect as much qualitative and quantitative data as possible. Collect information for every session or contact with the client. If the feedback loop of conceptualization, assessment, and analysis of intervention effects is to be useful, frequent, current data are necessary. As data are aggregated, different types of error tend to balance each other and have less of an effect; more data means that subsequent analyses can often be interpreted with more confidence. Continuous data collection can also help in the detection of treatment failure (Mash & Hunsley, 1993; Meier, 2003). Finally, data should be collected using as many different types of measurement as possible. The use of multiple methods avoids problems of (1) *mono-method bias*, results that include effects of the measurement method, thus interfering with test scores' ability to measure the construct of interest, and (2) *mono-operations bias*, results that reflect characteristics of the particular test used, again interfering with scores' ability to measure primarily the construct of interest.

Abramowitz (2002) collected baseline data for the three idiographic measures for three sessions, and continued to collect data after each of 13 subsequent treatment sessions. Table 7.3 lists values for the three measures by session.

Thus, Abramowitz (2002) produced a total of 48 ratings on these three scales, a considerable amount of quantitative data. The ratings included three baseline sessions and spanned the length of therapy. A quick glance at these data indicate a decrease in severity over time, suggesting improvement for Mr. F. As discussed in the next section, several analytic techniques can provide additional useful information related to the impact of the intervention and the validity of the three rating scales. Note also that Abramowitz (2002) employed multiple methods (i.e., self-reports and therapist ratings) whose findings converged in showing improvement over time for Mr. F.

Analyze Idiographic Data

A *time series* refers to collection, over a period of time, of data collected via a single measure. With counseling and psychotherapy, a time series usually consists of data collected over a period of multiple sessions. Often these data are displayed in a graph, as Abramowitz (2002) did when he constructed three separate graphs to display data resulting from therapist ratings of Mr. F's fear of thoughts, avoidance of situations, and neutralizing rituals. A *multivariate graphical time series*, however, displays data for two or more measures over time and can illustrate potential relations between these measures. For

TABLE 7.3. Three Therapist Idiographic Ratings for Mr. F

Session	Fear of thoughts	Avoidance	Rituals
Baseline Session 1	7	7	6
Baseline Session 2	6	6	5
Baseline Session 3	6	7	5
Session 1	5	5	4
Session 2	5	6	4
Session 3	4	5	1
Session 4	4	2	2
Session 5	3	2	1
Session 6	2	1	1
Session 7	2	0	1
Session 8	2	0	0
Session 9	1	0	1
Session 10	2	0	0
Session 11	1	1	1
Session 12	2	0	0
Session 13	1	0	0

Note. Therapist ratings on the scale could range from 0 (None) to 8 (Severe).

example, data from Abramowitz's (2002) three measures are displayed together in Figure 7.5.

Time series data also provide an opportunity to search for important events that may be linked to client change. Abramowitz (2002), for example, noted that Mr. F began practicing exposure to knives on his own after Session 8. Therapist ratings of avoidance, however, begin to show a sharp decrease after Sessions 5 and 6, suggesting that an additional event, perhaps the conceptualization of OCD shared by the therapist, sparked change.

Also of note in the graphical display is the high correspondence among the three clinical measures. In general, measures of different clinical constructs should provide different information. In the case of the three therapist ratings, the data appear highly correlated. In fact, ratings of fear of intrusive thoughts correlated at .92 with avoidance of situations and at .95 with neutralizing rituals, and avoidance and rituals correlated at .91. *Correlation coefficients* describe the extent to which two variables covary and can range from −1.00 to +1.00; a value of 0 indicates that no relationship exists between the two sets of scores. Thus, a correlation can provide useful information about the relatedness of scores on two or more measures. In the case of Mr. F, it appears that any one of the three measures could have been used in place of all three measures. Additional attention during the construct explication of the ratings might have led to greater differentiation of the resulting scores.

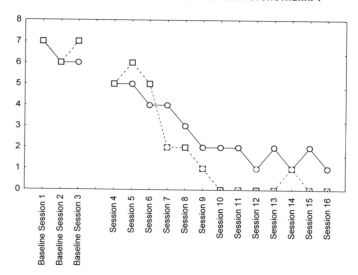

FIGURE 7.5. Change over time on three therapist ratings of Mr. F. Abramowitz (2002) rated Mr. F on three dimensions: Fear of intrusive thoughts (circles), avoidance of situations associated with intrusive thoughts (squares), and neutralizing rituals (diamonds), behaviors believed to lessen anxiety. Therapist ratings on the scale could range from 0 (None) to 8 (Severe). Over the course of therapy all three measures evidenced improvement.

Two other familiar descriptive statistics that may be of use in clinical data analyses are the mean and standard deviation. The *mean* is the average of a group of scores, and the *standard deviation* indicates the degree to which the scores vary around the mean. For Mr. F, it may be useful to examine the mean and standard deviations for all of the idiographic scores as well as selected time periods. In this approach the client functions as his or her own control, and scores for selected sessions are compared to evaluate such questions as whether baseline periods and final sessions differ from the entire set of observations.

Table 7.4 displays the mean and standard deviations for all 16 observations, the three baseline sessions and the final three sessions for Mr. F's three idiographic measures. One way to check for differences over time is to examine whether mean scores differ across comparison periods by at least one standard deviation. The *fear of intrusive thoughts* mean score for the three baseline sessions (6.33), for example, exceeds the mean score of all 16 observations (3.31) by greater than the standard deviation of all observations

TABLE 7.4. Descriptive Statistics for Mr. F's Idiographic Measures

Measure	All observations		Baseline		Final three sessions	
	X	SD	X	SD	X	SD
Fear of intrusive thoughts	3.31	1.99	6.33	.58	1.33	.58
Avoidance of situations	2.63	2.83	6.67	.58	.33	.58
Neutralizing rituals	2.00	2.07	5.33	.58	.33	.58

(3.02 > 1.99). The same holds for the *avoidance of situations* and the *neutralizing rituals* measures, suggesting that Mr. F began therapy with significantly greater distress than he experienced at later points. Comparing means of the final three sessions with data from the baseline period indicates that scores at the end of counseling are several standard deviations below the baseline. Taken together, these data suggest that Mr. F. evidenced significant improvement on the idiographic measures over the course of psychotherapy.

Consider Progress Notes for Process and Outcome Data

Abramowitz's (2002) case study is a useful example of a quantitative approach to process and outcome assessment. However, such an approach is often impractical for most cases because of the time required. One alternative is to employ data routinely collected in clinical settings, the most typical source being clinical or progress notes (Meier, 2003). Clinicians keep progress notes for each therapy session in the form of a general narrative or lists of important content (American Psychological Association, 1993; Sommers-Flanagan & Sommers-Flanagan, 1999). As shown in Table 7.5, Wiger (1999) provided a more detailed list of potential topics for progress notes.

Qualitative progress notes provide low-cost information relevant to case conceptualization constructs. More specifically, qualitative data in prog-

TABLE 7.5. Wiger's Suggested Content for Progress Notes

- How the session related to treatment plan objectives
- Interventions and techniques employed
- Important clinical observations (e.g., client cognition, behavior, affect)
- Recent progress or setbacks
- Diagnostic signs still present or now absent
- Treatment goals, including intermediate goals, met at this time
- Current medical necessity
- Work being done outside the session
- Current strengths and impairments

ress notes such as themes, stories, issues, and metaphors can be a key source of information about process factors, client outcomes, and the revelations between process and outcome (Meier, 2003). For example, an anxious client might express anxiety by frequently switching topics within and between sessions. A recording of these topics and related information might eventually provide data about when, how often, and why the client switches issues, thereby deepening the case conceptualization and providing more information relevant for subsequent intervention. Similarly, Meier and Davis (2005) provided examples of clients, (1) one of whom compared her problems to a box, with the size of the box indicating the client's perception of the intensity of her problems, and (2) another who offered the metaphor of a boxing match for his problems, with the round of the match indicating how much progress he had made.

Many qualitative methods involve rereading original material to perform careful comparisons, detect differences, note patterns, and identify trends (Miles & Huberman, 1990). *Grounded theory analysis* (Creswell, 2002; Strauss & Corbin, 1997), for example, involves a reader who makes explicit identification of important concepts in field notes. These identified concepts are then subjected to a coding scheme designed to organize them conceptually (Strauss & Corbin, 1997) in order to create theoretical constructs that explain the actions and processes occurring in a social setting.

For the purpose of outcome assessment, a thorough review of progress notes can produce outcome-related information that can be displayed in a table. *Tables* are a common means of displaying qualitative information and may be particularly useful for displaying important themes identified in a qualitative analysis of progress notes. For example, Meier (1999, 2003) presented a table extracting themes that emerged from a qualitative analysis of progress notes from an individual client presenting with depression. These themes could provide useful information for a case conceptualization in terms of potentially important process and outcome elements. In addition, outcomes could be tracked by examining the notes for signs of progress and setbacks over the course of therapy. Table 7.6 summarizes the major themes over 20 sessions of therapy.

With the wide availability of word-processing software, the clinician can easily highlight outcome information in progress notes or extracted themes. If outcomes for this depressed client consist of themes related to affect, they could be indicated by putting that information in bold type. Thus, relevant outcome information highlighted in Table 7.6 includes:

1. In Session 5 the client's anxiety is reported to have lessened considerably, and depression lessened moderately.

TABLE 7.6. Qualitative Analysis of Progress Notes with an Individual Client

Session no.	Key issues
1	Presenting problem centers on **depression and anxiety**; agrees to referral for possible medication; reports history of conflicted family relationships, particularly with long-deceased alcoholic father.
2	Has started medication and will continue counseling; reports difficulty at work with "crazy" customers; we establish a schedule of activities designed to increase positive reinforcement for him.
3	Reports *a history of trying to recreate a family life,* but with people other than immediate family of origin; for example, becomes a physical, emotional caretaker for distant relatives, older neighbors; reports no effect from reinforcement activities.
4	**Reports that he is very angry** with *many past incidents with family of origin,* particularly father, and some current events with mother.
5	**Much less anxious, moderately less depressed, but seems almost manic**; very strong emotional reactions to many current events.
6	He agrees to start a journal where he writes thoughts, feelings, and related events.
7	Reports that he has come to the conclusion that **he hates himself**; reading books about identity development; **now frequent, angry arguments with partner**.
8	Reports becoming **easily angry with coworkers**, even when their behavior does not affect him directly, as well as with partner and family members.
9	Reads for 30 minutes from a journal about *past family incidents* that provoked **anger, rage, and sadness in him**; question arises whether he should pursue family therapy with mother and siblings.
10	Notes that **he is angry with his mother,** *but cannot express those feelings* to her or even explore much in session; *family culture indicates that being angry with parents is equivalent to disobeying them.*
11	Despite father's death 15 years ago, reports that he still **wishes there was some way he could be emotionally close to father**; I confronted about this unrealistic idea; he later cancels next session.
12	Some processing in session of *how he experiences emotion*; relates stories that provide evidence (to him) that his role was to function as *emotional caretaker in his family; tried to protect mother from abusive, alcoholic father.*
13	No-show; later reported that he forgot about the session.
14	*Wondering whether to stay in current relationship*; debating financial security versus partner's treatment of him as a child.
15	Considering whether to leave town, start a new life elsewhere; now spending much time considering therapy issues between sessions.
16	Same issues as Session 15.
17	Ran into his brother's friend who had no idea that client's father was alcoholic; *confirmed for client that mother and siblings denied family difficulties*; I noted that in the past he had denied such problems as well.
18	Clearly has changed locus of responsibility for family conflict away from himself; **anger and rumination about family has decreased**; more focus on work, other people.
19	*Discusses buying a house with partner; one brother is now contacting him for social interactions.*
20	Termination; **client reports greater self-confidence, emotional independence from family**, stable work performance; describes himself as "better integrated."

Note. Bold text indicates material relevant to outcome, and *italicized* content relates to process. Data from Meier (1999, 2003). Reprinted by permission, Sage Publications.

2. Sessions 7 through 10 indicate that he is becoming aware of and experiencing anger.
3. Sessions 10 through 12 focus on the role of anger in his family and his awareness about how he experiences emotion.
4. After Session 14, client appears to be paying more attention to current problems, with anger and rumination about family issues clearly abating. He also appears to be doing considerable processing about important issues outside therapy sessions.
5. In Session 20 he concludes therapy by reporting greater self-confidence, emotional independence, and stable work performance, with depression no longer mentioned as a problem.

If depression and associated negative affect form the key outcome elements, the client's ideas about his role in the conflicted relationships of his family of origin and his continuing efforts to create a new family life appear to be important process elements (italicized in Table 7.6). Similarly, his tendency to avoid discussing and experiencing intense emotional material (and the resulting pace at which the therapist could focus on this material) may be important for conceptualizing potential interventions.

Summary and Implications

Idiographic approaches focus on the unique ways individuals experience and manifest psychological phenomena. This chapter presented just a few idiographic methods employed in clinical practice and research. Other approaches described in the literature, for example, include identification of an individual client's target complaints (Battle et al., 1966), goal attainment scaling (Kiresuk et al., 1994), validating the client's unique cognitive schemas (Mumma, 2004), idiographic role playing (Kern, 1991), and assessing self-scenarios (Muran & Segal, 1992).

Although they usually require more resources than nomothetic approaches, idiographic measures offer the potential for improving the quality of information provided to clinicians regarding client process and outcome in counseling and psychotherapy. *Potential* is the key word in the preceding sentence because procedures for evaluating the reliability and validity of idiographic measures are less developed than they are for nomothetic measures. In theory, idiographic measures should provide more precise information and feedback regarding important client attributes, particularly state effects, than nomothetic measures; idiographic measures may also improve the treatment utility of assessment as compared with nomothetic tests.

Considerable research is needed to evaluate idiographic approaches (Beutler & Hamblin, 1986). First, new methods of assessing reliability and validity estimates are needed with idiographic measures. Baselines and co-efficient alpha offer potentially useful procedures for evaluating reliability, for example, but further development of these and additional methods for evaluating the psychometric properties of idiographic measures is necessary. In addition, treatment utility might be evaluated by investigating whether idiographic measures provide information that helps therapists improve case formulations. Narrative therapy (NT) offers a number of new content areas to evaluate regarding process and outcome, although caution is in order because similar ideas presented in previous versions of NT, such as Neuro-linguistic Programming (Bandler & Grinder, 1975), either did not receive research support or were not evaluated from a research perspective. More contemporary research appears to have been conducted on methods that evaluate the meaning of client language. The word use research indicates that psychological improvements that result from writing about a traumat-ic event parallel the processes and outcomes expected to occur in talking therapies: Repeated exposure to an emotionally charged incident eventu-ally leads to the construction of a meaningful narrative and a lessening of negative affect.

Whatever type of data are collected over time, feedback to clients and therapists about progress would appear as important in idiographic approach-es as in nomothetic ones. One advantage of idiographic approaches is that an individual's case conceptualization can made more specific, even if derived from a empirically supported nomothetic theory, and that specificity can lead to selection of assessment targets unique to a particular client. Finally, computer technology allows for creation of a hybrid between nomothetic and idiographic testing approaches. A test administrator or client may select a subset of items from a longer list of nomothetic–generated items. That is, for any particular individual, a shorter list of items about specific problem areas may be more pertinent, and computer administration allows the selection and seamless display and scoring of responses to those items. The psycho-metric properties of item responses can be subsequently examined and the selected items and scores stored for future readministration.

General Measurement-Related Writing Assignment and Change-Related Writing Assignment

Note that the previous assignments have asked you to take a few steps into find-ing information relative to the psychometric properties of tests. For the next two class/time periods, finish the tables already started in previous assignments. That is, in whatever time frame is feasible, review the literature to find any additional information regarding theoretical definitions, test purpose, reliability estimates, and validity estimates. A reasonable goal in a graduate course is to include six to nine sources and reports (e.g., two to three reliability estimates per test) per table. If you have five or more reliability and validity estimates, plot them for comparison.

QUESTIONS AND EXERCISES

1. For 3 minutes, write down what you consider the major ideas of this section, chapter, or class. At the beginning of next week's class, share with the group.

2. The instructor should choose a short psychological test such as the State version of the State–Trait Anxiety Inventory. In class, but anonymously, students should complete all test items. Next, students should write a few notes beside each item describing how they made sense of the item (i.e., the item's meaning or on what basis they decided to answer the item). Without sharing their specific item response, students should then share their interpretation of the meaning of a few items with the rest of the group. Are the interpretations of each item's meaning or basis for response essentially the same (i.e., a nomothetic interpretation) or do students interpret the items in different ways (i.e., idiographically)?

3. Write brief definitions for the following terms: *baseline, criterion-reference, decay* and *drift, observational schedule, self-monitoring, micronarratives, seductive details, medical cost offset,* and *flexible feedback loop.*

CHAPTER 8

Summary, Integration, and Future Directions

Major Ideas
Initial Findings and Future Research
Conclusion

Major Ideas

The most persistent problems with psychological testing relate to issues of consistency, the assumption of the trait-based selection approach that individuals should evidence consistent behavior across situations and over time. This assumption is the foundation of the trait-based selection paradigm, for without an assumption of substantial consistency, one could not have confidence that measurements of characteristics such as cognitive ability would be able to predict future performance. Although research often supports a degree of consistency in human behavior, considerable evidence also exists that indicates that measured behavior can (1) be altered by situational, environmental, and contextual factors, as when a simple change in test instructions influences item responses, or (2) evidence too much consistency, as when a manager rates all of an employee's performances as excellent, demonstrating a *halo effect*.

These chronic consistency issues suggest that theories about testing, whether classical or item response theory (IRT), are incomplete in some important ways. Given the youthfulness of testing efforts, this is hardly surprising. What is more problematic is that the field continues to do what Fiske (1987) called "glossing over discrepancies ... avoiding attempts to understand the sources of discrepancies perpetuates contemporary difficulties in seeking dependable generalizations and in establishing the connections among constructs" (p. 303). Failing to address consistency problems has hindered theoretical and applied progress in testing. Again, quoting Fiske (1987): "It is certainly true that, without examination of current concepts and of the effects of current methods, social/behavioral science will continue its slow course and will accumulate only fragmentary knowledge" (p. 304).

Some clinicians and researchers have noticed what I would call, for lack of a better word, a *stuckness* in psychology and counseling. As noted in Chapter 1, Ronnestad and Skovholt's (2003) experienced counselors concluded that "there is a sense that there is not and will not be any significant new knowledge in the field" (p. 26). Scientists sometimes deal with difficult problems by not thinking about them (Bryson, 2003), and that would seem to be an apt description of how many clinicians and researchers have dealt with problems related to measurement issues that fall outside the selection paradigm. Bryson (2003) also provided examples of how researchers and scientific journals can ignore what was later recognized as important research (e.g., in the area of plate tectonics). Current scientific journals that publish research on psychological testing overwhelmingly favor the publication of research about traditional tests, such as the WAIS or the MMPI, as well as research employing traditional test development methodology, such as factor analysis. Researchers investigating new methods of outcome assessment are clearly swimming upstream.

A good example of this stuckness can be found with computer-based testing. At first glance the combination of psychological testing and computer applications would appear to be a domain ripe for innovation. Indeed, researchers and clinicians have proposed and investigated a variety of potentially interesting applications, including computer-adaptive testing for intellectual tests (Drasgow & Chuah, 2006), measuring response latency as part of the testing process (Ryman, Naitoh, & Englund, 1988), analysis of human speech to detect psychological constructs such as anxiety (Friedman & Sanders, 1992; Pennebaker et al., 2003), simulations of situations of clinical interest such as alcohol intake (Meier & Wick, 1991), and employing computer administration of interviews to minimize social desirability effects (Catania et al., 1990). Although computer-adaptive testing has had a significant impact on tests such as the SAT and GRE, an examination of scientific and commercial publications over the past three decades indicates that most efforts have been focused simply on converting traditional tests to computer format (Berger, 2006). Automated procedures have been created, for example, for the MMPI (Anderson, 1987; Butcher, 1987; Honaker,

1988), 16 Personality Factors (16PF; Harrell & Lombardo, 1984; Karson & O'Dell, 1987), Rorschach (Exner, 1987), Strong Interest Inventory (Hansen, 1987; Vansickle, Kimmel & Kapes, 1989), Self-Directed Search (Reardon & Loughead, 1988), and a variety of intelligence and aptitude tests (Elwood, 1972a, 1972b, 1972c, 1972d; Harrell, Honaker, Hetu, & Oberwager, 1987).

In this book I have reported on or suggested a number of options for moving psychological testing forward. Let me distill these options into four major ideas relevant to professionals who develop and use psychological tests. In essence, we should pay more attention to:

1. *Advancing the science and practice of counseling and psychotherapy with change-sensitive outcome measures.* A major theoretical issue with any test is its intended purpose(s), and professionals should learn to recognize the myth of *shared test purpose.* In many research and clinical reports, and even in test manuals, authors typically do not specify test purpose even though purpose should drive the test validation and interpretation process. Although selection tests have been economically important, researchers, test developers, and educators should not treat selection as the only purpose of interest. Criterion-referenced tests, for example, employ scores on some absolute measure of behavior to assess mastery of a learning task. The procedures for selecting items for criterion-referenced tests differ from those employed to select items for norm-based, selection tests. Similarly, change-sensitive tests require items that vary in conditions where a treatment or intervention has been delivered. Given that psychotherapy outcome research clearly demonstrates that counseling and psychotherapy produce change (e.g., Kazdin, 2000; Smith & Glass, 1977), developers of outcome assessments must employ item selection procedures during test construction and evaluation to find items that evidence change during intervention periods. Methods designed to select stable, trait-based items are ill-suited for detecting change.

The better data resulting from improved outcome assessments will be useful in day-to-day clinical systems only if employed in some type of feedback system. Researchers have also begun to demonstrate how data produced by nomothetic change-sensitive scales can be usefully employed in clinical settings (Lambert et al., 2001, 2005). Particularly with clients who were failing to improve, clinicians who received outcome information regularly have demonstrated improved outcomes. Given a substantial body of research that raises questions about the limitations of clinicians' judgments for a variety of tasks, including the assessment of client progress, the implementation of structured feedback systems may be as important to improving outcomes as designing and employing change-sensitive measures.

Cases with truly negative outcomes, such as those of Pat and Mary described in Chapter 1, will be much less likely in practice settings where therapists receive regular feedback about failing clients.

2. *Studying context effects.* Although method variance is the best known such effect, context effects include unintended biases resulting from influences such as how test takers interpret test instructions, items, and response formats, as well as situational characteristics such as the age and gender of an interviewer. Context effects become problematic when they are shared among test takers in a manner that causes them to become a source of test invalidity.

Professionals should also learn to refute the myth of *shared item meaning.* Although groups of individuals may interpret items similarly, in any large group individuals are likely to differ considerably in their interpretation of the meaning of a test item or task. Context effects created by differences between test developers' and test takers' age, gender, ethnicity, history, and relevant experiences may influence the gap between the intended meaning of a test item and the meaning as construed by the test taker. As Bartoshuk and colleagues' (2005) research suggests, in essence everyone employs at least a slightly different scale when perceiving and responding to tests of psychological constructs. This is comparable to a situation in which researchers studying global warming all employ at least slightly different thermometers to measure temperature. For counseling and psychotherapy practitioners and researchers, valid idiographic measures offer one alternative that needs further investigation.

3. *The default use of traditional methodological and analytical techniques.* It may be that many test developers and users will not seriously consider innovative methods until they become more aware of current tests' limitations. As noted in this text, many well-known and convenient measurement methods and analytic procedures evidence significant problems, including:

a. Self-reports and interviews that are subject to a long list of biases and errors that remain largely unexplained.

b. Use of coefficient alpha as the key indicator of reliability despite the fact that most scales that share a single method (e.g., self-report) appear to produce moderate to high alphas (e.g., .70 and above). This makes the use of alpha a relatively inefficient method for comparing reliability values of different tests that employ the same method.

c. Application of factor analysis to provide evidence of construct validity through the identification and labeling of factors that lack a substantial theoretical framework or other empirical foundation. Most test developers and users appear to assume that scales developed through factor analytic methods can be employed for any subsequent purpose. The primary use of factor analyses should be for the construction and evaluation of trait-based tests.

d. Correlation of scores on newly created scales with previously developed measures of similar constructs. This often occurs with so little theoretical foundation that it can be difficult to interpret whether the level of the found correlations provides evidence for discriminant *or* convergent validity.

e. Use of such labels as "good" or "high" when describing validity estimates for a test. The field needs to address the inability of educational and psychological tests (besides, arguably, intelligence or cognitive ability tests) to produce reliable distinctions beyond low, moderate, and high estimates of a construct. One step would be to integrate the concept of precision into validity and to develop additional analytic methods that can evaluate the precision of tests, including change-sensitive tests.

4. *Obtaining additional resources for testing or developing innovative methods that decrease costs and improve efficiency.* If clinicians were to employ outcome assessments and systematic feedback regularly, more resources would need to be devoted to testing in clinical settings. This would come at a cost (in terms of money and time) that the mental health professions currently do not possess. As noted in Chapter 2, little market incentive appears to exist for creating improved outcome measures. Nor does there appear to be many incentives for clinicians or insurance companies to implement outcome measures (but see Clement [1999], for an outstanding exception). Some method needs to be found to provide incentives to create the next generation of outcome measures; this might be provided by grants or simply by imitating other professions, such as medicine, where such accountability is taking hold. Once the benefits of the new psychological outcome measures were demonstrated, the forces of the marketplace might take hold.

Technology may offer another alternative. Computer-based approaches will be increasingly employed in the future if for no other reason than they can provide increased efficiency in test development, administration, scoring, and interpretation. To date, however, most automation in psychological testing has occurred with relatively little attention to such theoretical considerations as human factors issues (cf. Leeson, 2006; Meier & Lambert, 1991; Rosen, Sears, & Weil, 1987) or fully employing computer capabilities (such as the ability to measure response time) in the testing process. Computer-based testing does offer the promise of addressing context issues (such as with the Descriptor Differential Scale, described in Chapter 5) as well as more pragmatic problems such as assessing meaning in natural language (as described below in regard to idiographic measures).

Initial Findings and Future Research

Research and test development procedures related to the four major ideas presented above continue to appear. Clinicians and researchers who need better measures of process and outcome have reason for hope. Several potentially important discoveries with item-level test evaluations have been made, for example, that may explain long-standing issues about the equivalent effectiveness of difference psychotherapies and the lack of significant positive findings regarding counseling with children and adolescents conducted in community settings. And as noted above, the demonstration of improved outcomes using feedback in counseling and psychotherapy provides a practical direction for employing research results to improve practice efficacy.

Nomothetic Outcome Measures

As described in Chapter 7, initial research has provided empirical demonstrations that useful nomothetic change-sensitive measures can be constructed on the basis of item-level analyses (Meier, 2000, 2004; Meier et al., in press; Weinstock & Meier, 2003). These studies have shown that tests developed to detect change evidence larger effect sizes in response to psychosocial interventions than do measures developed with traditional methods; in other words, tests developed to detect change effects have enhanced power to do so. Research findings also suggest that change-sensitive items may be different for female and male child and adolescent clients and that brief measures of change-sensitive items can be constructed (e.g., Meier et al., in press).

Other intriguing results have been produced by examining change at the item level in nomothetic outcome measures. Meier and Vermeersch's (2007) examination of the change sensitivity of two comprehensive outcome measures completed by three separate clinical samples found that items assessing depression and anxiety demonstrated the largest change over time. They suggested that depression and anxiety represent a common outcome factor that will evidence change in all effective therapeutic interventions. As described in Chapter 6, if depression/anxiety improvements represent the largest common contribution to effect size calculations in meta-analyses of psychotherapy outcome, the depression/anxiety effect should also at least

partially explain the equivalent gains results widely found in the psychotherapy outcome literature.

A potentially important study for understanding puzzling findings in
the child and adolescent treatment literature was reported by Meier and
Schwartz (2007). Although psychotherapy has repeatedly been demonstrated as efficacious with children and adolescents in laboratory settings, very
few studies have been published demonstrating effectiveness in field settings
(Kazdin, 2000; Weisz et al., 1998). Meier and Schwartz (2007) examined
repeated assessments on brief outcome measures completed by 215 adolescents receiving counseling at several community mental health clinics.
Surprisingly, from intake to first follow-up adolescents reported an increase
in such behaviors as smoking cigarettes, cheating, and failing to tell an adult
when they go out. In contrast, parents of adolescents receiving psychosocial
interventions at the same mental health clinics reported improvement on
many problem behaviors. Meier and Schwartz's (2007) analysis of these data
suggested that adolescent clients may have underreported the frequency of
undesirable behaviors at intake but later admitted to greater frequencies at
follow-up. This social desirability bias parallels clinicians' recognition of adolescents' tendency to resist full self-disclosure in counseling (Orton, 1997;
Peterson, 2004) and could potentially be present in other client groups,
including some adults. This finding also suggests that valid analyses of outcome with children and adolescents may require an initial assessment that
occurs *after* such clients have developed a working alliance with a therapist
that allows these clients to more accurately report their undesirable behaviors.

Idiographic Outcome Measures

Although basic principles about the reliability and validity of idiographic
assessment have been proposed, considerable work about their application
and evaluation remains. First, the practicality and cost of idiographic measures remains a major concern. Multiple baseline measurements are routinely taken in idiographic behavioral approaches, yet baselines may require
too much time to be applicable in low-resource settings such as community mental health centers. Continuous or frequent monitoring using idiographic measures may not be feasible in some settings or with some clients,
although sampling schedules may help to alleviate this issue. When appropriate, self-monitoring may also help alleviate the assessment burden on
clinicians and staff.

Examination of clients' (and therapists') use of language presents a potentially important venue for examining change at an idiographic level (Pennebaker et al., 2003). Software that allows storage and analysis of the therapeutic conversation, for example, offers the possibility of a low-cost but potentially practical and useful approach to natural language research and clinical application. Here research is just beginning, as narrative therapists have offered a wide range of constructs to consider for process and outcome assessment. Key categories that would appear important in many narratives include affect and lessons learned, although an idiographic approach would suggest that categories and topics may be largely unique for each individual client. A therapist's progress notes provide another potential source of key categories that might be created and evaluated through content analysis or grounded theory research. Research on word use in writing procedures designed to alleviate trauma suggests that a relatively common sequence exists in which individuals construct a narrative over time that leads to meaningful resolutions of the trauma as well as a decrease in negative affect.

Context Effects

As described in Chapters 6, 7, and this chapter, ample opportunities exist to investigate problems related to test context. Testing theorists should incorporate such concepts as contexts and situations into their models. One approach to investigating method variance, for example, would be to examine the effects of perceived situations and contexts on test-related behaviors. In social contexts in counseling agencies, for example, adolescents may initially view all adults, including therapists, as individuals to whom one should report only socially desirable behaviors (Meier & Schwartz, 2007). Stereotype threat is a similar example of social context influencing test behavior (Steele, 1998). The potential influence of test takers' social roles, perceptions, and norms on test-taking behavior have received relatively little research attention.

Researchers who plan to investigate testing's contextual effects may wish to examine the philosophy and methods of generalizability theory (GT). Recall from Chapter 2 that GT proposes that with any particular test, a universe of conditions exist that may affect test scores. The concept of reliability is replaced by generalizability, the ability to generalize a score from one testing context to others. GT recognizes that error is not always random; systematic error can be identified by examining variability of measurement data over conditions, called facets. GT suggests that multiple sources, including persons, content, occasions, and observers, can affect measurement devices; GT provides a theoretical and statistical framework for identifying and estimating the magnitude of those sources. Given this information, researchers can then compare the relative effects of different measurement conditions. By knowing the most important sources of measurement variability, test developers can design measurement devices and procedures to minimize undesired sources.

Innovative Research Methods

As a scientific field, psychology is one of the newest sciences, and in contexts such as a research university, must function and compete for legitimacy alongside older, more advanced domains such as physics and medicine. It makes sense that psychological researchers would create and adopt methods such as factor analysis or structural equation modeling that appear to make our field a modern, legitimate science. But here I make the heretical suggestion that advanced statistical methods, in and of themselves, have done little to produce new, substantive knowledge. Note that factor analysis has been employed for decades in investigations of the construct validity of intelligence and related tests, and yet the field has yet to reach a consensus about what constitutes intelligence.

What would help psychology make substantive knowledge gains? It may be that to go forward, we need to make use of older, seemingly more basic methods. Researchers should consider employing new or different methodologies when they investigate context and other testing-related effects. Researchers interested in qualitative approaches, for example, could make a significant contribution by investigating the potential effects of narratives on roles and norms that are linked to test-related behaviors. Cognitive pilot tests, deconstruction procedures, increased structure for interviews, and rater training all provide avenues for investigating influences on and potentially improving the psychometric properties of process and outcome scales. Small groups of researchers are now investigating item meaning or employing single subjects in cognitive pilot tests. In the laboratories of the early experimental psychologists, subjects were not naive observers, but members of the research team or others able to observe psychological phenomena in a methodical manner (Danziger, 1990). There were good reasons for this practice. Danziger (1990) reviewed research in psychophysics documenting the difficulty individuals experience when quantifying perception. Danziger (1990) cited Boring (1942), who wrote that "the meaning of the judgment two is indeterminate unless the criterion has been established" (p. 482). In 1946, Cronbach suggested training for subjects to overcome response sets. Acquiescent students, for example, could increase their test-wiseness by learning how many false-marked-true errors they make. Cronbach (1946) similarly believed that "it is relatively easy to teach mature students what is desired in essay examination responses" (p. 489). In contemporary psychophysiological measurement, respondents first complete an adaptation or training period to allow stabilization of physiological variables (Sallis & Lichstein, 1979). Behavior therapists who teach their clients to self-monitor may instruct clients to keep a small notebook with them at all times, record incidents immediately after they occur, and record only a single response at a time (Hayes & Nelson, 1986). In all of these cases, test takers are selected, receive training, or employ procedures that increase their ability to perform the required measurement tasks.

Similarly, seminal work in such areas as learning, sensation and perception, and cognitive development has been performed using repeated observation of single subjects. The history of psychological science contains many examples (e.g., Fechner, Wundt, Piaget, Ebbinghaus, Pavlov, and Skinner) in which investigators' work with one or a few subjects produced data sufficient for the start of important research programs or for practical applications. Such research, although time-consuming, can be phenomenon-close: That is, the investigator observes the phenomenon as it occurs. The phenomenon may be multiply determined and the observer may commit errors. Nevertheless, systematic, repeated observation of a single subject, in naturalistic and experimental settings, is often the simplest available method with which to study a phenomenon. The data provided by methods such as single-subject designs, qualitative research, and protocol analysis are likely to be of sufficient quality to permit more precise construct explications. In contrast, an investigator who begins a research program by creating and administering a test to large groups may ultimately possess little sense of how the phenomenon operates, particularly when interpreting test scores influenced by multiple, difficult-to-identify factors related to context.

Researchers and test developers in outcome assessment and related areas may need to back away from psychological testing's emphasis on advanced quantitative methods and restart efforts at a descriptive, qualitative, and discovery level (Persons, 1991). History again provides a lesson here. Huler (2004) provided an account of the circumstances of how Admiral Beaufort, in the 1700s, helped to create the first accurate wind scale. Beaufort's work to create a wind scale occurred at a stage where most scientific efforts focused on observation, description, organization, and classification. Working with previous wind scales, Beaufort improved them by creating a scale that assigned numbers to easily observed sailing phenomena (see Table 8.1). The number 1, for example, was assigned to a light wind speed that

TABLE 8.1. A Portion of Beaufort's Wind Scale

Beaufort no.	Name	Miles per hour	Description of effects
0	Calm	<1	Calm; smoke rises vertically
1	Light air	1–3	Direction of wind shown by smoke but not by wind vanes
2	Light breeze	4–7	Wind felt on face; leaves rustle; ordinary vane moved by wind
3	Gentle breeze	8–12	Leaves and small twigs in constant motion; wind extends light flag
4	Moderate breeze	13–18	Raises dust and loose paper; small branches are moved
5	Fresh breeze	19–24	Small trees in leaf begin to sway; crested wavelets form on inland waters

enabled a sailor to steer a man-of-war sailing ship. Huler's description of the status of wind measurement in the 1700s and 1800s sounds reminiscent of psychological testing's current status. At least 20 other wind scales were in use then, and making sense of the results from different scales often was problematic. As Huler (2004) stated, "Like the man with two watches who is less certain of the time than the man with none, observers faced with a profusion of scales could actually find themselves more confused about how to describe the wind than they had been before the scale came along in the first place" (p. 159).

Conclusion

Panek (1998) noted that the history of science indicates that scientific instruments bring with them a point of view that can prevent researchers from noticing new phenomena:

> Whenever we couldn't conceive of what's out there, whenever we couldn't even begin to guess, it wasn't only because we still lacked the technology, and it wasn't only because we still lacked the information, but it was because we didn't yet understand what the preconceptions might be that were restricting our view. (p. 75)

Much of this book has focused on demonstrating the limitations of the selection paradigm for other testing purposes. In addition, the research paradigm that has guided psychotherapy outcome research has demonstrated its limitations. As noted in Chapter 1, Paul's (1967) question about psychotherapy efficacy, with its emphasis on such independent variables as treatment type, client characteristics, and therapist characteristics, has begun to exhibit signs of outliving its usefulness. Research guided by this question has returned robust but nonspecific results. Instead, it may be time to turn our collective attention to the other side of the research equation, dependent variables. If we can begin to understand *what* changes in counseling and psychotherapy, for example, will that help us develop better hypotheses about *why* those changes occur?

Signs of innovation continue to appear. Researchers have provided explanations for how psychological phenomena can demonstrate both trait and state effects (e.g., Cone, 1991; Tryon, 1991), thus laying a plausible theoretical foundation for measuring state effects associated with psychological interventions. Several journals have taken the risk of publishing innovative assessment approaches. The *Journal of Clinical Psychology*, for example, published a series of studies in 2005 on clinical feedback. *Measurement and Evaluation in Counseling and Development* has published research on new outcome assessment methodology. A professional group that has taken on the daunting task of investigating clinical outcomes in field settings is the Research Consortium of Counseling and Psychological Services in Higher Education (*www.utexas.edu/student/cmhc/research/rescon.html*). The U.S. college and university counseling centers represented by the consortium have collected a set of process and outcome data since the project began in 1990 and have published a set of monographs (available at the website) describing initial results.

Significant improvements in the validity of all clinical measures should be the goal of testing professionals. Ultimately, it is researchers' responsibility to create and evaluate such measures and clinicians' responsibility to employ the resulting data as compassionately as possible to improve the lives of patients and clients.

General Measurement-Related Writing Assignment and Change-Related Writing Assignment

Examine all the information gathered to decide which operation would be best for your intended purpose and sample. More specifically, answer the following questions, where relevant:

1. Is there a relation between the definitions you have found and the content validity of the tests? Is there an element in the definitions that is not assessed by the tests?

2. Have any of the tests been employed for the purpose for which you intend to use it?
3. Have any of the tests been employed with similar samples of persons with whom you intend to use it? In other words, how closely do the characteristics of your intended sample match the samples of persons who have already completed the test(s)?
4. Does one ofthe tests have higher reliability estimates than the others?
5. Does one of the tests have higher convergent validity estimates?
6. If you were able to find one or more estimates of discriminant validity, do the convergent validity values exceed the discriminant validity values for your chosen test?
7. For selection tests, does one test have higher predictive validity estimates?
8. For change-sensitive tests, is there evidence that one test is more sensitive to change?
9. Based on your responses to questions 1–8, which test is the best measure for your intended use?

This process should result in a first draft of a term paper. Instructors: If sufficient time exists, read the first drafts and provide feedback for a second, final draft.

QUESTIONS AND EXERCISES

1. For 3 minutes, write down what you consider the major ideas of this section, chapter, or class. At the beginning of next week's class, share with the group.

2. List three areas for future clinical assessment research with a justification for the importance of each.

3. This chapter describes four major ideas relevant to professionals who develop and use psychological tests. Which of the four make the most sense to you? The least?

References

Abler, R. M., & Sedlacek, W. E. (1986). Nonreactive measures in student affairs research (Research Rep. No. 5-86). College Park, MD: University of Maryland.

Abramowitz, J. S. (2002). Treatment of obsessive thoughts and cognitive rituals using exposure and response prevention. *Clinical Case Studies, 1,* 6–24.

Achenbach, T. M. (1994). Child Behavior Checklist and related instruments. In M. E. Maruish (Ed.), *The use of psychological testing for treatment planning and outcome assessment* (pp. 517–549). Hillsdale, NJ: Erlbaum.

Achenbach, T. M. (2006). As others see us: Clinical and research implications of cross-informant correlations for psychopathology. *Current Directions in Psychological Science, 15,* 94–98.

Agras, W. S., & Apple, R. F. (1997). *Overcoming eating disorders: Therapist guide.* New York: Graywind.

Aiken, L. R. (1989). *Assessment of personality.* Boston: Allyn & Bacon.

Alexander, A. F. O'D. (1962). *The planet Saturn.* New York: Dover Publications.

Alloy, L. B., & Abramson, L. Y. (1979). Judgment of contingency in depressed and nondepressed students: Sadder but wiser? *Journal of Experimental Psychology: General, 108,* 441–485.

Allport, G. W. (1937). *Personality.* New York: Henry Holt.

American Educational Research Association, American Psychological Association, and National Council on Measurement in Education. (1999). *Standards for educational and psychological testing.* Washington, DC: American Educational Research Association.

American Psychiatric Association. (2000). *Diagnostic and statistical manual of mental disorders* (4th ed., text rev.). Washington, DC: Author.

American Psychological Association. (1954). Technical recommendations for psychological tests and diagnostic techniques. *Psychological Bulletin, 51*(Suppl. 2), Pt. 2.

American Psychological Association. (1985). *Standards for educational and psychological tests.* Washington, DC: Author.

American Psychological Association. (1992). Call for book proposals for test instruments. *APA Monitor, 23,* 15.

American Psychological Association. (1993). Record keeping guidelines. *American Psychologist, 48,* 984–986.

Anastasi, A. (1985). Some emerging trends in psychological measurement: A fifty-year perspective. *Applied Psychological Measurement, 9,* 121–138.

Anastasi, A. (1986). Evolving concepts of test validation. *Annual Review of Psychology, 37,* 1–15.

Anastasi, A. (1992). A century of psychological science. *American Psychologist, 47,* 842.

Anderson, R.V. (1987). Computerization of a chemical dependency assessment. *Minnesota Medicine, 70,* 697–699.

Anderson, T. (2004). "To tell my story": Configuring interpersonal relations within narrative process. In L. E. Angus & J. McLeod (Eds.), *Handbook of narrative and psychotherapy* (pp. 315–329). Thousand Oaks, CA: Sage.

Angleitner, A., John, O. P., & Lohr, F. (1986). It's what you ask and how you ask it: An itemmetric analysis of personality questionnaires. In A. Angleitner & J. S. Wiggins (Eds.), *Personality assessment via questionnaires* (pp. 61–108). New York: Springer-Verlag.

Angus, L. E., & McLeod, J. (Eds.). (2004). *Handbook of narrative and psychotherapy.* Thousand Oaks, CA: Sage.

Anisman, H., & Zacharko, R. M. (1992). Depression as a consequence of inadequate neurochemical adaptation in response to stressors. *British Journal of Psychiatry, 160,* 36–43.

Arisohn, B., Bruch, M. A., & Heimberg, R. G. (1988). Influence of assessment methods of self-efficacy and outcome expectancy ratings of assertive behavior. *Journal of Counseling Psychology, 35,* 336–341.

Babor, T. F., Brown, J., & Del Boca, F. K. (1990). Validity of self-reports in applied research on addictive behaviors: Fact or fiction? *Behavioral Assessment, 12,* 5–31.

Babor, T. F., Stephens, R. S., & Marlatt, G. A. (1987). Verbal report methods in clinical research on alcoholism: Response bias and its minimization. *Journal of Studies on Alcohol, 48,* 410–424.

Baer, R. A., & Miller, J. (2002). Underreporting of psychopathology on the MMPI-2: A meta-analytic review. *Psychological Assessment, 14,* 16–26.

Bagby, R. M., Atkinson, L., Dickens, S., & Gavin, D. (1990). Dimensional analysis of the Attributional Style Questionnaire: Attributions of outcomes and events. *Canadian Journal of Behavioural Science, 22,* 140–150.

Bailey, J. M., & Bhagat, R. S. (1987). Meaning and measurement of stressors in the work environment: An evaluation. In S.V. Kasl & C. L. Cooper (Eds.),

Stress and health: Issues in research methodology (pp. 207–230). New York: Wiley.

Baker, T. B., & Brandon, T. H. (1990). Validity of self-reports in basic research. *Behavioral Assessment, 12,* 33–51.

Bales, J. (1990). Validity of assessment debated in courtrooms. *APA Monitor, 21,* 7.

Bandler, R., & Grinder, J. (1975). *The structure of magic I.* Palo Alto, CA: Science and Behavior Books.

Bandura, A. (1977). Self-efficacy: Toward a unifying theory of behavioral change. *Psychological Review, 84,* 191–215.

Bandura, A. (1986). Social foundations of thought and action: A social cognitive theory. Englewood Cliffs, NJ: Prentice-Hall.

Bandura, A. (1991). Human agency: The rhetoric and the reality. *American Psychologist, 46,* 157–162.

Bandura, A. (1997). *Self-efficacy: The exercise of control.* New York: Freeman.

Barlow, D. H. (1977). Behavioral assessment in clinical settings: Developing issues. In J. D. Cone & R. P. Hawkins (Eds.), *Behavioral assessment* (pp. 283–307). New York: Brunner/Mazel.

Barlow, D. H. (1981). On the relation of clinical research to clinical practice: Current issues, new directions. *Journal of Consulting and Clinical Psychology, 49,* 147–155.

Barlow, D. H., Hayes, S. C., & Nelson, R. O. (1984). *The scientist practitioner.* New York: Pergamon Press.

Barrett, L. B. (2006). Solving the motion paradox: Categorization and the experience of emotion. *2006 Personality and Social Psychology Review, 10,* 20–46.

Barrett, T. C., & Tinsley, H. E. A. (1977). Measuring vocational self-concept crystallization. *Journal of Vocational Behavior, 11,* 305–311.

Barton, K. A., Blanchard, E. B., & Veazy, C. (1999). Self-monitoring as an assessment strategy in behavioral medicine. *Psychological Assessment, 11,* 490–497.

Bartoshuk, L. M. (2000). Comparing sensory experiences across individuals: Recent psychophysical advances illuminate genetic variation in taste perception. *Chemical Senses, 25,* 447–460.

Bartoshuk, L. M., Fast, K., & Snyder, D. J. (2005). Differences in our sensory worlds: Invalid comparisons with labeled scales. *Current Directions in Psychological Science, 14,* 122–125.

Battle, C. C., Imber, S. D., Hoehn-Saric, R., Stone, A. R., Nash, E. R., & Frank, J. D. (1966). Target complaints as criteria of improvement. *American Journal of Psychotherapy, 20,* 184–192.

Beaber, R. J., Marston, A., Michelli, J., & Mills, M. J. (1985). A brief test for measuring malingering in schizophrenic individuals. *American Journal of Psychiatry, 142,* 1478–1481.

Beck, A. T., & Steer, R. A. (1987). *Manual for the revised Beck Depression Inventory.* San Antonio, TX: Psychological Corporation.

Beilock, S. L., & Carr, T. H. (2005). When high-powered people fail: Working memory and "choking under pressure" in math. *Psychological Science, 16,* 101–105.

Beilock, S. L., & McConnell, A. R. (2004). Stereotype threat and sport: Can athletic performance be threatened? *Journal of Sport and Exercise Psychology, 26,* 597–609.

Bem, D. J., & Allen, A. (1974). On predicting some of the people some of the time: The search for cross-situational consistencies in behavior. *Psychological Review, 81,* 506–520.

Benjamin, L. S. (1988). *SASB Short Form user's manual.* Madison, WI: INTREX Interpersonal Institute.

Berger, M. (2006). Computer assisted clinical assessment. *Child and Adolescent Mental Health, 11,* 64–75.

Berk, L. A., & Fekken, G. C. (1990). Person reliability evaluated in the context of vocational interest assessment. *Journal of Vocational Behavior, 37,* 7–16.

Berman, P. (1997). *Case conceptualization and treatment planning.* Thousand Oaks, CA: Sage.

Bernard, J. M., & Goodyear, R. K. (1992). *Fundamentals of clinical supervision.* Boston: Allyn & Bacon.

Bernreuter, R. G. (1933). Validity of the personality inventory. *Personality Journal, 11,* 383–386.

Berry, D. T. R., Wetter, M. W., Baer, R. A., Larsen, L., Clark, C., & Monroe, K. (1992). MMPI-2 random responding indices: Validation using a self-report methodology. *Psychological Assessment, 4,* 340–345.

Beutler, L. E., & Hamblin, D. L. (1986). Individualized outcome measures of internal change: Methodological considerations. *Journal of Consulting and Clinical Psychology, 54,* 48–53.

Beutler, L. E., & Harwood, T. M. (2000). *Prescriptive psychotherapy: A practical guide to systematic treatment selection.* Oxford, UK: Oxford University Press.

Bickman, L., Rosof-Williams, J., Salzer, M., Summerfelt, W. T., Noser, K., Wilson, S. J., et al. (2000). What information do clinicians value for monitoring adolescent client progress and outcomes? *Professional Psychology: Research and Practice, 31,* 70–74.

Biemer, P. P., Groves, R. M., Lyberg, L. E., Mathiowetz, N. A., & Sudman, S. (1991). *Measurement errors in surveys.* New York: Wiley.

Bilodeau, E. A., & Bilodeau, I. (1961). Motor skills learning. *Annual Review of Psychology, 12,* 243–280.

Blaney, P. H. (1992). Not personality scales, personality items. In W. Grove & D. Cicchetti (Eds.), *Thinking clearly about psychology: Personality and psychopathology* (Vol. 2, pp. 54–71). Minneapolis: University of Minnesota Press.

Block, J. (1977). Advancing the psychology of personality: Paradigmatic shift or improving the quality of research. In D. Magnusson & N. S. Endler

(Eds.), *Personality at the crossroads: Current issues in interactional psychology* (pp. 37–64). Hillsdale, NJ: Erlbaum.

Block, J. (1995). A contrarian view of the five-factor approach to personality description. *Psychological Bulletin, 117,* 187–215.

Bloom, L. A., Hursh, D., Wienke, W. D., & Wolf, R. K. (1992). The effects of computer assisted data collection on students' behavior. *Behavioral Assessment, 14,* 173–190.

Bloom, M., & Fischer, J. (1982). *Evaluating practice: Guidelines for the accountable professional.* Englewood Cliffs, NJ: Prentice-Hall.

Boice, R. (1983). Observational skills. *Psychological Bulletin, 93,* 3–29.

Boothe, B., & Von Wyl, A. (2004). Story dramaturgy and personal conflict. In L. E. Angus & J. McLeod (Eds.), *Handbook of narrative and psychotherapy* (pp. 283–296). Thousand Oaks, CA: Sage.

Boring, E. G. (1942). *Sensation and perception in the history of experimental psychology.* New York: Appleton-Century-Crofts.

Boring, E. G. (1957). *A history of experimental psychology* (2nd ed.). New York: Appleton-Century-Crofts.

Botcheva, L., White, C. R., & Huffman, L. C. (2002). Learning culture and outcomes measurement practices in community agencies. *American Journal of Evaluation, 23,* 421–434.

Botwin, M. D., & Buss, D. M. (1989). Structure of act-report data: Is the five-factor model of personality recaptured? *Journal of Personality and Social Psychology, 56,* 988–1001.

Bowers, K. S. (1973). Situationism in psychology: An analysis and a critique. *Psychological Review, 80,* 307–336.

Bradburn, N. M., Rips, L. J., & Shevell, S. K. (1987). Answering autobiographical questions: The impact of memory and inference on surveys. *Science, 236,* 157–161.

Brennan, R. L. (2005). *Generalizability theory.* New York: Springer.

Bridge, R. G., Reeder, L. G., Kanouse, D., Kinder, D. R., Nagy, J. T., & Judd, C. M. (1977). Interviewing changes attitudes sometimes. *Public Opinion Quarterly, 41,* 56–64.

Briggs, S. R. (1992). Assessing the five-factor model of personality description. *Journal of Personality, 60,* 253–293.

Brody, G. H., & Forehand, R. (1986). Maternal perceptions of child maladjustment as a function of the combined influence of child behavior and maternal depression. *Journal of Consulting and Clinical Psychology, 54,* 237–240.

Brown, G. S., & Jones, E. R. (2005). Implementation of a feedback system in a managed care environment: What are patients teaching us? *Journal of Clinical Psychology, 61,* 187–198.

Brown, J. L., & Vanable, P. A. (2005, October). *Measurement of sexual behaviors: What computer assisted self-interviews have to offer HIV/AIDS risk assessments.* Paper presented at the 43rd annual Gardner Conference, Auburn, NY.

Brown, R. E., & Reed, C. S. (2002). An integral approach to evaluating outcome evaluation training. *American Journal of Evaluation, 23*, 1–17.

Bryson, B. (2003). *A short history of nearly everything.* New York: Broadway Books.

Burisch, M. (1984). Approaches to personality inventory construction. *American Psychologist, 39,* 214–227.

Burlingame, G. M., Lambert, M. J., Reisinger, C. W., Neff, W. M., & Mosier, J. (1995). Pragmatics of tracking mental health outcomes in a managed care setting. *Journal of Mental Health Administration, 22,* 226–236.

Buros, O. K. (Ed.). (1970). *Personality tests and reviews:* I. Highland Park, NJ: Gryphon.

Buss, D. M., & Craik, K. H. (1983). The act frequency approach to personality. *Personality Review, 90,* 105–126.

Buss, D. M., & Craik, K. H. (1985). Why not measure that trait? Alternative criteria for identifying important dispositions. *Journal of Personality and Social Psychology, 48,* 934–946.

Butcher, J. N. (1987). Computerized clinical and personality assessment using the MMPI. In J. N. Butcher (Ed.), *Computerized psychological assessment* (pp. 161–197). New York: Basic Books.

Butcher, J. N. (1990). *MMPI-2 in psychological treatment.* New York: Oxford University Press.

Campbell, D. P. (1971). Handbook for the Strong Vocational Interest Blank. Stanford, CA: Stanford University Press.

Campbell, D. T. (1950). The indirect assessment of social attitudes. *Psychological Bulletin, 47,* 15–38.

Campbell, D. T., & Fiske, D. W. (1959). Convergent and discriminant validity by the multitrait–multimethod matrix. *Psychological Bulletin, 56,* 81–105.

Campbell, R. S., & Pennebaker, J. W. (2003). The secret life of pronouns: Flexibility in writing style and physical health. *Psychological Science, 14,* 60–65.

Carver, C. S., & Scheier, M. F. (1981). The self-attention-induced feedback loop and social facilitation. *Journal of Experimental Social Psychology, 17,* 545–568.

Cash, T. F., Grant, J. R., Shovlin, J. M., & Lewis, R. J. (1992). Are inaccuracies in self-reported weight motivated distortions? *Perceptual and Motor Skills, 74,* 209–210.

Catania, J. A., Gibson, D. R., Chitwood, D. D., & Coates, T. J. (1990). Methodological problems in AIDS behavioral research: Influences on measurement error and participation bias in studies of sexual behavior. *Psychological Bulletin, 108,* 339–362.

Cattell, R. B. (1946). Confirmation and clarification of primary personality factors. *Psychometrika, 12,* 197–220.

Cattell, R. B., & Scheier, I. H. (1961). *The meaning and measurement of neuroticism.* New York: Ronald Press.

Ceci, S. J. (1991). How much does schooling influence intellectual development and its cognitive components?: A reassessment of the evidence. *Developmental Psychology, 27,* 703–722.

Chafetz, G. S., & Chafetz, M. E. (1994). *Obsession: The bizarre relationship between a prominent Harvard psychiatrist and her suicidal patient.* New York: Crown.

Chaplin, W. F., & Goldberg, L. R. (1984). A failure to replicate the Bem and Allen study of individual differences in cross-situational consistency. *Journal of Personality and Social Psychology, 47,* 1074–1090.

Cheek, J. M. (1982). Aggregation, moderator variables, and the validity of personality tests: A peer-rating study. *Journal of Personality and Social Psychology, 43,* 1254–1269.

Christensen, A., Margolin, G., & Sullaway, M. (1992). Interparental agreement on child behavior problems. *Psychological Assessment, 4,* 419–425.

Church, A. T., Katigbak, M. S., & Castaneda, I. (1988). The effects of language of data collection on derived conceptualizations of healthy personality with Filipino bilinguals. *Journal of Cross-cultural Psychology, 19,* 178–192.

Claiborn, C. D., & Goodyear, R. K. (2005). Feedback in therapy. *Journal of Clinical Psychology, 61,* 209–217.

Clement, P. W. (1994). Quantitative evaluation of 26 years of private practice. *Professional Psychology: Research and Practice, 25,* 173–176.

Clement, P. W. (1999). *Outcomes and incomes.* New York: Guilford Press.

Cohen, S., & Edwards, J. R. (1989). Personality characteristics as moderators of the relationship between stress and disorder. In R. W. J. Neufeld (Ed.), *Advances in the investigation of psychological stress* (pp. 235–283). New York: Wiley.

Collins, L. M. (1991). Measurement in longitudinal research. In L. M. Collins & J. L. Horn (Eds.), *Best methods for the analysis of change* (pp. 137–148). Washington, DC: American Psychological Association.

Cone, J. D. (1988). Psychometric considerations and the multiple models of behavioral assessment. In A. S. Bellack & M. Hersen (Eds.), *Behavioral assessment: A practical handbook* (3rd ed., pp. 42–66). Elmsford, NY: Pergamon Press.

Cone, J. D. (1991). Foreword. In W. W. Tryon, *Activity measurement in psychology and medicine.* New York: Plenum Press.

Cone, J. D. (1999). Introduction to the special section on self-monitoring: A major assessment method in clinical psychology. *Psychological Assessment, 11,* 411–414.

Cone, J. D., & Foster, S. L. (1991). Training in measurement: Always the bridesmaid. *American Psychologist, 46,* 653–654.

Connell, J. P., & Thompson, R. (1986). Emotion and social interaction in the strange situation: Consistencies and asymmetric influences in the second year. *Child Development, 57,* 733–745.

Conners, C. K. (1994). Conners Rating Scales. In M. E. Maruish (Ed.), *The use of psychological testing for treatment planning and outcome assessment* (pp. 550–578). Hillsdale, NJ: Erlbaum.

Contrada, R. J., & Krantz, D. S. (1987). Measurement bias in health psychology research designs. In S. V. Kasl & C. L. Cooper (Eds.), *Stress and health: Issues in research methodology* (pp. 57–78). New York: Wiley.

Conyne, R. K., & Clack, R. J. (1981). *Environmental assessment and design.* New York: Praeger.

Cook, T., & Campbell, D. (1979). *Quasi-experimentation.* Chicago: Rand Mc-Nally.

Coombs, C. H., Dawes, R. M., & Tversky, A. (1970). *Mathematical psychology.* Englewood Cliffs, NJ: Prentice-Hall.

Cooper, H. (1981). Ubiquitous halo. *Psychological Bulletin, 90,* 218–244.

Costello, C., & Comrey, A. (1967). Scales for measuring depression and anxiety. *Journal of Psychology, 66,* 303–313.

Craske, M. G., & Tsao, J. C. (1999). Self-monitoring with panic and anxiety disorders. *Psychological Assessment, 11,* 466–479.

Creswell, J. W. (2002). *Educational research.* Upper Saddle River, NJ: Merrill Prentice-Hall.

Crocker, L., & Algina, J. (1986). *Introduction to classical and modern test theory.* New York: Holt, Rinehart & Winston.

Cronbach, L. J. (1946). Response sets and test validity. *Educational and Psychological Measurement, 6,* 475–494.

Cronbach, L. J. (1949). *Essentials of psychological testing.* New York: Harper.

Cronbach, L. J. (1950). Further evidence on response sets and test design. *Educational and Psychological Measurement, 10,* 3–31.

Cronbach, L. J. (1957). The two disciplines of scientific psychology. *American Psychologist, 12,* 671–684.

Cronbach, L. J. (1970). *Essentials of psychological* testing (3rd ed.). New York: Harper & Row.

Cronbach, L. J. (1975a). Beyond the two disciplines of scientific psychology. *American Psychologist, 30,* 116–127.

Cronbach, L. J. (1975b). Five decades of public controversy over mental testing. *American Psychologist, 30,* 1–14.

Cronbach, L. J. (1984). *Essentials of psychological testing* (4th ed.). New York: Harper & Row.

Cronbach, L. J. (1989). Construct validation after thirty years. In R. L. Linn (Ed.), *Intelligence: Measurement, theory and public policy* (pp. 147–171). Urbana: University of Illinois Press.

Cronbach, L. J. (1991a). Methodological studies—a personal retrospective. In R. E. Snow & D. E. Wiley (Eds.), *Improving inquiry in social science* (pp. 385–400). Hillsdale, NJ: Erlbaum.

Cronbach, L. J. (1991b). Emerging views on methodology. In T. D. Wachs & R. Plomin (Eds.), *Conceptualization and measurement of organism-environment interaction* (pp. 87–104). Washington, DC: American Psychological Association.

Cronbach, L. J. (1992, August). Validation concepts and strategies. In W. J. Camara

(Chair), *One hundred years of psychological testing.* Symposium conducted at the convention of the American Psychological Association, Washington, DC.

Cronbach, L. J., Ambron, S. R., Dornbursch, S. M., Hess, R. D., Hornik, R. C., Phillips, D. C., et al. (1980). *Toward reform of program evaluation.* San Francisco: Jossey-Bass.

Cronbach, L. J., & Gleser, G. C. (1965). *Psychological tests and personnel decisions* (2nd ed.). Urbana: University of Illinois Press.

Cronbach, L. J., Gleser, G. C., Nanda, H., & Rajaratnam, N. (1972). *The dependability of behavioral measurements: Theory of generalizability for scores and profiles.* New York: Wiley.

Cronbach, L. J., & Meehl, P. E. (1955). Construct validity in psychological tests. *Psychological Bulletin, 52,* 281–302.

Cronbach, L. J., & Snow, R. E. (1977). *Aptitudes and instructional methods.* New York: Wiley.

Cross, K. P., & Angelo, T. A. (1988). *Classroom assessment techniques.* Ann Arbor, MI: National Center for Research to Improve Postsecondary Teaching and Learning.

Crowne, D., & Marlowe, D. (1964). *The approval motive.* New York: Wiley.

Cummings, N. A., O'Donohue, W. T., & Ferguson, K. E. (Eds.). (2002). *The impact of medical cost offset on practice and research: Making it work for you: A report of the first Reno Conference on Medical Cost Offset* (Rep. No. IX, pp. 145–165). Reno, NV: Context Press.

Cutrona, C. E., Russell, D., & Jones, R. (1984). Cross-situational consistency in causal attributions: Does attributional style exist? *Journal of Personality and Social Psychology, 47,* 1043–1058.

Cyr, J. J., McKenna-Foley, J. M., & Peacock, E. (1985). Factor structure of the SCL-90–R: Is there one? *Journal of Personality Assessment, 49,* 571–578.

Dahlstrom, W. G. (1969). Recurrent issues in the development of the MMPI. In J. Butcher (Ed.), *MMPI: Research developments and clinical applications* (pp. 1–40). New York: McGraw Hill.

Dahlstrom, W. G. (1985). The development of psychological testing. In G. A. Kimble & K. Schlesinger (Eds.), *Topics in the history of psychology* (Vol. 2, pp. 63–113). Hillsdale, NJ: Erlbaum.

Dahlstrom, W. G. (1993). Tests: Small samples, large consequences. *American Psychologist, 48,* 393–399.

Danziger, K. (1990). *Constructing the subject.* Cambridge, UK: Cambridge University Press.

Dar, R. (1987). Another look at Meehl, Lakatos, and the scientific practices of psychologists. *American Psychologist, 42,* 145–151.

Darley, J., & Fazio, R. (1980). Expectancy confirmation processes arising in the social interaction sequence. *American Psychologist, 35,* 867–881.

Davis, S. R., & Meier, S. T. (2001). *The elements of managed care.* Pacific Grove, CA: Brooks/Cole.

Dawis, R. V. (1987). Scale construction. *Journal of Counseling Psychology, 34,* 481–489.

Dawis, R. V. (1992). The individual differences tradition in counseling psychology. *Journal of Counseling Psychology, 39,* 7–19.

Dawis, R. V., & Lofquist, L. H. (1984). A psychological theory of work adjustment: An individual-differences model and its application. Minneapolis: University of Minnesota Press.

Dempsey, P. (1964). A unidimensional depression scale for the MMPI. *Journal of Consulting Psychology, 28,* 364–370.

Derogatis, L. R. (1983). *SCL-90–R: Administration, scoring, and procedural manual—II.* Baltimore: Clinical Psychometric Research.

DeWitt, K. N., Kaltreider, N. B., Weiss, D. S., & Horowitz, M. J. (1983). Judging change in psychotherapy: Reliability of clinical formulations. *Archives of General Psychiatry, 40,* 1121–1128.

Dickinson, T. L., & Baker, T. A. (1989, August). *Training to improve rating accuracy: A meta-analysis.* Paper presented at the annual convention of the American Psychological Association, New Orleans.

Diener, E., & Larsen, R. J. (1984). Temporal stability and cross-situational consistency of affective, behavioral, and cognitive responses. *Journal of Personality and Social Psychology, 47,* 871–883.

Digman, J. M. (1990). Personality structure: Emergence of the five-factor model. *Annual Review of Psychology, 41,* 417–440.

Dillman, D. A. (1978). *Mail and telephone surveys: The total design method.* New York: Wiley.

Dimaggio, G., & Semerari, A. (2004). Disorganized narratives. In L. E. Angus & J. McLeod (Eds.), *Handbook of narrative and psychotherapy* (pp. 263–282). Thousand Oaks, CA: Sage.

Dix, T. (1993). Attributing dispositions to children: An interactional analysis of attribution in socialization. *Personality and Social Psychology Bulletin, 19,* 633–643.

Doleys, D. M., Meredith, R. L., Poire, R., Campbell, L. M., & Cook, M. (1977). Preliminary examination of assessment of assertive behavior in retarded persons. *Psychological Reports, 41,* 855–859.

Domino, G. (1971). Interactive effects of achievement orientation and teaching style on academic achievement. *Journal of Educational Psychology, 62,* 427–431.

Drasgow, F., & Chuah, S. (2006). Computer-based testing. In M. Eid & E. Diener (Eds.), *Handbook of multimethod measurement in psychology* (pp. 87–100). Washington, DC: American Psychological Association.

Duff, F. L. (1965). Item subtlety in personality inventory scales. *Journal of Consulting Psychology, 29,* 565–570.

Dunning, D., Heath, C., & Suls, J. M. (2004). Flawed self-assessment. *Psychological Science in the Public Interest, 5,* 69–106.

Easterbrook, J. A. (1959). The effect of emotion on cue utilization and the organization of behavior. *Psychological Review, 3,* 183–201.

Eastman, C., & Marzillier, J. (1984). Theoretical and methodological difficulties in Bandura's self-efficacy theory. *Cognitive Therapy and Research, 8,* 213–229.

Edwards, A. (1953). The relationship between the judged desirability of a trait and the probability that the trait will be endorsed. *Journal of Consulting Psychology, 24,* 90–93.

Edwards, A. (1970). *The measurement of personality traits by scales and inventories.* New York: Holt, Rinehart and Winston.

Ekkekakis, P., Hall, E. E., & Petruzzello, S. J. (1999). Measuring state anxiety in the context of acute exercise using the State Anxiety Inventory: An attempt to resolve the brouhaha. *Journal of Sport and Exercise Psychology, 21,* 205–229.

Ellis, B. (1967). Measurement. In P. Edwards (Ed.), *Encyclopedia of philosophy* (Vol. 5, pp. 241–250). New York: Macmillan.

Ellis, M. V., & Blustein, D. L. (1991). The unificationist view: A context for validity. *Journal of Counseling and Development, 69,* 561–563.

Elwood, D. L. (1972a). Validity of an automated measure of intelligence in borderline retarded subjects. *American Journal of Mental Deficiency, 77,* 90–94.

Elwood, D. L. (1972b). Test retest reliability and cost analyses of automated and face to face intelligence testing. *International Journal of Man–Machine Studies, 4,* 1–22.

Elwood, D. L. (1972c). Automated versus face-to-face intelligence testing: Comparison of test–retest reliabilities. *International Journal of Man–Machine Studies, 4,* 363–369.

Elwood, D. L. (1972d). Automated WAIS testing correlated with face-to-face WAIS testing: A validity study. *International Journal of Man–Machine Studies, 4,* 129–137.

Endicott, J., & Spitzer, R. L. (1978). A diagnostic interview: The schedule for affective disorders and schizophrenia. *Archives of General Psychiatry, 35,* 837–844.

Endicott, J., Spitzer, R. L., Fleiss, J. L., & Cohen, J. (1976). The global assessment scale: A procedure for measuring overall severity of psychiatric disturbance. *Archives of General Psychiatry, 33,* 766–771.

Epstein, S. (1979). The stability of behavior: I. On predicting most of the people much of the time. *Journal of Personality and Social Psychology, 37,* 1097–1126.

Epstein, S. (1980). The stability of behavior: II. Implications for psychological research. *American Psychologist, 35,* 790–806.

Epstein, S. (1983). The stability of confusion: A reply to Mischel and Peake. *Psychological Review, 90,* 179–184.

Epstein, S. (1990). Comment on the effects of aggregation across and within occasions on consistency, specificity, and reliability. *Methodika, 4,* 95–100.

Erford, B. T. (2007). Basic assessment concepts. In B. T. Erford (Ed.), *Assessment for counselors* (pp. 1–43). Boston: Lahaska Press.

Estes, W. K. (1992). Ability testing. *Psychological Science, 3,* 278.

Exner, J. E., Jr. (1987). Computer assistance in Rorschach interpretation. In J. N. Butcher (Ed.), *Computerized psychological assessment* (pp. 218–235). New York: Basic Books.

Eyde, L. D., & Kowal, D. M. (1984). *Ethical and professional concerns regarding computerized test interpretation services and users.* Paper presented at the convention of the American Psychological Association, Toronto.

Fairbanks, C. M. (1992). Labels, literacy, and enabling learning: Glenn's story. *Harvard Educational Review, 62,* 475–493.

Falmagne, J. (1992). Measurement theory and the research psychologist. *Psychological Science, 3,* 88–93.

Fancher, R. E. (1966). Explicit personality theories and accuracy in person perception. *Journal of Personality, 34,* 252–261.

Fancher, R. E. (1967). Accuracy versus validity in person perception. *Journal of Consulting Psychology, 31,* 264–269.

Fancher, R. E. (1985). *The intelligence men: Makers of the IQ controversy.* New York: Norton.

Finn, J. D., Pannozzo, G. M., & Voelkl, K. E. (1995). Disruptive and inattentive–withdrawn behavior and achievement among fourth graders. *Elementary School Journal, 95,* 421–434.

Fisher, K. M., & Lipson, J. H. (1985). Information processing interpretation of errors in college science learning. *Instructional Science, 14,* 49–74.

Fiske, D. (1979). Two worlds of psychological phenomena. *American Psychologist, 34,* 733–740.

Fiske, D. W. (1987). Construct invalidity comes from method effects. *Educational and Psychological Measurement, 47,* 285–307.

Fiske, D. W., & Rice, L. (1955). Intra-individual response variability. *Psychological Bulletin, 52,* 217–250.

Fiske, S., & Taylor, S. (1984). *Social cognition.* New York: Random House.

Foa, E., & Kozak, M. (1986). Emotional processing of fear: Exposure to corrective information. *Psychological Bulletin, 99,* 20–35.

Foa, E., & Riggs, D. (1993). Post-traumatic stress disorder in rape victims. In J. Oldham, M. B. Riba, & A. Tasman (Eds.), *American Psychiatric Press review of psychiatry* (Vol. 12, pp. 273–303). Washington, DC: American Psychiatric Press.

Forbes, R. J., & Dijksterhuis, E. J. (1963). *A history of science and technology* (Vol. 1). Baltimore: Penguin Books.

Forzi, M. (1984). Generalizability and specificity of self-schemata. *Bollettino di Psicologia Applicata, 170,* 3–12 [Abstract].

Frederiksen, N. (1986). Toward a broader conception of human intelligence. *American Psychologist, 41,* 445–452.

Freeman, F. N. (1926). *Mental tests.* New York: Houghton Mifflin.

Freeman, F. S. (1955). *Theory and practice of psychological testing* (rev. ed.). New York: Henry Holt.

Fremer, J. (1992). High stakes testing and gate-keeper uses of assessment. In W. J. Camara (Chair), *One hundred years of psychological testing.* Symposium conducted at the convention of the American Psychological Association, Washington, DC.

Friedman, E. H., & Sanders, G. G. (1992). Speech timing of mood disorders. *Computers in Human Services, 8,* 121–142.

Froyd, J. E., Lambert, M. J., & Froyd, J. D. (1996). A review of practices of psychotherapy outcome measurement. *Journal of Mental Health, 5,* 11–15.

Fulton, R. T., Larson, A. D., & Worthy, R. C. (1983). The use of microcomputer technology in assessing and training communication skills of young hearing-impaired children. *American Annals of the Deaf, 128,* 570–576.

Funder, D. C., & Colvin, C. R. (1991). Explorations in behavioral consistency: Properties of persons, situations, and behaviors. *Journal of Personality and Social Psychology, 60,* 773–794.

Fuqua, D. R., Johnson, A. W., Newman, J. L., Anderson, M. W., & Gade, E. M. (1984). Variability across sources of performance ratings. *Journal of Counseling Psychology, 31,* 249–252.

Fuqua, D. R., Newman, J. L., Scott, T. B., & Gade, E. M. (1986). Variability across sources of performance ratings: Further evidence. *Journal of Counseling Psychology, 33,* 353–356.

Galassi, J. P., Frierson, H. T., Jr., & Sharer, R. (1981). Concurrent versus retrospective assessment in test anxiety research. *Journal of Consulting and Clinical Psychology, 49,* 614–615.

Garb, H. N. (1992). The trained psychologist as expert witness. *Clinical Psychology Review, 12,* 451–467.

Garb, H. N. (1998). Studying the clinician: Judgment research and psychological assessment. Washington, DC: American Psychological Association.

Geen, R. G. (1987). Test anxiety and behavioral avoidance. *Journal of Research in Personality, 21,* 481–488.

Gelso, C. J. (1979). Research in counseling: Methodological and professional issues. *Counseling Psychologist, 8,* 7–35.

Gentile, J. R. (1990). *Educational psychology.* Dubuque, IA: Kendall/Hunt.

Gerbert, B., Bronstone, A., Pantilat, S., McPhee, S., Allerton, M., & Moe, J. (1999). When asked, patients tell: Disclosure of sensitive health-risk behaviors. *Medical Care, 37,* 104–111.

Gibbs, D., Napp, D., Jolly, D., Westover, B., & Uhl, G. (2002). Increasing evaluation capacity within community-based HIV prevention programs. *Evaluation and Program Planning, 25,* 216–269.

Gleser, G. C., Green, B. L., & Winget, C. N. (1978). Quantifying interview data on psychic impairment of disaster survivors. *Journal of Nervous and Mental Diseases, 166,* 209–216.

Goldberg, L. R. (1990). An alternative "description of personality": The Big-Five factor structure. *Journal of Personality and Social Psychology, 59,* 1216–1229.

Goldberg, L. R. (1993). The structure of phenotypic personality traits. *American Psychologist, 48,* 26–34.

Golden, C. J., Sawicki, R. F., & Franzen, M. D. (1984). Test construction. In G. Goldstein & M. Hersen (Eds.), *Handbook of psychological assessment* (2nd ed., pp. 21–40). New York: Pergamon Press.

Golding, S. L. (1975). Flies in the ointment: Methodological problems in the analysis of the percentage of variance due to persons and situations. *Psychological Bulletin, 82,* 278–288.

Goldstein, G., & Hersen, M. (1990). Historical perspectives. In G. Goldstein & M. Hersen (Eds.), *Handbook of psychological assessment* (2nd ed., pp. 3–17). New York: Pergamon Press.

Golembiewski, R. T., Billingsley, K., & Yeager, S. (1976). Measuring change and persistence in human affairs: Types of change generated by OD designs. *Journal of Applied Behavioral Science, 12,* 133–157.

Goodenough, F. L. (1950). *Mental testing.* New York: Rinehart.

Goodstein, L. (1978). *Consulting with human service systems.* Reading, MA: Addison-Wesley.

Gottman, J. M., & Leiblum, S. R. (1974). *How to do psychotherapy and how to evaluate it.* New York: Holt, Rinehart and Winston.

Gould, S. J. (1981). *The mismeasure of man.* Norton: New York.

Gracely, R. H., & Kwilosz, D. M. (1988). The Descriptor Differential Scale: Applying psychophysical principles to clinical pain assessment. *Pain, 35,* 279–288.

Gracely, R. H., & Naliboff, B. D. (1996). Measurement of pain sensation. In L. Kruger (Ed.), *Pain and touch* (pp. 243–313). San Diego: Academic Press.

Graham, J. R. (1990). *MMPI-2: Assessing personality and psychopathology.* New York: Oxford University Press.

Gray, G. V., & Lambert, M. J. (2001). Feedback: A key to improving therapy outcomes. *Behavioral Healthcare Tomorrow, 10,* 25–45.

Greaner, J. L., & Penner, L. A. (1982). The reliability and validity of Bem and Allen's measure of cross-situational consistency. *Social Behavior and Personality, 10,* 241–244.

Greenberg, L. S., & Angus, L. E. (2004). The contributions of emotion processes to narrative chance in psychotherapy: A dialectical constructivist approach. In L. E. Angus & J. McLeod (Eds.), *Handbook of narrative and psychotherapy* (pp. 331–364). Thousand Oaks, CA: Sage.

Gregory, R. J. (1992). *Psychological testing.* Boston: Allyn & Bacon.

Gresham, F. M., & Elliott, S. N. (1990). *Social skills rating system manual.* Circle Pines, MN: American Guidance Service.

Grice, P. (1991). *Studies in the way of words.* Cambridge, MA: Harvard University Press.

Gronlund, N. E. (1985). *Measurement and evaluation in teaching* (5th ed.). New York: Macmillan.

Gronlund, N. E. (1988). *How to construct achievement tests* (4th ed.). Englewood Cliffs, NJ: Prentice-Hall.

Groth-Marnat, G. (1990). *Handbook of psychological assessment* (2nd ed.). New York: Wiley.

Guastello, S. J., & Rieke, M. L. (1990). The Barnum effect and validity of computer-based test interpretations: The Human Resource Development Report. *Psychological Assessment, 2,* 186–190.

Guilford, J. P. (1946). New standards for test evaluation. *Educational and Psychological Measurement, 6,* 427–439.

Guilford, J. P. (1967). *The nature of human intelligence.* New York: McGraw-Hill.

Guion, R. M. (1976). Recruiting, selection, and job placement. In M. D. Dunnette (Ed.), *Handbook of industrial and organizational psychology* (pp. 777–828). Chicago: Rand McNally.

Gulliksen, H. (1950). Intrinsic validity. *American Psychologist, 5,* 511–517.

Guskey, T. R., & Passaro, P. D. (1994). Teacher efficacy: A study of construct dimensions. *American Educational Research Journal, 31,* 627–643.

Guyatt, G., Walter, S., & Norman, G. (1987). Measuring change over time: Assessing the usefulness of evaluative instruments. *Journal of Chronic Disease, 40,* 171–178.

Gynther, M. D., & Green, S. B. (1982). Methodological problems in research with self-report inventories. In P. C. Kendall & J. N. Butcher (Eds.), *Handbook of research methods in clinical psychology* (pp. 355–386). New York: Wiley.

Halmi, K. A., Sunday, S., Puglisi, A., & Marchi, P. (1989). Hunger and satiety in anorexia and bulimia nervosa. In L. H. Schneider, S. J. Cooper, & K. A. Halmi (Eds.), *The psychobiology of human eating disorders: Preclinical and clinical perspectives* (pp. 431–445). New York: New York Academy of Sciences.

Hambleton, R. K., Swaminathan, H., & Rogers, H. J. (1991). *Fundamentals of item response theory.* Newbury Park, CA: Sage.

Hannan, C., Lambert, M. J., Harmon, C., Nielsen, S. L., Smart, D. W., Shimokawa, K., et al. (2005). A lab test and algorithms for identifying clients at risk for treatment failure. *Journal of Clinical Psychology, 61,* 155–163.

Hansen, J. C. (1987). Computer-assisted interpretation of the Strong Interest Inventory. In J. N. Butcher (Ed.), *Computerized psychological assessment* (pp. 292–324). New York: Basic Books.

Hardtke, K. K., & Angus, L. E. (2004). The Narrative Assessment Interview. In L. E. Angus & J. McLeod (Eds.), *Handbook of narrative and psychotherapy* (pp. 247–262). Thousand Oaks, CA: Sage.

Harmon, C., Hawkins, E. J., Lambert, M. J., Slade, K., & Whipple, J. L. (2005). Improving outcomes for poorly responding clients: The use of clinical support tools and feedback to clients. *Journal of Clinical Psychology, 61,* 175–185.

Harp, S. F., & Mayer, R. E. (1998). How seductive details do their damage: A theory of cognitive interest in science learning. *Journal of Educational Psychology, 90,* 414–434.

Harrell, T. H., Honaker, L. M., Hetu, M., & Oberwager, J. (1987). Computerized versus traditional administration of the Multidimensional Aptitude Battery—Verbal Scale: An examination of reliability and validity. *Computers in Human Behavior, 3,* 129–137.

Harrell, T. H., & Lombardo, T. A. (1984). Validation of an automated 16PF administrative procedure. *Journal of Personality Assessment, 48,* 638–642.

Harris, T. O. (1991). Life stress and illness: The question of specificity. *Annals of Behavioral Medicine, 13,* 211–219.

Hartman, D. P. (1984). Assessment strategies. In D. H. Barlow & M. Hersen (Eds.), *Single case experimental designs* (pp. 107–139). New York: Pergamon Press.

Hathaway, S. (1972). Where have we gone wrong? The mystery of the missing progress. In J. N. Butcher (Ed.), *Objective personality assessment* (pp. 24–44). New York: Academic Press.

Haverkamp, B. E. (1993). Confirmatory bias in hypothesis testing for client-identified and counselor self-generated hypotheses. *Journal of Counseling Psychology, 40,* 305–315.

Hayes, S. C., & Cavior, N. (1977). Multiple tracking and the reactivity of self-monitoring: I. Negative behaviors. *Behavior Therapy, 8,* 819–831.

Hayes, S. C., & Cavior, N. (1980). Multiple tracking and the reactivity of self-monitoring: II. Positive behaviors. *Behavioral Assessment, 2,* 283–296.

Hayes, S. C., & Nelson, R. O. (1986). Assessing the effects of therapeutic interventions. In R. O. Nelson & S. C. Hayes (Eds.), *Conceptual foundations of behavioral assessment* (pp. 430–460). New York: Guilford Press.

Haymaker, J. C., & Erwin, F. W. (1980). *Investigation of applicant responses and falsification detection procedures for the Military Applicant Profile* (Final Project Report, Work Unit No. DA644520). Alexandria, VA: U.S. Army Research Institute for the Behavioral and Social Sciences.

Haynes, S. N. (1993). Treatment implications of psychological assessment. *Psychological Assessment, 5,* 251–253.

Haynes, S. N. (2001). Clinical applications of analogue behavioral observation: Dimensions of psychometric evaluation. *Psychological Assessment, 13,* 73–85.

Haynes, S. N., Spain, E. H., & Oliveira, J. (1993). Identifying causal relationships in clinical assessment. *Psychological Assessment, 5,* 281–291.

Hazlett-Stevens, H., Ullman, J. B., & Craske, M. G. (2004). Factor structure of the Penn State Worry Questionnaire. *Assessment, 11,* 361–370.

Hedges, L. (1987). The meta-analysis of test validity studies: Some new approaches. In H. Wainer & H. Braun (Eds.), *Test validity for the 1990's and beyond* (pp. 191–212). Hillsdale, NJ: Erlbaum.

Heidbreder, E. (1933). *Seven psychologies.* Englewood Cliffs, NJ: Prentice-Hall.

Helfrich, H. (1986). On linguistic variables influencing the understanding of questionnaire items. In A. Angleitner & J. S. Wiggins (Eds.), *Personality assessment via questionnaires* (pp. 178–190). New York: Springer-Verlag.

Helms, J. E. (1992). Why is there no study of cultural equivalence in standardized cognitive ability testing? *American Psychologist, 47,* 1083–1101.

Helzer, J. E. (1983). Standardized interviews in psychiatry. *Psychiatric Developments, 2,* 161–178.

Hembree, R. (1988). Correlates, causes, effects, and treatment of test anxiety. *Review of Educational Research, 5,* 47–77.

Heppner, P. P., Kivlighan, D. M., & Wampold, B. E. (1992). *Research design in counseling.* Pacific Grove, CA: Brooks/Cole.

Heppner, P. P., Kivlighan, D. M., & Wampold, B. E. (1999). *Research design in counseling* (2nd ed.). Pacific Grove, CA: Brooks/Cole.

Herman, K. C. (1993). Reassessing predictors of therapist competence. *Journal of Counseling and Development, 72,* 29–32.

Hill, C. E. (1982). Counseling process researcher: Philosophical and methodological dilemmas. *Counseling Psychologist, 10,* 7–20.

Hill, C. E. (1991). Almost everything you ever wanted to know about how to do process research on counseling and psychotherapy but didn't know who to ask. In C. Watkins & L. Schneider (Eds.), *Research in counseling* (pp. 85–118). Hillsdale, NJ: Erlbaum.

Hill, C. E., & Lambert, M. J. (2004). Methodological issues in studying psychotherapy processes and outcomes. In M. J. Lambert (Ed.), *Bergin and Garfield's handbook of psychotherapy and behavior change* (5th ed., pp. 84–135). New York: Wiley.

Hoffman, B., & Meier, S. T. (2001). An individualized approach to managed mental health care in colleges and universities: A case study. *Journal of College Student Psychotherapy, 15,* 49–64.

Hogan, R., & Nicholson, R. A. (1988). The meaning of personality test scores. *American Psychologist, 43,* 621–626.

Holden, R. R. (1989). Disguise and the structured self-report assessment of psychopathology: II. A clinical replication. *Journal of Clinical Psychology, 45,* 583–586.

Holden, R. R., & Jackson, D. N. (1979). Item subtlety and face validity in personality assessment. *Journal of Consulting and Clinical Psychology, 47,* 459–468.

Holland, J. L. (1959). A theory of vocational choice. *Journal of Counseling Psychology, 6,* 35–45.

Holland, J. L. (1985). *Making vocational choices: A theory of vocational personalities and work environments* (2nd ed.). Englewood Cliffs, NJ: Prentice-Hall.

Holloway, E. L. (1995). *Clinical supervision: A systems approach.* Thousand Oaks, CA: Sage.

Honaker, L. M. (1988). The equivalency of computerized and conventional

MMPI administration: A critical review. *Clinical Psychology Review, 8,* 561–577.

Horvath, A. O., & Greenberg, L. S. (1989). Development and validation of the Working Alliance Inventory. *Journal of Counseling Psychology, 36,* 223–233.

Hoshmand, L. L. S. (1994). *Orientation to inquiry in a reflective professional psychology.* Albany, NY: SUNY Press.

Hough, L. A., Eaton, N. K., Dunnette, M. D., Kamp, J. D., & McCloy, R. A. (1990). Criterion-related validities of personality constructs and the effect of response distortion on those validities. *Journal of Applied Psychology, 75,* 581–595.

Howard, K. I., Moras, K., Brill, P. C., Martinovich, Z., & Lutz, W. (1996). Evaluation of psychotherapy: Efficacy, effectiveness, and patient progress. *American Psychologist, 51,* 1059–1064.

Hser, Y.-I., Anglin, M. D., & Chou, C.-P. (1992). Reliability of retrospective self-report by narcotics addicts. *Psychological Assessment, 4,* 207–213.

Huebner, L. (1979). Redesigning campus environments. In U. Delworth & G. Hanson (Eds.), *New directions for student services* (pp. 1–22). San Francisco: Jossey-Bass.

Huler, S. (2004). *Defining the wind.* New York: Crown.

Humphreys, L. G. (1992). Commentary: What both critics and users of ability tests need to know. *Psychological Science, 3,* 271–274.

Hunter, J. E., & Hunter, R. F. (1984). The validity and utility of alternative predictors of job performance. *Psychological Bulletin, 96,* 72–98.

Jackson, D. N. (1970). A sequential system for personality scale development. In C. Spielberger (Ed.), *Current topics in clinical and community psychology* (Vol. 2, pp. 61–96). New York: Academic Press.

Jackson, D. N. (1971). The dynamics of structured personality tests. *Psychological Review, 78,* 229–248.

Jackson, D. N. (1975). Multimethod factor analysis: A reformulation. *Multivariate Behavioral Research, 10,* 259–275.

Jackson, D. N. (1992). One hundred years of personality and intelligence testing. In W. J. Camara (Chair), *One hundred years of psychological testing.* Symposium conducted at the convention of the American Psychological Association, Washington, DC.

Jackson, D. N., & Messick, S. (1969). A distinction between judgments of frequency and of desirability as determinants of response. *Educational and Psychological Measurement, 29,* 273–293.

Jackson, J. L. (1999). Psychometric considerations in self-monitoring assessment. *Psychological Assessment, 11,* 439–447.

Jenkins, H. M., & Ward, W. C. (1965). Judgment of contingency between responses and outcomes. *Psychological Monographs: General and Applied, 79,* 17.

Jennings, T. E., Lucenko, B. A., Malow, R. M., & Devieux, J. G. (2002). Audio-CASI vs. interview method of administration of an HIV/STD risk of exposure screening instrument for teenagers. *International Journal of STD and AIDS, 13,* 781–784.

Jessor, R., & Hammond, K. R. (1957). Construct validity and the Taylor Anxiety Scale. *Psychology Bulletin, 54,* 161–170.

John, O. P., Angleitner, A., & Ostendorf, F. (1988). The lexical approach to personality: A historical review of trait taxonomic research. *European Journal of Personality, 2,* 171–205.

Johnson, A. M., Copas, A. J., Erens, B., Mandalia, S., Fenton, K., Korovessis, C., et al. (2001). Effect of computer-assisted self-interviews on reporting of sexual HIV risk behaviours in a general population sample: A methodological experiment. *AIDS, 15,* 111–115.

Johnson, C. W., Hickson, J. F., Fetter, W. J., & Reichenbach, D. R. (1987). Microcomputer as teacher/researcher in a nontraditional setting. *Computers in Human Behavior, 3,* 61–70.

Johnson, T. P., Jobe, J. B., O'Rourke, D., Sudman, S., Warnecke, R. B., Chavez, N., et al. (1997). Dimensions of self-identification among multicultural and multiethnic respondents in survey interviews. *Evaluation Review, 21,* 671–687.

Jones, E. E., & Nisbett, R. E. (1971). The actor and the observer: Divergent perceptions of the causes of behavior. In E. E. Jones, D. E. Kanouse, H. H. Kelly, R. E. Nisbett, S. Valins, & B. Weiner (Eds.), *Attribution* (pp. 79–94). Morristown, NJ: General Learning Press.

Jones, E. E., Rock, L., Shaver, K. G., Goethals, G. R., & Ward, L. M. (1968). Pattern of performance and ability attribution: An unexpected primacy effect. *Journal of Personality and Social Psychology, 10,* 317–340.

Joreskog, K. G. (1974). Analyzing psychological data by structural analysis of covariance matrices. In R. C. Atkinson, D. H. Krantz, R. D. Luce, & P. Suppes (Eds.), *Contemporary developments in mathematical psychology* (Vol. 2, pp. 1–56). San Francisco: Freeman.

Judge, T. A., Higgins, C. A., & Cable, D. M. (2000). The employment interview: A review of recent research and recommendations for future research. *Human Resource Management Review, 10,* 383–406.

Judson, H. F. (1980). *The search for solutions.* New York: Holt, Rinehart and Winston.

Kagan, J. (1988). The meanings of personality predicates. *American Psychologist, 43,* 614–620.

Kahn, J. S., & Meier, S. T. (2001). Children's definitions of family power and cohesion affect scores on the Family System Test. *American Journal of Family Therapy, 2,* 141–155.

Kahn, J. S., Meier, S. T., Steinberg, B., & Sackett, R. (2000). *The effects of global versus specific language on the Outcome Questionnaire (OQ-45).* Unpublished manuscript, University at Buffalo, NY.

Kantor, J. R. (1924). *Principles of psychology* (Vol. 1). Bloomington, IN: Principia Press.

Kaplan, A. (1964). *The conduct of inquiry.* San Francisco: Chandler.

Karcher, M. J., & Finn, L. (2005). How connectedness contributes to experimental smoking among rural youth: Developmental and ecological analyses. *Journal of Primary Prevention, 26,* 25–36.

Karson, S., & O'Dell, J. W. (1987). Computer-based interpretation of the 16PF: The Karson Clinical Report in contemporary practice. In J. N. Butcher (Ed.), *Computerized psychological assessment* (pp. 198–217). New York: Basic Books.

Katz, I. (1964). Review of evidence relating to effects of desegregation on the intellectual performance of Negroes. *American Psychologist, 19,* 381–399.

Kazdin, A. E. (1974). Self-monitoring and behavior change. In M. J. Mahoney & C. E. Thorsen (Eds.), *Self-control: Power to the person* (pp. 218–246). Monterey, CA: Brooks-Cole.

Kazdin, A. E. (1980). *Research design in clinical psychology.* New York: Harper & Row.

Kazdin, A. E. (1985). Selection of target behaviors: The relationship of the treatment focus to clinical dysfunction. *Behavioral Assessment, 7,* 33–48.

Kazdin, A. E. (1988). *Child psychotherapy: Developing and identifying effective treatments.* New York: Pergamon Press.

Kazdin, A. E. (1994). Psychotherapy for children and adolescents. In A. E. Bergin & S. L. Garfield (Eds.), *Handbook of psychotherapy and behavior change* (4th ed., pp. 543–594). New York: Wiley.

Kazdin, A. E. (2000). *Psychotherapy for children and adolescents: Directions for research and practice.* New York: Oxford University Press.

Kelly, M. A. R., Roberts, J. E., & Ciesla, J. A. (2005). Sudden gains in cognitive behavioral treatment for depression: When do they occur and do they matter? *Behavior Research and Therapy, 43,* 703–714.

Kendall, P. C., Hollon, S. D., Beck, A. T., Hammen, C. L., & Ingram, R. E. (1987). Issues and recommendations regarding use of the Beck Depression Inventory. *Cognitive Therapy and Research, 3,* 289–299.

Kendall, P. C., Kipnis, D., & Otto-Salaj, L. (1992). When clients don't progress: Influences on and explanations of therapeutic progress. *Cognitive Therapy and Research, 16,* 269–281.

Kenny, D. A., & Kashy, D. A. (1992). Analysis of the multitrait–multimethod matrix by confirmatory factor analysis. *Psychological Bulletin, 112,* 165–172.

Kern, J. M. (1991). An evaluation of a novel role-play methodology: The standardized idiographic approach. *Behavior Therapy, 22,* 13–29.

Kiresuk, T., Choate, R. O., Cardillo, J. E., & Larsen, N. (1994). Training in goal attainment scaling. In T. J. Kiresuk, A. Smith, & J. E. Cardillo (Eds.), Goal attainment scaling: Applications, theory, and measurement (pp. 105–118). Hillsdale, NJ: Erlbaum.

Kiresuk, T. J., Smith, A., & Cardillo, J. E. (Eds.). (1994). *Goal attainment scaling: Applications, theory, and measurement.* Hillsdale, NJ: Erlbaum.

Kleinmuntz, B. (1967). *Personality measurement: An introduction.* Homewood, IL: Dorsey.

Kline, P. (1998). *The new psychometrics.* London: Routledge.

Kluger, A. N., & DeNisi, A. (1996). The effects of feedback interventions on performance: A historical review, a meta-analysis, and a preliminary feedback intervention theory. *Psychological Bulletin, 119,* 254–284.

Kluger, A. N., & DeNisi, A. (1999). Feedback interventions: Toward the understanding of a double-edged sword. *Current Directions in Psychological Science, 7,* 67–72.

Kopta, S. M., Howard, K. I., Lowry, J. L., & Beutler, L. E. (1994). Patterns of symptomatic recovery in psychotherapy. *Journal of Consulting and Clinical Psychology, 62,* 1009–1016.

Korotitsch, W. J., & Nelson-Gray, R. O. (1999). An overview of self-monitoring research in assessment and treatment. *Psychological Assessment, 11,* 415–425.

Krantz, D. H., Luce, R. D., Suppes, P., & Tversky, A. (1971). *Foundations of measurement: Vol. I. Additive and polynomial representations.* New York: Academic Press.

Kraut, R. E., & McConahay, J. B. (1973). How being interviewed affects voting: An experiment. *Public Opinion Quarterly, 36,* 398–406.

Krech, D., & Crutchfield, R. (1948). *Theory and problems in social psychology.* New York: McGraw-Hill.

Kuhn, T. S. (1970). *The structure of scientific revolutions.* Chicago: University of Chicago Press.

Kuncel, R. B. (1973). Response processes and relative location of subject and item. *Educational and Psychological Measurement, 33,* 545–563.

Kurth, A. E., Martin, D. P., Golden, M. R., Weiss, N. S., Heagerty, P. J., Spielberg, F., et al. (2004). A comparison between audio computer-assisted self-interviews and clinician interviews for obtaining the sexual history. *Sexually Transmitted Diseases, 31,* 719–726.

Lambert, M. J. (1994). Use of psychological tests for outcome assessment. In M. E. Maruish (Ed.), *The use of psychological testing for treatment planning and outcome assessment* (pp. 75–97). Hillsdale, NJ: Erlbaum.

Lambert, M. J. (1998). Manual-based treatment and clinical practice: Hangman of life or promising development? *Clinical Psychology-Science & Practice, 5,* 391–395.

Lambert, M. J., & Finch, A. E. (1999). The Outcome Questionnaire. In M. G. Maruish (Ed.), *The use of psychological testing for treatment planning and outcomes assessment* (2nd ed., pp. 831–869). Hillsdale, NJ: Erlbaum.

Lambert, M. J., Garfield, S. L., & Bergin, A. E. (2004). Overview, trends, and future issues. In M. J. Lambert (Ed.), *Bergin and Garfield's handbook of psychotherapy and behavior change* (5th ed., pp. 805–821). New York: Wiley.

Lambert, M. J., Harmon, C., Slade, K., Whipple, J. L., & Hawkins, E. J. (2005).

Providing feedback to psychotherapists on their patients' progress: Clinical results and practice suggestions. *Journal of Clinical Psychology, 61,* 165–174.

Lambert, M. J., Hatch, D. R., Kingston, M. D., & Edwards, B. C. (1986). Zung, Beck, and Hamilton Rating Scales as measures of treatment outcome: A meta-analytic comparison. *Journal of Consulting and Clinical Psychology, 54,* 54–59.

Lambert, M. J., & Hill, C. E. (1994). Assessing psychotherapy outcomes and processes. In A. E. Bergin & S. L. Garfield (Eds.), *Handbook of psychotherapy and behavior change* (4th ed., pp. 72–13). New York: Wiley.

Lambert, M. J., & Lambert, J. M. (2004). Use of psychological tests for assessing treatment outcome. In M. E. Maruish (Ed.), *The use of psychological testing for treatment planning and outcome assessment* (pp. 115–151). Hillsdale, NJ: Erlbaum.

Lambert, M. J., Whipple, J. L., Smart, D. W., Vermeesch, D. A., Nielsen, S. L., & Hawkins, E. J. (2001). The effects of providing therapists with feedback on patient progress during psychotherapy: Are outcomes enhanced? *Psychotherapy Research, 11,* 49–68.

Lambert, N. M. (1991). The crisis in measurement literacy in psychology and education. *Educational Psychologist, 26,* 23–35.

Lamiell, J. T. (1990). Explanation in the psychology of personality. *Annals of Theoretical Psychology, 6,* 153–192.

Landy, F. J. (1986). Stamp collecting versus science: Validation as hypothesis testing. *American Psychologist, 41,* 1183–1192.

Lang, P. J. (1968). Fear reduction and fear behaviour: Problems in treating a construct. In J. M. Shlien (Ed.), *Research in psychotherapy* (Vol. 3, pp. 90–102). Washington, DC: American Psychological Association.

Lanning, K. (1988). Individual differences in scalability: An alternative conception of consistency for personality theory and measurement. *Journal of Personality and Social Psychology, 55,* 142–148.

Larson, L. M., Suzuki, L. A., Gillespie, K. N., Potenza, M. T., Bechtel, M. A., & Toulouse, A. L. (1992). Development and validation of the Counseling Self-Estimate Inventory. *Journal of Counseling Psychology, 39,* 105–120.

Lautenschlager, G. J., & Atwater, D. C. (1986). *Controlling response distortion on an empirically keyed biodata questionnaire.* Unpublished manuscript.

Lee, C. (1984). Accuracy of efficacy and outcome expectations in predicting performance in a simulated assertiveness task. *Cognitive Therapy and Research, 8,* 37–48.

Leeson, H. V. (2006). The mode effect: A literature review of human and technological issues in computerized testing. *International Journal of Testing, 6,* 1–24.

Levitt, H. M., & Rennie, D. L. (2004). Narrative activity. In L. E. Angus & J. McLeod (Eds.), *Handbook of narrative and psychotherapy* (pp. 299–313). Thousand Oaks, CA: Sage.

Lewin, K. (1935). *A dynamic theory of personality.* New York: McGraw-Hill.

Lewin, K. (1951). *Field theory in social science: Selected theoretical papers.* New York: Harper.

Lewis, J. D., & Magoon, T. M. (1987). Survey of college counseling centers' follow-up practices with former clients. *Professional Psychology: Research and Practice, 18,* 128–133.

Lichstein, E. (1970). Techniques for assessing outcomes of psychotherapy. In P. McReynolds (Ed.), *Advances in psychological assessment* (Vol. 2, pp. 178–197). Palo Alto, CA: Science and Behavior Books.

Licht, M. H., Paul, G. L., & Power, C. T. (1986). Standardized direct-multivariate DOC systems for service and research. In G. L. Paul (Ed.), *Assessment in residential treatment settings* (pp. 223–266). Champaign, IL: Research Press.

Lipsey, M. (1990). *Design sensitivity.* Newbury Park, CA: Sage.

Lipsey, M. (1998). Design sensitivity: Statistical power for applied experimental research. In L. Bickman and D. J. Rog (Eds.), *Handbook of applied social research methods* (pp. 39–68). Thousand Oaks, CA: Sage.

Lipsey, M. W. (1983). A scheme for assessing measurement sensitivity in program evaluation and other applied research. *Psychological Bulletin, 94,* 152–165.

Lockhead, G. R. (1992). Psychophysical scaling: Judgments of attributes or objects? *Behavioral and Brain Sciences, 15,* 543–558.

Lockhead, G. R. (1995). Context defines psychology. In F. Kessel (Ed.), *Psychology, science, and human affairs: Essays in honor of William Bevan* (pp. 125–137). Boulder, CO: Westview Press.

Loevinger, J. (1957). Objective tests as instruments of psychological theory [Monograph]. *Psychological Reports, 3,* 635–694.

Lofquist, L. H., & Dawis, R. V. (1969). *Adjustment to work: A psychological view of man's problems in a work-oriented society.* New York: Appleton-Century-Crofts.

Lohman, R. L. (1989). Human intelligence: An introduction to advances in theory and research. *Review of Educational Research, 59,* 333–373.

Lord, F. M., & Novick, M. R. (1968). Statistical theories of mental test scores. Reading, MA: Addison-Wesley.

Lord, R. G., & Hanges, P. J. (1987). A control system model of organizational motivation: Theoretical development and applied implications. *Behavioral Science, 32,* 161–178.

Lubin, B., Larsen, R. M., & Matarazzo, J. D. (1984). Patterns of psychological test usage in the United States: 1935–1982. *American Psychologist, 39,* 451–454.

Lueger, R. J. (1998). Using feedback on patient progress to predict the outcome of psychotherapy. *Journal of Clinical Psychology, 54,* 383–393.

Lykken, D. T. (1971). Multiple factor analysis and personality research. *Journal of Experimental Research in Personality, 5,* 161–170.

MacGregor, D., Lichtenstein, S., & Slovic, P. (1988). Structuring knowledge retrieval: An analysis of decomposed quantitative judgments. *Organizational Behavior and Human Decision Processes, 42,* 303–323.

Magnusson, D., & Endler, N. S. (1977). *Personality at the crossroads: Current issues in interactional psychology.* Hillsdale, NJ: Erlbaum.

Mahoney, M. J. (1977). Some applied issues in self-monitoring. In J. D. Cone & R. P. Hawkins (Eds.), *Behavioral assessment: New directions in clinical psychology* (pp. 241–254). New York: Brunner/Mazel.

Maloney, M. P., & Ward, M. P. (1976). *Psychological assessment: A conceptual approach.* New York: Oxford University Press.

Marin, G., Triandis, H. C., Betancourt, H., & Kashima, Y. (1983). Ethnic affirmation versus social desirability: Explaining discrepancies in bilinguals' responses to a questionnaire. *Journal of Cross-cultural Psychology, 14,* 173–186.

Mariotto, M. J., & Licht, M. H. (1986). Ongoing assessment of functioning with DOC systems: Practical and technical issues. In G. L. Paul (Ed.), *Assessment in residential treatment settings* (pp. 191–224). Champaign, IL: Research Press.

Mark, M., Rabinowitz, J., Kindler, S., Rabinowitz, S., Munitz, H., & Bleich, A. (1991). A system for improving psychiatric record keeping. *Hospital and Community Psychiatry, 42,* 1163–1166.

Marmar, C. R., Marziali, E., Horowitz, M. J., & Weiss, D. S. (1986). The development of the therapeutic alliance rating system. In L. S. Greenberg & W. M. Pinsof (Eds.), *The psychotherapeutic process: A research handbook* (pp. 367–390). New York: Guilford Press.

Marsh, W. W., Dowson, M., Pietsch, J., & Walker, R. (2004). Why multicollinearity matters: A reexamination of relations between self-efficacy, self-concept, and achievement. *Journal of Educational Psychology, 96,* 518–522.

Martin, R. A. (1989). Techniques for data acquisition and analysis in field investigations of stress. In R. W. J. Neufeld (Ed.), *Advances in the investigation of psychological stress* (pp. 195–234). New York: Wiley.

Martin, R. P. (1988). *Assessment of personality and behavior problems.* New York: Guilford Press.

Mash, E. J., & Hunsley, J. (1993). Assessment considerations in the identification of failing psychotherapy: Bringing the negatives out of the darkroom. *Psychological Assessment, 5,* 292–301.

Maslach, C., & Jackson, S. (1981). The measurement of experienced burnout. *Journal of Occupational Behavior, 2,* 99–113.

Matarrazo, J. D. (1983). The reliability of psychiatric and psychological diagnosis. *Clinical Psychology Review, 3,* 103–145.

Matarazzo, J. D. (1987). There is only one psychology, no specialties, but many applications. *American Psychologist, 42,* 893–903.

Mattaini, M. A. (1993). *More than a thousand words: Graphics for clinical practice.* Washington, DC: NASW Press.

May, T. M., & Scott, K. J. (1989). *Assessment in counseling psychology: Do we practice what we preach?* Paper presented at the American Psychological Association convention, New Orleans.

Mayer, R. E., Heiser, J., & Lonn, S. (2001). Cognitive constraints on multimedia learning: When presenting more material results in less understanding. *Journal of Educational Psychology, 93,* 187–198.

Mayfield, E., Brown, S., & Hamstra, W. (1980). Selection interviews in the life insurance industry: An update of research and practice. *Personnel Psychology, 33,* 225–239.

McAdams, D. P. (1996). Personality, modernity, and the storied self: A contemporary framework for studying persons. *Psychological Inquiry, 7,* 295–321.

McArthur, C. (1968). Comment on studies of clinical versus statistical prediction. *Journal of Counseling Psychology, 15,* 172–173.

McCall, R. B. (1991). So many interactions, so little evidence. Why? In T. D. Wachs & Robert Plomin (Eds.), *Conceptualization and measurement of organism–environment interaction* (pp. 142–161). Washington, DC: American Psychological Association.

McCall, R. J. (1958). Face validity in the D scale of the MMPI. *Journal of Clinical Psychology, 14,* 77–80.

McCrae, R. R., & Costa, P. T., Jr. (1983). Social desirability scales: More substance than style. *Journal of Consulting and Clinical Psychology, 51,* 882–888.

McCrae, R. R., & Costa, P. T., Jr. (1985). Updating Norman's "adequate taxonomy": Intelligence and personality dimensions in natural language and in questionnaires. *Journal of Personality and Social Psychology, 49,* 710–721.

McCrae, R. R., & Costa, P. T., Jr. (1987). Validation of the five-factor model of personality across instruments and observers. *Journal of Personality and Social Psychology, 52,* 81–90.

McCrae, R. R., & Costa, P. T., Jr. (1989). The structure of interpersonal traits: Wiggins' circumplex and the five-factor model. *Journal of Personality and Social Psychology, 56,* 586–595.

McFall, R. M., & Marston, A. (1970). An experimental investigation of behavior rehearsal in assertive training. *Journal of Abnormal Psychology, 76,* 295–303.

McFall, R. M., & McDonel, E. C. (1986). The continuing search for units of analysis in psychology: Beyond persons, situations, and their interactions. In R. O. Nelson & S. C. Hayes (Eds.), *Conceptual foundations of behavioral assessment* (pp. 201–241). New York: Guilford Press.

McIntyre, R. M., Smith, D. E., & Hassett, C. E. (1984). Accuracy of performance ratings as affected by rater training and perceived purpose of rating. *Journal of Applied Psychology, 69,* 147–156.

Meehl, P. E. (1954). *Clinical versus statistical prediction: A theoretical analysis and a review of the evidence.* Minneapolis: University of Minnesota Press.

Meehl, P. E. (1957). When shall we use our heads instead of formula? *Journal of Counseling Psychology, 4,* 268–273.

Meehl, P. E. (1965). Seer over sign: The first good example. *Journal of Experimental Research in Personality, 1,* 27–32.

Meehl, P. E. (1967). Theory testing in psychology and in physics: A methodological paradox. *Science, 34,* 103–115.

Meehl, P. E. (1973). Why I do not attend case conferences. In P. E. Meehl,

Psychodiagnosis: Selected papers (pp. 225–302). Minneapolis: University of Minnesota Press.

Meehl, P. E. (1991). Why summaries of research on psychological theories are often uninterpretable. In R. E. Snow & D. E. Wiley (Eds.), *Improving inquiry in social science* (pp. 13–59). Hillsdale, NJ: Erlbaum.

Meier, S. T. (1984). The construct validity of burnout. *Journal of Occupational Psychology, 57,* 211–219.

Meier, S. T. (1988). Predicting individual differences in performance on computer-administered tests and tasks: Development of the Computer Aversion Scale. *Computers in Human Behavior, 4,* 175–187.

Meier, S. T. (1991). Tests of the construct validity of occupational stress measures with college students: Failure to support discriminant validity. *Journal of Counseling Psychology, 38,* 91–97.

Meier, S. T. (1994). *The chronic crisis in psychological measurement and assessment.* New York: Academic Press.

Meier, S. T. (1997). Nomothetic item selection rules for tests of psychological interventions. *Psychotherapy Research, 7,* 419–427.

Meier, S. T. (1998). Evaluating change-based item selection rules. *Measurement and Evaluation in Counseling and Development, 31,* 15–27.

Meier, S. T. (1999). Training the practitioner–scientist: Bridging case conceptualization, assessment, and intervention. *Counseling Psychologist, 27,* 846–869.

Meier, S. T. (2000). Treatment sensitivity of the PE Form of the Social Skills Rating Scales: Implications for test construction procedures. *Measurement and Evaluation in Counseling and Development, 33,* 144–156.

Meier, S. T. (2003). *Bridging case conceptualization, assessment, and intervention.* Thousand Oaks, CA: Sage.

Meier, S. T. (2004). Improving design sensitivity through intervention-sensitive measures. *American Journal of Evaluation, 25,* 321–334.

Meier, S. T., & Davis, S. R. (1990). Trends in reporting psychometric properties of scales used in counseling psychology research. *Journal of Counseling Psychology, 37,* 113–115.

Meier, S. T., & Davis, S. R. (2005). *The elements of counseling* (5th ed.). Pacific Grove, CA: Brooks/Cole.

Meier, S. T., & Lambert, M. E. (1991). Psychometric properties and correlates of three computer aversion scales. *Behavior Research Methods, Instruments, and Computers, 23,* 9–15.

Meier, S. T., & Letsch, E. (2000). Data collection issues in an urban community mental health center: What is necessary and sufficient information for outcome assessment? *Professional Psychology: Research and Practice, 31,* 409–411.

Meier, S. T., McCarthy, P., & Schmeck, R. (1984). Validity of self-efficacy as a predictor of writing performance. *Cognitive Therapy and Research, 8,* 107–120.

Meier, S. T., McDougal, J., & Bardos, A. (in press). Development of a change-sensitive outcome measure for children. *Canadian Journal of School Psychology.*

Meier, S. T., & Schwartz, E. (2007). *Negative change in treated and untreated adolescents: Implications for design sensitivity of program evaluations. Manuscript submitted for publication,*

Meier, S. T., & Vermeersch, D. (2007). *What changes in counseling and psychotherapy?* Unpublished manuscript, University at Buffalo.

Meier, S. T., & Wick, M. T. (1991). Computer-based unobtrusive measurement: Potential supplements to reactive self-reports. *Professional Psychology: Research and Practice, 22,* 410–412.

Mergenthaler, E. (1996). Emotion-abstraction patterns in verbatim protocols: A new way of describing psychotherapeutic processes. *Journal of Consulting and Clinical Psychology, 64,* 1306–1315.

Messick, S. (1980). Test validity and the ethics of assessment. *American Psychologist, 35,* 1012–1027.

Messick, S. (1989a). Validity. In R. L. Linn (Ed.), *Educational measurement* (3rd ed., pp. 13–103). Washington, DC: American Council on Education and National Council on Measurement in Education.

Messick, S. (1989b). Meaning and values in test validation: The science and ethics of assessment. *Educational Researcher, 18,* 5–11.

Messick, S. (1991). Psychology and methodology of response styles. In R. E. Snow & D. E. Wiley (Eds.), *Improving inquiry in social science* (pp. 161–200). Hillsdale, NJ: Erlbaum.

Meyer, M. (1926). Special reviews. *Psychological Bulletin, 23,* 261–276.

Miles, M. B., & Huberman, A. M. (1990). *Qualitative data analysis.* Thousand Oaks, CA: Sage.

Miller, S. D., Duncan, B. L., Sorrell, R., & Brown, G. S. (2005). The Partners for Change Outcome Management System. *Journal of Clinical Psychology, 61,* 199–208.

Millsap, R. E. (1990). A cautionary note on the detection of method variance in multitrait–multimethod data. *Journal of Applied Psychology, 75,* 350–353.

Miner, G. G., & Miner, J. B. (1979). *Employee selection within the law.* Washington, DC: Bureau of National Affairs.

Mischel, W. (1968). *Personality and assessment.* New York: Wiley.

Mischel, W., & Peake, P. K. (1982). Beyond deja vu in the search for cross-situational consistency. *Psychological Review, 89,* 730–755.

Moos, R. (1973). Conceptualizations of human environments. *American Psychologist, 28,* 652–665.

Moos, R. (1979a). Evaluating educational environments. San Francisco: Jossey-Bass.

Moos, R. (1979b). Improving social settings by social climate measurement and feedback. In R. Munoz, L. Snowden, & J. Kelly (Eds.), *Social and psychological research in community settings* (pp. 145–182). San Francisco: Jossey-Bass.

Moras, K., Di Nardo, P. A., & Barlow, D. H. (1992). Distinguishing anxiety and depression: Reexamination of the reconstructed Hamilton Scales. *Psychological Assessment, 4,* 224–227.

Morrison, R. L. (1988). Structured interviews and rating scales. In A. S. Bellack & M. Hersen (Eds.), *Behavioral assessment* (3rd ed., pp. 252–278). New York: Pergamon Press.

Mosier, C. I. (1947). A critical examination of the concepts of face validity. *Educational Psychological Measurement, 7,* 191–205.

Mumma, G. (2004). Validation of idiosyncratic cognitive schema in cognitive case formulations: An intraindividual idiographic approach. *Psychological Assessment, 16,* 211–230.

Muran, J. C., & Segal, Z. V. (1992). The development of an idiographic measure of self-schemas: An illustration of the construction and use of self-scenarios. *Psychotherapy: Theory, Research, Practice, Training, 29,* 524–535.

Murphy, J. T., Hollon, P. W., Zitzewitz, J. M., & Smoot, J. C. (1986). *Physics.* Columbus, OH: Merrill.

Murphy, K. R., & Davidshofer, C. O. (1988). *Psychological testing.* Englewood Cliffs, NJ: Prentice-Hall.

Murray, H. A. (1938). *Explorations in personality.* New York: Oxford University Press.

National Institute of Mental Health. (1976). *Putting knowledge to use: A distillation of the literature regarding transfer and change.* Rockville, MD: Author.

Naveh-Benjamin, M., McKeachie, W. J., & Lin, Y. (1987). Two types of test-anxious students; Support for an information processing model. *Journal of Educational Psychology, 79,* 131–136.

Nay, W. R. (1979). *Multimethod clinical assessment.* New York: Gardner Press.

Needleman, L. D. (1999). *Cognitive case conceptualization.* Mahway, NJ: Erlbaum.

Nelson, L. D., & Cicchetti, D. (1991). Validity of the MMPI Depression Scale for outpatients. *Psychological Assessment, 3,* 55–59.

Nelson, L. D., Pham, D., & Uchiyama, C. (1996). Subtlety of the MMPI-2 Depression Scale: A subject laid to rest? *Psychological Assessment, 8,* 331–333.

Nelson, M. L., & Neufeldt, S. A. (1998). The pedagogy of counseling: A critical examination. *Counselor Education and Supervision, 38,* 70–88.

Nelson, R. O. (1977a). Methodological issues in assessment via self-monitoring. In J. D. Cone & R. P. Hawkins (Eds.), *Behavioral assessment: New directions in clinical psychology* (pp. 217–254). New York: Brunner/Mazel.

Nelson, R. O. (1977b). Assessment and therapeutic functions of self-monitoring. In M. Hersen, R. M. Eisler, & P. M. Miller (Eds.), *Progress in behavior modification* (Vol. 5, pp. 263–308). New York: Brunner/Mazel.

Nelson, R. O., & Hayes, S. C. (1986). The nature of behavioral assessment. In R. O. Nelson & S. C. Hayes (Eds.), *Conceptual foundations of behavioral assessment* (pp. 1–41). New York: Guilford Press.

Neufeld, R. W. J. (1977). *Clinical quantitative methods.* New York: Grune & Stratton.

Nisbett, R. E., & Wilson, J. D. (1977). The halo effect: Evidence for unconscious alteration of judgments. *Journal of Personality and Social Psychology, 35,* 250–256.

Norcross, J. C. (2004). Tailoring the therapy relationship to the individual patient: Evidence-based practices. *Clinician's Research Digest, 30*(Suppl. Bulletin), 1–2.

Norenzayan, A., & Schwarz, N. (1999). Telling what they want to know: Participants tailor causal attributions to researchers' interests. *European Journal of Social Psychology, 29,* 1011–1020.

Norman, W. T. (1963). Toward an adequate taxonomy of personality attributes: Replicated factor structure in peer nomination personality ratings. *Journal of Abnormal and Social Psychology, 66,* 574–583.

Norman, W. T. (1969). "To see ourselves as others see us!": Relations among self-perceptions, peer-perceptions, and expected peer-perceptions of personality attributes. *Multivariate Behavioral Research, 4,* 417–443.

Nunnally, J. C. (1967). *Psychometric theory.* New York: McGraw-Hill.

Nunnally, J. C. (1978). *Psychometric theory* (2nd ed.). New York: McGraw-Hill.

O'Muircheartaigh, C. (1997). Measurement error in surveys: A historical perspective. In L. Lyberg, P. Biemer, M. Collins, E. D. De Leeuw, C. Dippo, N. Schwartz, et al. (Eds.), *Survey measurement and process quality* (pp. 1–28). New York: Wiley.

Ong, J. (1965). *The opposite-form procedure in inventory construction and research.* New York: Vantage Press.

Orton, G. L. (1997). *Strategies for counseling with children and their parents.* Pacific Grove, CA: Brooks/Cole.

Pajares, F. (1996). Self-efficacy beliefs in academic settings. *Review of Educational Research, 66,* 533–578.

Palmer, R. H. (1986). Does quality assurance improve ambulatory care? Implementing a randomized controlled trial in sixteen group practices. *Journal of Ambulatory Care Management, 9,* 1–15.

Panek, R. (1998). *Seeing and believing.* New York: Viking Penguin.

Parducci, A. (1965). Category judgment: A range frequency model. *Psychological Review, 72,* 407–418.

Parkinson, B., Briner, R. B., Reynolds, S., & Totterdell, P. (1995). Time frames for mood: Relations between monetary and generalized ratings of affect. *Personality and Social Psychology Bulletin, 21,* 331–339.

Parsons, F. (1909). *Choosing a vocation.* Boston: Houghton Mifflin.

Paul, A. (2004). *The cult of personality testing: How personality tests are leading us to miseducate our children, mismanage our companies, and misunderstand ourselves.* New York: Free Press.

Paul, G. L. (1967). Strategy of outcome research in psychotherapy. *Journal of Consulting Psychology, 31,* 109–118.

Paul, G. L. (Ed.). (1986). *Assessment in residential treatment settings.* Champaign, IL: Research Press.

Paul, G. L., Mariotto, M. J., & Redfield, J. P. (1986a). Assessment purposes, domains, and utility for decision making. In G. L. Paul (Ed.), *Assessment in residential treatment settings* (pp. 1–26). Champaign, IL: Research Press.

Paul, G. L., Mariotto, M. J., & Redfield, J. P. (1986b). Sources and methods for gathering information in formal assessment. In G. L. Paul (Ed.), *Assessment in residential treatment settings* (pp. 27–62). Champaign, IL: Research Press.

Paulhus, D. L. (1991). Measurement and control of response bias. In J. P. Robinson, P. R. Shaver, & L. S. Wrightsman (Eds.), *Measures of personality and social psychological attitudes* (Vol. 1, pp. 17–59). New York: Academic Press.

Paulman, R. G., & Kennelly, J. J. (1984). Test anxiety and ineffective test taking: Different names, same constructs? *Journal of Educational Psychology, 76,* 279–288.

Pelham, W. E., Fabiano, G. A., & Massetti, G. (2005). Evidence-based assessment of attention deficit hyperactivity disorder in children and adolescents. *Journal of Clinical Child and Adolescent Psychology, 34,* 449–476.

Pennebaker, J. W. (1993). Putting stress into words: Health, linguistic, and therapeutic implications. *Behaviour Research and Therapy, 31,* 539–548.

Pennebaker, J. W., Mehl, M. R., & Niederhoffer, K. G. (2003). Psychological aspects of natural language use: Our words, our selves. *Annual Review of Psychology, 54,* 547–577.

Persons, J. B. (1989). *Cognitive therapy in practice: A case formulation approach.* New York: Norton.

Persons, J. B. (1991). Psychotherapy outcome studies do not accurately represent current models of psychotherapy: A proposed remedy. *American Psychologist, 46,* 99–106.

Persons, J. B., & Mikami, A. Y. (2002). Strategies for handling treatment failure successfully. *Psychotherapy: Theory / Research / Practice / Training, 39,* 139–151.

Pervin, L. A. (1984). Idiographic approaches to personality. In N. S. Endler & J. M. Hunt (Eds.), *Personality and the behavioral disorders* (2nd ed., pp. 261–282). New York: Wiley.

Peterson, D. R. (1968). *The clinical study of social behavior.* New York: Appleton-Century-Crofts.

Peterson, J. (2004). The individual counseling process. In A. Vernon (Ed.), *Counseling children and adolescents* (3rd ed., pp. 35–74). Denver, CO: Love.

Pines, A. (1981). Burnout: A current problem in pediatrics. *Current Problems in Pediatrics, 11,* 1–32.

Piotrowski, C., & Keller, J. W. (1984). Psychological testing: Trends in master's level counseling psychology programs. *Teaching of Psychology, 11,* 244–245.

Piotrowski, C., & Keller, J. W. (1989). Psychological testing in outpatient mental health facilities: A national study. *Professional Psychology: Research and Practice, 20,* 423–425.

Piotrowski, C., & Lubin, B. (1990). Assessment practices of health psychologists: Survey of APA Division 38 clinicians. *Professional Psychology Research and Practice, 21,* 99–106.

Platt, J. R. (1977). Strong inference. In H. S. Broudy, R. H. Ennis, & L. I. Krimerman (Eds.), *Philosophy of educational research* (pp. 203–217). New York: Wiley.

Pleh, C. (2003). Thoughts on the distribution of thoughts: Memes or epidemies. *Journal of Cultural and Evolutionary Psychology, 1,* 21–51.

Polkinghorne, D. E. (2004). Narrative therapy and postmodernism. In L. E. Angus & J. McLeod (Eds.), *Handbook of narrative and psychotherapy* (pp. 53–67). Thousand Oaks, CA: Sage.

Popham, W. J. (1993). Educational testing in America: What's right, what's wrong? *Educational Measurement: Issues and Practice, 12,* 11–14.

Posavac, E. J., & Carey, R. G. (2003). *Program evaluation: Methods and case studies.* Upper Saddle River, NJ: Prentice-Hall.

Powell, M. P., & Vacha-Haase, T. (1994). Issues related to research with children: What counseling psychologists need to know. *Counseling Psychologist, 22,* 444–453.

Project Match Research Group (1997). Matching alcoholism treatments to client heterogeneity: Project MATCH Posttreatment drinking outcomes. *Journal of Studies on Alcohol, 58,* 7–29.

Public Broadcasting System (2005). *The testing industry's Big Four.* Retrieved August 16, 2006, from *www.pbs.org/wgbh/pages/frontline/shows/schools/testing/companies.html.*

Quarm, D. (1981). Random measurement error as a source of discrepancies between the reports of wives and husbands concerning marital power and task allocation. *Journal of Marriage and the Family, 43,* 521–535.

Rachman, S., & Hodgson, R. (1974). Synchrony and desynchrony in fear and avoidance. *Behaviour Research and Therapy, 12,* 311–318.

Reardon, R., & Loughead, T. (1988). A comparison of paper-and-pencil and computer versions of the Self-Directed Search. *Journal of Counseling and Development, 67,* 249–252.

Riley, W. T., Carson, S. C., Martin, N., Behar, A., Forman-Hoffman, V. L., & Jerome, A. (2005). Initial feasibility of a researcher configurable computerized self-monitoring system. *Computers in Human Behavior, 21,* 1005–1018.

Robins, L. N., Helzer, J. E., Croughan, J., & Ratcliff, K. S. (1981). National Institute of Mental Health Diagnostic Interview Schedule: Its history, characteristics, and validity. *Archives of General Psychiatry, 38,* 381–389.

Rodebaugh, T. L., Woods, C. M., & Heimberg, R. G. (2007). The reverse of social anxiety is not always the opposite: The reverse-scored items of the Social Interaction Anxiety Scale do not belong. *Behavior Therapy, 38,* 192–206.

Roediger, H. L., & Karpicke, J. D. (2006). The power of testing memory. *Perspectives on Psychological Science, 1,* 181–210.

Rogers, R., Bagby, R. M., & Dickens, S. E. (1992). *Test manual for the Structured Interview of Reported Symptoms (SIRS).* Tampa, FL: Psychological Assessment Resources.

Ronnestad, M. H., & Skovholt, T. M. (2003). The journey of the counselor and therapist: Research findings and perspectives on professional development. *Journal of Career Development, 30,* 5–44.

Rosen, L. D., Sears, D. C., & Weil, M. M. (1987). Computerphobia. *Behavior Research Methods, Instruments, and Computers, 19,* 167–179.

Rosenthal, R. (1976). *Experimenter effects in behavioral research* (rev. ed.). New York: Halsted Press.

Ross, L. (1977). The intuitive psychologist and his shortcomings: Distortions in the attribution process. In L. Berkowitz (Ed.), *Advances in experimental social psychology* (Vol. 10, pp. 174–221). New York: Academic Press.

Rounds, J. B., & Tinsley, H. E. (1984). Diagnosis and treatment of vocational problems. In S. D. Brown & R. W. Lent (Eds.), *Handbook of counseling psychology* (pp. 137–177). New York: Wiley.

Rushton, J. P., Brainerd, C. J., & Pressley, M. (1983). Behavioral development and construct validity: The principle of aggregation. *Psychological Bulletin, 94,* 18–38.

Rushton, J. P., Jackson, D. N., & Paunonen, S. V. (1981). Personality: Nomothetic or idiographic?: A response to Kentrick and Stringfield. *Psychological Review, 88,* 582–589.

Ryman, D. H., Naitoh, P., & Englund, C. E. (1988). Minicomputer-administered tasks in the study of effects of sustained work on human performance. *Behavior Research Methods, Instruments, and Computers, 16,* 256–261.

Saal, F. E., Downey, R. G., & Lahey, M. A. (1980). Rating the ratings: Assessing the psychometric quality of rating data. *Psychological Bulletin, 88,* 413–428.

Sallis, J. F., & Lichstein, K. L. (1979). The frontal electromyographic adaptation response: A potential source of confounding. *Biofeedback and Self-Regulation, 4,* 337–339.

Sapyta, J. (2004). *The effect of the provision of information on client status toward clinician behavior and outcome: A meta-analysis.* Manuscript submitted for publication.

Sapyta, J., Riemer, M., & Bickman, L. (2005). Feedback to clinicians: Theory, research, and practice. *Journal of Clinical Psychology, 61,* 145–153.

Sarason, I. G. (1961). Test anxiety, experimental instructions, and verbal learning. *American Psychologist, 16,* 374.

Sarason, I. G. (1972). Experimental approaches to test anxiety: Attention and the uses of information. In C. D. Spielberger (Ed.), *Anxiety: Current trends in theory and research* (Vol. 2, pp. 381–403). New York: Academic Press.

Schatz, P., & Browndyke, J. (2002). Applications of computer-based neuropsychological assessment. *Journal of Head Trauma Rehabilitation. 17,* 395–410.

Schmidt, F. L., & Hunter, J. E. (1977). Development of a general solution to the problem of validity generalization. *Journal of Applied Psychology, 62,* 529–540.

Schmitt, N., & Stults, D. M. (1986). Methodology review: Analysis of multitrait–multimethod matrices. *Applied Psychological Measurement, 10,* 1–22.

Schrader, A. D., & Osburn, H. G. (1977). Biodata faking: Effects of induced subtlety and position specificity. *Personnel Psychology, 30,* 395–404.

Schretlen, D. (1986). *Malingering: Use of a psychological test battery to detect two kinds of simulation.* Ann Arbor, MI: University Microfilms International.

Schroeder, D. H., & Costa, P. T. (1984). Influence of life event stress on physical illness: Substantive effects or methodological flaws. *Journal of Personality and Social Psychology, 46,* 853–863.

Schroeder, H. E., & Rakos, R. F. (1978). Effects of history on the measurement of assertion. *Behavior Therapy, 9,* 965–966.

Schuman, H., & Presser, S. (1981). *Questions and answers in attitude surveys.* New York: Academic Press.

Schwab, D. P., & Heneman, H. G. (1969). Relationship between interview structure and inter-interview reliability in an employment situation. *Journal of Applied Psychology, 53,* 214–217.

Schwarz, N. (1990). Assessing frequency reports of mundane behaviors: Contributions of cognitive psychology to questionnaire construction. In C. Hendrick & M. S. Clark (Eds.), *Research methods in personality and social psychology: Review of personality and social psychology* (Vol. 11, pp. 98–119). Beverly Hills, CA: Sage.

Schwarz, N. (1997). Questionnaire design: The rocky road from concepts to answers. In L. Lyberg, P. Biemer, M. Collins, E. D. De Leeuw, C. Dippo, N. Schwartz, et al. (Eds.), *Survey measurement and process quality* (pp. 29–46). New York: Wiley.

Schwarz, N. (1999). Self-reports: How the questions shape the answers. *American Psychologist, 54,* 93–105.

Schwarz, N., Knauper, B., Hippler, H. J., Noelle-Neumann, E., & Clark, F. (1991). Rating scales: Numeric values may change the meaning of scale labels. *Public Opinion Quarterly, 55,* 570–582.

Schwarz, N., & Oyserman, D. (2001). Asking questions about behavior: Cognition, communication, and questionnaire construction. *American Journal of Evaluation, 22,* 127–160.

Schwarz, N., Strack, F., & Mai, H. P. (1991). Assimilation and contrast effects in part–whole question sequences: A conversational logic analysis. *Public Opinion Quarterly, 55,* 3–23.

Schwarz, N., Strack, F., Muller, G., & Chassein, B. (1988). The range of response alternatives may determine the meaning of the question: Further evidence on informative functions of response alternatives. *Social Cognition, 6,* 107–117.

Scott, W. A. (1968). Attitude measurement. In G. Lindzey & E. Aronson (Eds.), *Handbook of social psychology* (pp. 204–273). Reading, MA: Addison-Wesley.

Scriven, M. (1969). Psychology without a paradigm. In L. Breger (Ed.), *Clinical-cognitive psychology: Models and integrations* (pp. 9–24). Englewood Cliffs, NJ: Prentice-Hall.

Sedlacek, W., Bailey, B., & Stovall, C. (1984). Following directions: An unobtrusive measure of student success. *Journal of College Student Personnel, 25,* 556.

Shavelson, R. J., & Webb, N. M. (1991). *Generalizability theory.* Newbury Park, CA: Sage.

Shavelson, R. J., Webb, N. M., & Rowley, G. L. (1989). Generalizability theory. *American Psychologist, 44,* 922–932.

Shertzer, B., & Stone, S. C. (1980). *Fundamentals of counseling* (3rd ed.). Boston: Houghton Mifflin.

Siegman, A. W. (1956). The effect of manifest anxiety on a concept formation task, a nondirected learning task, and on timed and untimed intelligence tests. *Journal of Consulting Psychology, 20,* 176–178.

Silva, F. (1993). *Psychometric foundations and behavioral assessment.* New York: Sage.

Singer, J. A., & Blagov, P. S. (2004). Self-defining memories, narrative identity, and psychotherapy: A conceptual model, empirical investigation, and case report. In L. E. Angus & J. McLeod (Eds.), *Handbook of narrative and psychotherapy* (pp. 229–246). Thousand Oaks, CA: Sage.

Smith, G. P., & Burger, G. (1993). *Detection of malingering: A validation study of the SLAM test.* Paper presented at the annual convention of the American Psychological Association, Toronto.

Smith, M. L., & Glass, G. V. (1977). Meta-analysis of psychotherapy outcome studies. *American Psychologist, 32,* 752–760.

Smyth, J. M. (1998). Written emotional expression: Effect sizes, outcome types, and moderating variables. *Journal of Consulting and Clinical Psychology, 66,* 174–184.

Snow, R. E. (1991). Aptitude–treatment interaction as a framework for research on individual differences in psychotherapy. *Journal of Consulting and Clinical Psychology, 59,* 205–216.

Snow, R. E., & Lohman, D. F. (1984). Toward a theory of cognitive aptitude for learning from instruction. *Journal of Educational Psychology, 76,* 347–376.

Snow, R. E., & Wiley, D. E. (1991). Straight thinking. In R. E. Snow & D. E. Wiley (Eds.), *Improving inquiry in social science* (pp. 1–12). Hillsdale, NJ: Erlbaum.

Sommers-Flanagan, J., & Sommers-Flanagan, R. (1999). *Clinical interviewing* (2nd ed.). Boston: Allyn & Bacon.

Speer, D. C., & Newman, F. L. (1996). Mental health services outcome evaluation. *Clinical Psychology: Science and Practice, 3,* 105–129.

Spielberger, C. D. (1991). *State–Trait Anger Expression Inventory.* Odessa, FL: Psychological Assessment Resources.

Spielberger, C. D., Gorsuch, R. L., & Lushene, R. (1970). *Manual for the State–Trait Anxiety Inventory (STAI).* Palo Alto, CA: Consulting Psychologists Press.

Spielberger, C. D., Sydeman, S., Owen, A. E., & Marsh, B. J. (1997). Measuring anxiety and anger with the State–Trait Anxiety Inventory (STAI) and State–Trait Anger Expression Inventory (STAXI). In M. Maruish (Ed.), *The use of psychological testing for treatment planning and outcome assessment* (2nd ed., pp. 993–1022). Mahwah, NJ: Erlbaum.

Staats, A. W. (1983). *Psychology's crisis of disunity: Philosophy and method for a unified science*. New York: Praeger Press.

Staats, A. W. (1988, August). *Personality as basic behavioral processes: A critical bridging theory*. Paper presented at the American Psychological Association convention, Atlanta.

Stagner, R. (1984). Trait psychology. In N. S. Endler & J. M. Hunt (Eds.), *Personality and the behavioral disorders* (2nd ed., Vol. 1, pp. 3–28). New York: Wiley.

Stattin, H. (1984). Developmental trends in the appraisal of anxiety-provoking situations. *Journal of Personality, 52,* 46–57.

Staw, B. M., & Ross, J. (1985). Stability in the midst of change: A dispositional approach to job attitudes. *Journal of Applied Psychology, 70,* 469–480.

Steege, M. W., Davin, T., & Hathaway, M. (2001). Reliability and accuracy of a performance-based behavioral recording procedure. *School Psychology Review, 30,* 252–261.

Steele, C. M. (1998). Stereotyping and its threat are real. *American Psychologist, 53,* 680–681.

Steele, C. M., & Aronson, J. (1995). Stereotype threat and the intellectual test performance of African Americans. *Journal of Personality and Social Psychology, 69,* 797–811.

Steele, F. (1973). *Physical settings and organization development*. Reading, MA: Addison–Wesley.

Sterling-Turner, H. E., Robinson, S. L., & Wilczynski, S. M. (2001). Functional assessment of distracting and disruptive behaviors in the school setting. *School Psychology Review, 30,* 211–226.

Sternberg, R. J. (1984). A contextualist view of the nature of intelligence. *International Journal of Psychology, 19,* 307–334.

Sternberg, R. J., & Williams, W. M. (1998). You proved our point better than we did: A reply to our critics. *American Psychologist, 53,* 576–577.

Stevens, S. S. (1951). Mathematics, measurement and psychophysics. In S. S. Stevens (Ed.), *Handbook of experimental psychology* (pp. 1–41). New York: Wiley.

Stice, E., Fisher, M., & Lowe, M. R. (2004). Are dietary restraint scales valid measures of acute dietary restriction? Unobtrusive observational data suggest not. *Psychological Assessment, 16,* 51–59.

Stiffman, A. R., Orme, J. G., Evans, D. A., Feldman, R. A., & Keeney, P. A. (1984). A brief measure of children's behavior problems: The Behavior Rating Index for Children. *Measurement and Evaluation in Counseling and Development, 16,* 83–90.

Stoltenberg, C. D., & Delworth, U. (1987). *Supervising counselors and therapists*. San Francisco: Jossey-Bass.

Stone, E. F. (1978). *Research methods in organizational behavior.* Santa Monica, CA: Goodyear.

Stone, E. F., Stone, D. L., & Gueutal, H. G. (1990). Influence of cognitive ability on responses to questionnaire measures: Measurement precision and missing response problems. *Journal of Applied Psychology, 75,* 418–427.

Strack, F., Schwarz, N., & Gschneidinger, E. (1985). Happiness and reminiscing: The role of time perspective, mood, and mode of thinking. *Journal of Personality and Social Psychology, 49,* 1460–1469.

Strauss, A., & Corbin, J. (Eds.). (1997). *Grounded theory in practice.* Thousand Oaks, CA: Sage.

Streiner, D. L. (1998). Thinking small: Research designs appropriate for clinical practice. *Canadian Journal of Psychiatry, 43,* 737–741.

Strong, E. K., Jr. (1943). *Vocational interests of men and women.* Stanford, CA: Stanford University Press.

Strupp, H. H., Horowitz, L. M., & Lambert, M. J. (Eds.). (1997). *Measuring patient changes in mood, anxiety, and personality disorders: Toward a core battery.* Washington, DC: American Psychological Association.

Sudman, S., & Bradburn, N. (1982). *Asking questions: A practical guide to questionnaire design.* San Francisco: Jossey-Bass.

Sudman, S., Bradburn, N., & Schwarz, N. (1996). *Thinking about answers: The application of cognitive processes to survey methodology.* San Francisco: Jossey-Bass.

Super, D. E. (1957). *Psychology of careers.* New York: Harper.

Swanson, J. L., & Hansen, J. C. (1988). Stability of vocational interests on 4-year, 8-year, and 12-year intervals. *Journal of Vocational Behavior, 33,* 185–202.

Swezey, R. W. (1981). *Individual performance assessment: An approach to criterion-referenced test development.* Reston, VA: Reston.

Taft, R. (1955). The ability to judge people. *Psychological Bulletin, 52,* 1–23.

Tellegen, A. (1985). Structures of mood and personality and their relevance to assessing anxiety, with an emphasis on self-report. In A. H. Tuma & J. D. Master (Eds.), *Anxiety and the anxiety disorders* (pp. 681–706). Hillsdale, NJ: Erlbaum.

Tellegen, A. (1988). The analysis of consistency in personality assessment. *Journal of Personality, 56,* 621–663.

Tenopyr, M. L. (1992). Court decisions and psychological assessment. In W. J. Camara (Chair), *One hundred years of psychological testing.* Symposium conducted at the convention of the American Psychological Association, Washington, DC.

Terman, L. M., & Merrill, M. A. (1937). *Measuring intelligence.* Boston: Houghton-Mifflin.

Terman, L. M., & Miles, C. C. (1936). *Sex and personality.* New York: McGraw-Hill.

Thayer, C. E., & Fine, A. H. (2001). Evaluation and outcome measurement in the non-profit sector: Stakeholder participation. *Evaluation and Program Planning, 24,* 103–108.

Thorndike, E. L. (1920). A constant error in psychological ratings. *Journal of Applied Psychology, 4,* 25–29.

Thorndike, R. L. (1949). *Personnel selection.* New York: Wiley.

Thorndike, R. L. (1969). Helping teachers use tests. *NCME Measurement in Education: A series of special reports of the National Council on Measurement in Education, 1.*

Thorndike, R. L., & Hagen, E. (1961). *Measurement and evaluation in psychology and education* (2nd ed.). New York: Wiley.

Tichenor, V., & Hill, C. E. (1989). A comparison of six measures of working alliance. *Psychotherapy, 26,* 195–199.

Torgerson, W. S. (1958). *Theory and methods of scaling.* New York: Wiley.

Trapnell, P. D., & Wiggins, J. S. (1990). Extension of the Interpersonal Adjective Scales to include the Big Five dimensions of personality. *Journal of Personality and Social Psychology, 59,* 781–790.

Trent, T. T., Atwater, D. C., & Abrahams, N. M. (1986). Biographical screening of military applicants: Experimental assessment of item response distortion. In G. E. Lee (Ed.), *Proceedings of the Tenth Annual Symposium of Psychology in the Department of Defense* (pp. 96–100). Colorado Springs, CO: U.S. Air Force Academy, Department of Behavioral Sciences and Leadership.

Trochim, W. (1999). *The research methods knowledge base.* www.atomicdog.com/trochim.

Truscott, S. D., Baumgart, M. B., & Rogers, K. M. (2004). Financial conflicts of interest in the school psychology assessment literature. *School Psychology Quarterly, 19,* 166–178.

Tryon, W. W. (1991). *Activity measurement in psychology and medicine.* New York: Plenum Press.

Tschannen-Moran, M., & Hoy, A. W. (2001). Teacher efficacy: Capturing an elusive construct. *Teaching and Teacher Education, 17,* 783–805.

Tupes, E., C., & Christal, R. E. (1961). *Recurrent personality factors based on trait ratings (ASD-TR-61-97).* Lackland Air Force Base, TX: Aeronautical Systems Division, Personnel Laboratory.

Tversky, A., & Kahneman, D. (1974). Judgment under uncertainty: Heuristics and biases. *Science, 185,* 1124–1131.

Tymofievich, M., & Leroux, J. A. (2000). Counselors' competencies in using assessments. *Measurement and Evaluation in Counseling and Development, 33,* 50–59.

Umphress, V. J., Lambert, M. J., Smart, D. W., Barlow, S. H., & Clouse, G. (1997). Concurrent and construct validity of the outcome questionnaire. *Journal of Psychoeducational Assessment, 15,* 40–55.

Vansickle, T. R., Kimmel, C., & Kapes, J. T. (1989). Test–retest equivalency of the computer-based and paper–pencil versions of the Strong Campbell

Interest Inventory. *Measurement and Evaluation in Counseling and Development, 22,* 88–83.

VanZandt, C. E. (1990). Professionalism: A matter of personal initiative. *Journal of Counseling and Development, 68,* 243–245.

Vermeersch, D. A., Lambert, M. J., & Burlingame, G. M. (2000). Outcome Questionnaire: Item sensitivity to change. *Journal of Personality Assessment, 74,* 242–261.

Vermeersch, D. A., Whipple, J. L., Lambert, M. J., Hawkins, E. J., Burchfield, C. M., & Okiishi, J. C. (2004). Outcome Questionnaire: Is it sensitive to changes in counseling center clients? *Journal of Counseling Psychology, 51,* 38–49.

Vernon, P. E. (1934). The attitude of the subject in personality testing. *Journal of Applied Psychology, 18,* 165–177.

Vernon, P. E. (1964). *Personality assessment.* London: Methuen.

Violato, C., & Travis, L. D. (1988). An application of generalizability theory to the consistency–specificity problem: The transsituational consistency of behavioral persistence. *Journal of Psychology, 122,* 389–407.

Vogt, W. P. (1993). *Dictionary of statistics and methodology.* Newbury Park, CA: Sage.

Wachtel, P. (1973). Psychodynamics, behavior therapy, and the implacable experimenter: An inquiry into the consistency of personality. *Journal of Abnormal Psychology, 82,* 321–334.

Walsh, W. B. (1973). *Theories of person–environment interaction: Implications for the college student.* Iowa City, IA: American College Testing Program.

Walsh, W. B., & Betz, N. E. (1985). *Tests and assessment.* Englewood Cliffs, NJ: Prentice-Hall.

Wampold, B. E. (2001). *The great psychotherapy debate: Models, methods, and findings.* Mahwah, NJ: Erlbaum.

Waters, L. K. (1965). A note on the "fakability" of forced-choice scales. *Personnel Psychology, 18,* 187–191.

Watson, D. (1988). The vicissitudes of mood measurement: Effects of varying descriptors, time frames, and response formats on measures of positive and negative affect. *Journal of Personality and Social Psychology, 55,* 128–141.

Watson, D., & Pennebaker, J. W. (1989). Health complaints, stress and distress: Exploring the central role of negative affectivity. *Psychological Review, 96,* 234–254.

Webb, E., Campbell, D., Schwartz, R., Sechrest, L., & Grove, J. (1981). *Nonreactive measures in the social sciences.* Boston: Houghton Mifflin.

Webster-Stratton, C. (1996). Early onset conduct problems: Does gender make a difference? *Journal of Consulting and Clinical Psychology, 64,* 540–551.

Wedding, D., & Faust, D. (1989). Clinical judgment and decision making in neuropsychology. *Archives of Clinical Neuropsychology, 4,* 233–265.

Weiner, B. (1985). *Human motivation.* New York: Springer-Verlag.

Weinstock, M., & Meier, S. T. (2003). A comparison of two item selection methodologies for measuring change in university counseling center clients. *Measurement and Evaluation in Counseling and Development, 36,* 66–75.

Weiss, D. S. (2004). Structured clinical interview techniques for PTSD. In J. P. Wilson & T. M. Keane (Eds.), *Assessing psychological trauma and PTSD* (2nd ed., pp. 103–121). New York: Guilford Press.

Weisz, J. R., Huey, S. J., & Weersing, V. R. (1998). Psychotherapy outcome research with children and adolescents: The state of the art. In T. H. Ollendick & R. J. Prinz (Eds.), *Advances in clinical child psychology* (Vol. 20, pp. 49–91). New York: Plenum Press.

Weisz, J. R., Weiss, B., & Donenberg, R. R. (1992). The lab versus the clinic: Effects of child and adolescent psychotherapy. *American Psychologist, 47,* 1578–1585.

Weisz, J. R., Weiss, B., Han, S. S., Granger, D. A., & Morton, T. (1995). Effects of psychotherapy with children and adolescents revisited: A meta-analysis of treatment outcome studies. *Psychological Bulletin, 177,* 450–468.

West, S. G., & Graziano, W. G. (1989). Long-term stability and change in personality: An introduction. *Journal of Personality, 57,* 175–194.

Wetter, M., Baer, R., Berry, D., Smith, G., & Larsen, L. (1992). Sensitivity of MMPI-2 validity scales to random responding and malingering. *Psychological Assessment, 4,* 369–374.

White, M. (2004). Folk psychology and narrative practices. In L. E. Angus & J. McLeod (Eds.), *Handbook of narrative and psychotherapy* (pp. 15–52). Thousand Oaks, CA: Sage.

White, P. A. (2000). Causal judgment from contingency information: Relation between subjective reports and individual tendencies in judgment. *Memory and Cognition, 28,* 415–426.

Wiener, D. N. (1948). Subtle and obvious keys for the Minnesota Multiphasic Personality Inventory. *Journal of Consulting Psychology, 12,* 164–170.

Wiesner, W. H., & Cronshaw, S. F. (1988). A meta-analytic investigation of the impact of interview format and degree of structure on the validity of the employment interview. *Journal of Occupational Psychology, 61,* 275–290.

Wiger, D. (1999). *The psychotherapy documentation primer.* New York: Wiley.

Wiggins, J. S. (1973). *Personality and prediction: Principles of personality assessment.* Reading, MA: Addison-Wesley.

Wiggins, J. S. (1982). Circumplex models of interpersonal behavior in clinical psychology. In P. S. Kendall & J. N. Butcher (Eds.), *Handbook of research methods in clinical psychology* (pp. 183–221). New York: Wiley.

Wiggins, J. S., & Pincus, A. L. (1989). Conceptions of personality disorders and dimensions of personality. *Psychological Assessment, 1,* 305–316.

Wiley, D. (1991). Test validity and invalidity reconsidered. In R. E. Snow & D. E. Wiley (Eds.), *Improving inquiry in social science* (pp. 75–108). Hillsdale, NJ: Erlbaum.

Williams, J. M. (1996). Depression and the specificity of autobiographical memory. In D. C. Rubin (Ed.), *Remembering our past: Studies in autobiographical memory* (pp. 244–267). Cambridge, UK: Cambridge University Press.

Wilson, G. T., & Vitousek, K. M (1999). Self-monitoring in the assessment of eating disorders. *Psychological Assessment, 11,* 480–489.

Wissler, C. (1901). The correlation of mental and physical tests. *Psychological Review Monographs, 3*(6).

Wolf, T. H. (1973). *Alfred Binet.* Chicago: University of Chicago Press.

Worthen, B. R., Borg, W. R., & White, K. R. (1993). *Measurement and evaluation in the schools.* New York: Longman.

Wright, P. M., Lichtenfels, P. A., & Pursell, E. D. (1989). The structured interview: Additional studies and a meta-analysis. *Journal of Occupational Psychology, 62,* 191–199.

Yeaton, W. H., & Sechrest, L. (1981). Critical dimensions in the choice and maintenance of successful treatments: Strength, integrity, and effectiveness. *Journal of Consulting and Clinical Psychology, 49,* 156–167.

Zigler, E., & Glick, M. (1988). Is paranoid schizophrenia really camouflaged depression? *American Psychologist, 43,* 284–290.

Zinn, J. (2006). I'm like, so fat: Helping your teen make healthy choices about eating and exercise in a weight-obsessed world. *Eating Disorders: The Journal of Treatment and Prevention, 14,* 171–172.

Ziskin, J. Z. (1995). *Coping with psychiatric and psychological testimony* (Vol. 1, 5th ed.). Los Angeles: Law and Psychology Press.

Zuckerman, M., Koestner, R., DeBoy, T., Garcia, T., Maresca, B. C., & Sartoris, J. M. (1988). To predict some of the people some of the time: A reexamination of the moderator variable approach in personality theory. *Journal of Personality and Social Psychology, 54,* 1006–1019.

Author Index

Subject Index

About the Author

Scott T. Meier, PhD, is a licensed psychologist and Professor and Chair of the Department of Counseling, School, and Educational Psychology at the University at Buffalo, The State University of New York. His main research and teaching are in the areas of psychological measurement (particularly outcome assessment), research methods (program evaluation), and counseling skills (integration of case conceptualization and assessment with intervention). Dr. Meier is a member of the American Evaluation Association, the Association for Psychological Science, and the Association for Behavioral and Cognitive Therapies. He is the author or coauthor of four books (including *The Elements of Counseling*) and has published in the journals *American Psychologist, Journal of Counseling Psychology, Measurement and Evaluation in Counseling and Development,* and the *American Journal of Evaluation.*